MAKING SENSE OF A NEW WORLD: LEARNING TO READ IN A SECOND LANGUAGE

Eve Gregory is Senior Lecturer in Education at Goldsmiths' College, University of London where she works with students on undergraduate, postgraduate and research degrees. Her own research interests are focused on cultural contexts and the literacy practices of young children, bilingualism and early literacy and family involvement in children's learning. She has directed a number of projects investigating children's out-of-school reading and the transfer of cognitive strategies between home and school, and has published extensively from these. Both her research and her teaching call upon her former experience as an Early Years teacher in multilingual classrooms.

Making Sense of a New World:
Learning to read in a second language

Eve Gregory

P·C·P
Paul Chapman
Publishing Ltd

Dedication
To my parents and to all the children who appear in this book.

Paul Chapman Publishing Ltd
144 Liverpool Road
London
N1 1LA

British Library Cataloguing in Publication Data
Gregory, Eve
    Making sense of a new world : learning to read in a second
    language
    1. Reading (Elementary) 2. Bilingual children
    I. Title
    372.4

    ISBN 1 85396 263 5

Typeset by Dorwyn Ltd
Printed and bound in Great Britain

A   B   C   D   E   F   G   H   9   8   7   6

Contents

Preface

This book is written for colleagues working with young children who must embark on learning a new language and culture as they enter the school gate. It is for colleagues who are fascinated by the different strategies these children use as they set about the task of learning to read for the first time in a language they must also learn to speak. Like myself, these colleagues may well be frustrated that, according to most studies on the reading process, the special strengths of these children (which teachers observe on a daily basis) simply do not exist.

I hope that this book begins to fill the gap I myself find as I teach both emergent bilinguals and those who are about to become their future teachers. I hope, too, that the book may contribute to the debate on the role of linguistic and cultural difference as an important area of study and will lead to further books on emergent bilinguals and the curriculum. The book aims to appeal to anyone who has the opportunity of working with emergent bilinguals in an Early Years setting. While writing this book, I have been privileged in working with colleagues from a number of countries and I hope that the ideas presented are equally relevant to teachers in Europe and abroad. Although computers, audio and videotapes and attractive books are a bonus, the approaches suggested do not depend upon any specialist equipment which cannot be made by teachers. My aim is to offer general principles for good practice. No special mention is made of the requirements of any particular national curriculum as these principles should be flexible enough to be used within the guidelines of a number of countries.

In Britain, it is still easy to feel 'cocooned' within a monolingual world. Yet, even within Europe, frontiers are collapsing and families, like that of Nicole whom we meet in this book, are simply choosing to live in another country and, of course, taking their young children with them. Our mainland European colleagues view the whole area of migration and second language learning as one of rapidly increasing significance which is an important subject of initial teacher and in-service education in its own right. As the number of those seeking refuge in wealthier countries continues to grow, there is every reason to believe that the age of the emergent bilingual has scarcely yet begun.

Eve Gregory
Lenzkirch, Baden-Württemberg, Germany
July 1995

Acknowledgements

This book owes its existence to a number of people. First and foremost, I thank the families, community teachers and teachers who invited me into their homes and classrooms and gave their time generously. I also thank the teachers in the schools where the work was based, particularly Rani Shamas and the teachers at Canon Barnett School in the London Borough of Tower Hamlets. I owe much to the patience of Nasima Rashid who worked with me visiting families and community classes and teaching the children in school. In the nicest way possible, she pointed out the cultural bias in many of my own ideas. Discussions with my colleague Margaret Spencer and with colleagues at NALDIC (National Association for Language Development in the Curriculum) and Hertfordshire Section 11 team helped me formulate and clarify my thoughts. Colleagues from the IEDPE (European Institute for Developing the Potential of all Children) as well as visits from ERASMUS students and tutors have enabled me to understand perspectives in different European countries. I should also like to thank Pamela Oberhuemer from the State Institute for Early Childhood Education, Bavaria, for the material used in her dual language stories project; Herr Auberli, Oberstudienrat in Baden-Württemberg, for information on teaching German to young second language learners; and Dinah Volk and Jeff Schultz who introduced me to the latest work at the Californian Centre for Cultural Diversity and Second Language Learning. My thanks are also due to Viv Edwards for titles of books available for early second language work, to Maica Bernal and her colleagues from the University of Vic, Catalonia, Spain, for the use of their book *Ventafocs* and to Penguin for the use of *Rapunzel*. Laurie Mullett of Goldsmiths' College gave me much-needed help with the graphics and I should like to express my thanks. I am grateful to Ann Williams of Reading University and to Karl Kimmig for their suggestions in improving the manuscript. Last, but by no means least, I thank my Chinese 'sister' Yueping Zhang for teaching me never to assume that my own culture is superior to others.

Work leading to this book has been financially supported by Goldsmiths' College, University of London, The Paul Hamlyn Foundation and the ESRC (R000221186).

The 'Stages of Learning' in *Patterns of Learning* (CLPE 1990, pp. 40–1), and in *Guide to the Primary Learning Record* (CLPE 1993, pp. 71–2) have been reproduced by kind permission of Hilary Hester at the Centre for Language in Primary Education, Webber Row, London SE1 8QW. The development of the 'Stages' and the theory and practice underpinning them are described in the two publications.

1

Setting the Scene

Jessica and Tony are five and have just started school in Britain together. Both children were born locally. One child is a native English speaker; the other speaks only Cantonese at home. Their classroom has many attractive books from which the children choose in order to share the story with the teacher. Many of these books will become their first reading material. On this occasion, both choose a book by the same author: a 'Mr Men' book by Roger Hargreaves:

Jessica: Mr Jelly. Oh, I've got this story anyway. It's a good one. Mr Jelly was in bed fast asleep when a leaf fell off a tree and hit against his window. It made him wake up. He said, 'My house is falling down'. He quickly went under the duvet. (turns page) When he went downstairs, he quickly pulled out some Rice Krispies and he put some yoghurt on and they went Snap, Crackle, Pop! 'Oh no, There's someone shooting me!' So he quickly crept underneath the table. I've got this story.
Teacher: Have you?
Jessica: (before turning the page) He goes out for a walk, doesn't he? He went for a walk in the woods. A worm popped his head out and he jumped into the air in fright. Then . . . is that all it says? The worm woke up and said 'Hallo!' Is that all it says? He came out of the other side of the wood . . . and, is that all it says? I know some of it, but I'm forgetting some of it. He fell down on the ground and he shut his eyes. A tramp picked him up. He asked him what his name was. 'Mr Jelly.' He waved 'Bye, bye' to the tramp. He said to Mr Jelly 'Just count up 1,2,3,4,5,6,7 and it'll be all right'. When he was walking through the woods, he saw a little twig. 'Oh, I'm not afraid . . .' and he changed into a different person. And he wasn't afraid anymore. He changed his name to Mr Happy. He sat in his chair and he relaxed.

Tony points to all the little figures on the back cover, asking 'What's his name?' before choosing Mr Fussy.

Tony: What's his name?
Teacher: Mr Fussy.

Tony: Mr Fussy. (he repeats four times using different intonation)
  Mr Fussy is in the house. (turns page)
  Mr Fussy . . . What's that?
Teacher: It's a glass . . . Oh no, it's a jar of marmalade.
Tony: Jar marmalade?
Teacher: Yes . . . to put on your bread . . . you know, in the morning.
Tony: Here's . . . (mumbles inaudibly) What's his name?
Teacher: It's Mr Fussy's hand, I think.
Tony: That's Mr Fussy's hand. What's he touch . . . his hand?
Teacher: It's an iron.
Tony: (turns back a page) What's he touch?
Teacher: He's touching the grass outside.
Tony: He's . . . What's his name?
Teacher: Mr Fussy

And so they continue until Tony becomes impatient and quickly turns the pages to the end.

It is not difficult to spot which child is the native English speaker. Jessica is already very familiar with the *lexis* and *syntax* of her first language. Closer examination of her text shows some of the skills involved in this: she uses four tense forms in both the positive and negative sense (the simple present 'can, goes, etc.', the present continuous 'I'm forgetting, etc.', the simple past 'went, pulled, etc.' and the past continuous 'was walking, etc.'); she accurately uses a variety of prepositions (in, on, off, against, under, out, underneath, up, down, through, into, etc.) and she knows which prepositions to use after verbs (to fall down, to fall out, to fall off, to go down, to pick up, to wake up, to count up, to go out, to pop out, to jump into, etc.). She uses adverbs (quickly), pronouns (he, his, him), interrogatives (what?) and inversions (doesn't he?), a variety of nouns (twig, person, duvet, woods, ground, etc.) and verbs (jump, pop, forget, relax, change, etc.).

She is also beginning to use the special language of books; note the position of 'quickly' in 'he quickly went, pulled and crept', lexis such as 'quivered' and phrases like 'in fright'. Her introduction to the story contains an adverbial clause – 'Mr Jelly was in bed fast asleep *when* a leaf fell off a tree and hit against his window' – and her use of direct speech shows how successfully she combines entering into the text, 'My house is falling down', while still remaining the narrator, 'He quickly went under the duvet'. She is able to predict events from her prior knowledge of the story – 'He goes out for a walk, doesn't he?' – and her telling has a beginning (Mr Jelly was fast asleep), a climax (Mr Jelly's ordeal) and a resolution or ending (He sat in his chair and relaxed). Finally, Jessica shows how she and Mr Jelly inhabit the same world. It is a world of duvets and Rice Krispies for breakfast which go 'Snap, Crackle, Pop!'. It is a world of leaves and twigs and trees and where worms live in holes in woods. It is also a world shared by her teacher. As they tackle texts together, both know they can rely on shared experiences to make predictions. Jessica may well feel confident as she steps into reading in school.

But what of Tony? His strategies in making sense of the story are quite different from those of Jessica. Rather than bringing prior linguistic and story knowledge to the task, we see him actively asking the teacher to tell him what he cannot yet say in English. His method seems to be constantly to question, 'What's his name?', 'What's that?', 'What's he touch?' and then repeatedly to practise, sometimes using different intonation, as if rehearsing, e.g. 'Mr Fussy' (four times). His questions become more insistent as the story goes on, perhaps because he forgets the answer or perhaps because the answer appears insufficient to him. But language is only part of Tony's difficulties as illustrated in his question 'Jar marmalade?'. Even as she replies, his teacher realises the inadequacy of her explanation – 'Yes . . . to put on your bread . . . you know, in the morning'. Unlike Jessica, Tony does not inhabit Mr Fussy's world.

DIFFERENT COUNTRIES, DIFFERENT CONTEXTS

As they set about making sense of this new world, children like Tony will have very different experiences according to where they happen to live and go to school. In most of Europe, Tony will be exceptional while Jessica remains the norm. But in many parts of the world, children will expect to learn to read and write in a language which is not their own. We need to remember that a large majority of countries in the world are multilingual. Between four and five thousand languages are spoken in fewer than two hundred different states; in Nigeria over five hundred languages are spoken natively, while India claims over sixteen hundred mother-tongues. In some countries, literacies in several languages and scripts will stand side-by-side in different types of schools; Street (1984) explains how this takes place in Iran, and Wagner, Messick and Spratt (1986) describe parallel but totally different schools in Morocco where learning takes place in either French or modern or classical Arabic. In many multilingual countries there will be one *lingua franca* or common language for formal education which only the more affluent will use for business or commerce in later life. In some former colonial countries all children may be faced with the task of making sense of literacy in an unknown language. In Zambia, for example, initial literacy teaching takes place in English, a language which many children have no means of practising outside the classroom. However unpromising the conditions, then, we know that children can and do learn to read for the first time in languages which they cannot yet speak and that this need not be regarded as something strange.

Circumstances in some parts of the world will be more favourable than those outlined above. Countries which have two official languages hold out more promise to strangers because they need to ensure early bilingual competence for all children through carefully planned immersion programmes. In Singapore, for example, it is taken for granted that children will be able to learn to speak, read and write simultaneously in languages using very different scripts (English and Mandarin). Within Europe, linguistic regions such as Wales or Catalonia hold out similar expectations for children. Although school language programmes are directed at developing bilingualism in two languages only (English/Welsh or

Spanish/Catalan), children with minority languages (largely Arabic speakers in Catalonia and speakers of South Asian languages in Wales) will benefit from the focus placed on language through immersion programmes. Second language teaching will also be high on the agenda of initial and in-service teacher education courses and an integral part of National Curriculum requirements.

Even within officially monolingual countries, provision made for non-native speakers like Tony will vary greatly. If he moves to the USA, he will join 24 per cent of the population (at the time of the 1990 census) who belong to a language minority and speak a language other than English at home. His schooling will be influenced by the US Supreme Court's crucial decision in the *Lau v. Nichols case* (1974) which stated that 'there is no equality of treatment merely by providing students with the same facilities, textbooks, teachers and curriculum; for students who do not understand English are effectively foreclosed from any meaningful education'. From this time, *minority language submersion* (in other words, no support of any kind) was made illegal in schools. A variety of different programmes now exist which combine immersion into the new language with mother-tongue maintenance. If he lives in one of twelve states which have a high number of language minority students, Tony should now have access to some means of bilingual education. Some of these programmes will also include monolingual children like Jessica, should this be the choice of her parents.

At the end of the twentieth century provision of second language tuition has become a matter of urgency for a number of European countries which have seen large increases in their immigrant population. Germany has become host to many non-native speakers who may be guest-workers (largely from Europe and Turkey), ethnic Germans (largely from the Soviet Union) or political asylum seekers. Most wish to remain permanently in the country. If he were to join these families in the southern German region of Baden-Württemberg, children like Tony may expect to enter a full-time immersion class for up to one year, where structured tuition following the normal curriculum will provide him with enough German to join the ordinary class as soon as possible. He will be spared from tests in German until considered fluent. If he belongs to one of the larger minorities his consulate should provide mother-tongue teaching and it will be the duty of the school to ensure collaboration between the mother-tongue and class teacher for joint curriculum planning and assessment of each child. If he were a Turkish speaker (the largest minority group) in neighbouring Bavaria, he should be able to participate in pilot projects promoting bilingual education (in Turkish and German) for all. If he moves across the border to either Austria or Switzerland, he may be sure that sections of the national or local curricula will be devoted to ways of combining second language with subject content teaching backed up by specialist initial and in-service education for those who will teach him.

Recognition of his mother-tongue, however, will disappear abruptly should he move to France. Here the emphasis will be on teaching him to become a French citizen with an excellent knowledge of the language and culture as quickly as possible. Equality here is interpreted as providing the same curriculum, which should be uniformly of a high quality, for everyone. Later in this book, we shall meet Nicole, an English child living in France, and see how she enters a new world at the school gate, leaving behind her English mother-tongue in an endeavour to learn all that is French. Like the rest of her class, she will strive for perfection of pronunciation and learn to read words by intensively practising sounds and syllables. Like all children, she will sit a national test or 'Evaluation' at age eight and, should her work prove inadequate, she will repeat the year and try the test again.

CHANGING CONTEXTS IN BRITAIN

Apart from Nicole, all the children appearing in this book begin school in Britain. Here, provision made for their incipient bilingualism as they step into a new world will have passed through very different phases during the second half of the twentieth century. These are most clearly displayed through references in official education reports during each decade. At the time of the Plowden Report (HMSO 1967) such references are largely negative. The report reminds us of research which highlights the dichotemy of 'positive' and 'negative' bilingualism according to the social class of the family and the circumstances in which the new language has been learned. 'Elite' bilingualism (where the learner chooses to learn a second language) is contrasted with 'folk' bilingualism learned in a *diglossic situation* (where the first language is of an inferior status and the new language has to be learned for survival in the new country). Studies on 'élite' bilingualism are said to show many positive cognitive effects which have not been replicated with children of unskilled or semi-skilled immigrant workers.

The argument in the report runs as follows: 'Immigrant children' are 'deprived' and at a disadvantage in school owing to the poor education of their families. In addition, they will be 'handicapped' by their unfamiliarity with the new language and culture, and are consequently likely to suffer a 'culture shock' upon entering British schools. The solution to children's needs during the 1960s was, therefore, seen to lie in *assimilation* of immigrants through tighter controls on new arrivals, through *bussing* children to other schools when the proportion of immigrants reached 33 per cent and through providing a *'compensating environment'* by *'enriched intellectual nourishment'*.

The 1970s mark a distinct shift from compensation and separation to a recognition of linguistic and cultural pluralism in schools. This is symbolised by the now famous quotation from the Bullock Report (HMSO 1975): 'No child should be expected to cast off the language and culture of the home as he crosses the school threshold, nor to live and act as though school and home represent two totally separate and different cultures which have to be kept firmly apart. The curriculum should reflect many elements of that part of his life which a child lives outside school' (para. 20.5). The report goes on to stress the importance of sustained and specialist language assistance for children well past the initial stages of learning, for the language specialist to work closely with the class teacher and for *all* teachers to become responsible for children's language learning.

Attitudes towards mother-tongue teaching were also largely optimistic during the 1970s. The Bullock Report preceded a Directive (1977) from the European Commission which strongly urged member states to make provision for mother-tongue teaching for the children of all migrant workers on the grounds that bilingual teaching improves the educational performance of linguistic minority children. Children's incipient bilingualism began to be seen as positive and this is also reflected in the Bullock Report. Forward-looking statements such as: 'Their . . . bilingualism is of great importance . . . to society as a whole. As a linguistically conscious nation in the modern world, we should see it as an asset, as something to be nurtured and one of the agencies that should nurture it is the school' (para. 20.17) inspired some schools to invite parents and community leaders into school on an informal basis to give mother-tongue tuition. In 1979 The Department of Education and Science set up The Linguistic Minorities Project (the findings of which were published in 1985), a research project to provide an account of changing patterns of bilingualism in a representative selection of areas in England which was expected to assist new policy implementation. In 1978 it instigated a pilot project (The Bradford Project) to investigate mother-tongue teaching for young Panjabi speaking children within the mainstream school. At the same time, Bedfordshire Education Authority assisted by European Community funds set up the Bedford Project to provide bilingual education for Italian speakers.

However, these initiatives came to an abrupt halt during the 1980s. The Bedford Project was terminated in 1980 when the European Community grant ran out for the reason that it was too expensive (Tosi 1984). The Bradford Project had not been set up to evaluate the maintenance of mother-tongue and the development of bilingualism, but to test *how far mother-tongue teaching would speed up acquisition of English*. Within this narrow remit, the research team was unable to prove clearly that one curriculum was more effective than another, and this project, too, came to an end at the beginning of the 1980s (Fitzpatrick 1987). The image of high cost provision together with a lack of positive effect on the learning of English contributed to the official policy decision not to fund bilingual education within the state system. This decision was made clear in the report of the Swann Committee on the Education of Children from Ethnic Minority Groups (*Education for All*, HMSO 1985) which states that 'community languages' are best taken care of by the communities themselves and taught outside the state school system. By the end of the 1980s, then, positive initiatives from the 1970s had left their mark in that the bilingualism of minority group children was no longer presented as a deficit as during the 1960s, but neither was it treated as an asset; findings on the widespread bilingualism and multilingualism of linguistic minority children reported in the Linguistic Minorities Project consequently never attracted much political or educational interest in the planning of a multicultural curriculum.

The Education Reform Act 1988 marked the beginning of ar
National Curriculum 'will be taking account of ethnic and cul'
ensuring that the curriculum provides equal opportunities for a.. ,
less of ethnic origin or gender' (National Curriculum Council 1988, p.
claim for equal opportunities is reiterated by the School Examinations and As
sessment Council with the claim that the SATs (standard assessment tasks) avoid
race, culture or gender bias, that they should be amenable to translation into
another language other than English or Welsh and that they would not contain
material to put pupils from ethnic minorities at a disadvantage (SEAC 1989).
Finally, the special status of equal opportunities is fleshed out in two NCC
documents *Curriculum Guidance 3: The Whole Curriculum* (1990) and *Starting
Out with the National Curriculum* (1992) which state that equal opportunities
should underpin every area of the curriculum and, as such, must be an explicit
part of the policy of every school and integral to the planning, development and
evaluation of a school's curriculum.

The key question is: can we really ensure equality of opportunity simply by
providing the *same* curriculum for all children? If not, what type of provision
might ensure equal opportunities for children who enter school unable to speak
the host language? How far, and in what ways, should we recognise linguistic and
cultural differences? Is the situation in Britain unique or do we have much to
share with others, both in Europe and abroad? There is every reason to believe
that the twenty-first century will see major joint European initiatives in minority
education. Collaborative action-research projects between European colleagues
are on the agenda for future European Commission funding. Britain will have
much to offer these projects. The combination of established Language Centres
such as NALDIC (National Association for Language Development in the Curriculum), The Reading and Language Information Centre in Reading and CLPE
(Centre for Language in Primary Education) in London and interest shown by
the School Curriculum and Assessment Authority (SCAA) *Teaching and Learning English as an Additional Language: New Perspectives* (1995) may mark the
beginning of a new era for innovational practice in Britain.

WHAT'S IN A WORD?

Words used to describe children like Tony reflect current official educational
policy in different countries. In France, the term is simple and has not changed
during recent years. Tony will be described as 'non-francophone' (non-French
speaker). In Austria and Germany there is a subtle change to 'Schüler mit
nichtdeutscher Muttersprache' or 'non *mother-tongue* German speaker'. In Britain, we find that the '*immigrants*' or '*non-English speakers*' of the Plowden
Report in 1967 become '*non-native speakers*' or '*English second language
learners*' (ESL) in the Bullock Report of 1975, '*bilingual children*' of the late
1970s and in the Cox Report of 1988 and '*children with English as an additional
language*' during the 1990s.

ciding upon a satisfactory term to describe the children in this book was not
y. Use of the term 'bilingual' in educational circles in Britain during the 1980s
ɔ describe children like Tony signalled acceptance of a wider definition of the
word to mean those at any stage of second language learning. Yet to refer to
Tony as 'bilingual' contradicts both common understanding and dictionary definition which describes a bilingual as 'able to speak two languages, especially with
fluency' (*Collins English Dictionary* 1992). Clearly, children like Tony are not
fluent (or anywhere near it) in their new language. If they were, there would be
little point in writing a book about them. Indeed, there is a danger that use of the
term 'bilingual' might deflect attention from the fact that the children need help
as they go about learning in a new language. For this very reason, the term has
been rejected in the USA (where 'non-native speakers', 'English second language speakers', 'minority language speakers' or sometimes 'non mother-tongue
English speakers' are used) and Australia (where the terms 'English second
language' alongside 'children with languages other than English' (LOTE) are
preferred). Yet 'bilingualism' is Tony's aim and terms like 'second' or 'additional
language learner' do not adequately reflect this. Really, the children are just
beginning on the road to bilingualism. But 'beginner bilingual' implies that they
need to be taught, step-by-step. This is obviously not the case. Luckily, children
are also learning informally, from their classmates, the television and life generally. For this reason, I refer to Tony and all the children in this book as
'*emergent bilinguals*'.

So how might we define 'emergent bilinguals'? I do not wish to imply that
Tony's learning of a new language 'just happens'. This may well occur over many
years, but our children cannot afford such a luxury. They will usually have to
achieve the same level of literacy after a very short time as their monolingual
peers. Rather, I want to emphasise a joint process of formal and informal learning *where the teacher and her teaching does matter*. Emergent bilinguals are
children who are the first generation in their family to receive formal schooling
in the new country, who do not speak the language of the host country at home
and who are consequently at the early stages of second language learning (see
Appendix 1 for a fuller description of the children's stage in second language
learning). All the children have just entered school and are learning to read in a
language they cannot yet speak. The children in this book have come from very
different linguistic and cultural backgrounds. Some have recently entered the
country, others have been born in the host country. Despite their differences, the
children share an important task during the coming infant school years: they
must lose their 'strangeness', not only to the new language, but to a strange
culture through experiencing everyday new routines and ways of life. Their
ultimate aim is to become *bilingual* which I understand as:

> *being able to function in two (or more) languages, either in monolingual or bilingual
> communities, in accordance with the sociocultural demands made on an individual's
> communicative and cognitive competence by these communities and by the individual
> herself, at the same level as native speakers, and being able positively to identify with both
> (or all) language groups (and cultures) or parts of them.*
>
> (*Skutnabb-Kangas 1984, p. 90*)

As they step into school, Jessica and Tony seem miles apart. Yet in some countries, such as England and France, tests at seven and eight will measure how far each has mastered nouns such as 'funfair', 'bumper cars', 'ghost train', 'blaze', 'crowd', 'Catherine wheels' 'delight', etc., verbs such as 'remind', 'gather', 'buy', 'reflect', etc., adverbs such as 'briskly' as well as a familiarity with the passive voice 'so that they could be seen' (examples taken from the UK standard assessment tasks in 1993). But familiarity with the language is not all. They will first need to sort out the characters in the texts of the test: are Pat and Jo boys or girls? Or is one a boy and one a girl? Which is which and does it matter? Then comes the world of hotdogs, ghost trains and 'greens' (which are not vegetables, but 'where fires are lit'). It all appears a formidable task to master in just two years. Yet some children show us that it can be done. What still largely remains a mystery is whether there might be any patterns to their success or tuition they have received.

Emergent bilinguals are largely absent from research into reading. Studies on the reading process, methods of teaching and materials tend to assume either some oral fluency in the language in which tuition takes place or some literacy skills in the first language. Can we, as teachers, assume that learning to read in English is the same for Jessica and Tony? Or might young children who are simultaneously learning spoken and written English approach the task differently? If so, what special strengths might the children have? How do we provide 'culturally responsive' teaching which considers the expectations and interpretations of both children and their families? If these children do use special strategies, what implications might we draw for our teaching methods? Might we need to investigate different ways of analysing our interaction with the child as we keep records and hear reading?

A PLAN OF THE BOOK

This book aims to provide a framework for observing, teaching and assessing young children learning to read in a second language. Examples from years of classroom observations, taped reading interactions, interviews with mainstream and community teachers and work with parents are seated within the findings from research on second language learning and learning to read. The book assumes no specialist knowledge on the part of the reader. It is written for teachers, student teachers, bilingual instructors and all those interested in young children entering into a new language in school. There is no claim to provide simple solutions. Rather, the book illustrates the complexity of the dual task of learning a new skill in a new language and a new language through a new skill.

The argument put forward is that young learners in a new language do have particular strengths as they step into reading in school; strengths which are not accounted for in 'mainstream' studies on reading. Throughout the book, case studies and taped interactions are used to urge teachers to question how far existing studies on the reading process suffice to explain the strategies used by emergent bilinguals in their own classrooms. The book aims to encourage teachers to examine carefully their own strategies as they work with the children and makes practical suggestions for linking the teaching of English with beginning reading, listening to children read, assessing their English and working with parents and community schools. Above all, the book aims to highlight the importance of an awareness of different strengths (and weaknesses) if we are to provide equal acces to literacy to the emergent bilinguals in our classrooms.

The book attempts to link theory and practice throughout. Nevertheless, the focus is different in each section. Part One examines the scope of existing theories of beginning reading and studies on the reading process in explaining the task ahead for these emergent bilinguals. Chapter 2 focuses on the way young emergent bilinguals learn to situate themselves in the social context of reading. It investigates the interpretations of 'reading' held by parents, teachers and children as they enter school and presents a cross-cultural perspective of the role of the caregiver in structuring learning and initiating children into reading in the home. It goes on to examine the implications of different interpretations and practices for teacher/child interaction in the classroom. Chapter 3 investigates reading as a mental and linguistic activity. It draws upon both existing research and classroom examples to examine the strengths and weaknesses children have as they use different clues to make sense of the reading task in school.

Part Two moves into the classroom and focuses on ways in which teachers might use their knowledge of current research to inform practice, both in classroom reading lessons and in their work with children's families and community teachers. Using the findings from Part One, Chapters 4 and 5 outline two different but complementary approaches for beginning reading in the classroom. Chapter 6 draws upon case studies to suggest particular strategies for listening to children read and record-keeping. Finally, I return to the children's interpretations of reading as they reach the end of the primary school. How do they remember learning to speak and read English? To conclude the book, the words and opinions of the British teachers are joined by those of their colleagues in Europe. How do they view the challenges they face in the twenty-first century?

Throughout the book, readers are asked to question their own beliefs on what reading is and how it is learned. Cocooned within the membership of a professional group in one culture and education system, it is easy to believe established theories and ideas to be 'natural' and unchangeable. Yet we do not have to travel far to realise that our beliefs on how children learn to read are determined by our own cultural group. Our neighbours in Europe all have young emergent bilinguals in their schools and all have different approaches to introducing them to reading. Ultimately, teachers will aim at a 'joint culture creation' (Bruner 1986) within their classroom, yet to be authentic, this will need to be culturally responsive to all the children in the class. Rather than devoting a single chapter to reading and emergent bilinguals in different European countries, I make reference throughout the book to definitions and approaches in Europe. This means I really beg the question posed at the end of the book: will there be any such children in the next century? In Catalonia in Spain and Baden-

Württemberg in Germany, there is a growing belief that the twenty-first century will see migration within Europe on a scale which will affect us all. It is a belief we cannot afford to ignore as we make the promise of 'equal opportunity' to young children learning a second, third or even fifth language in school.

Further reading

Alladina, S. and Edwards, V. (eds.) (1991) *Multilingualism in the British Isles, Africa, the Middle East and Asia*, London: Longman.

Bourne, J. (1989) *Moving into the Mainstream: LEA Provision for Bilingual Pupils*, Windsor: NFER Nelson.

Edwards, V. and Redfern, A. (1992) *The World in a Classroom*, Clevedon: Multilingual Matters.

Mills, R. W. and Mills, J. (1993) *Bilingualism in the Primary School*, London: Routledge.

Part One

Emergent Bilinguals and the Reading Process:
Understanding Cultures, Codes and Contexts

2

Interpreting the Social Context

The setting is a narrow, inner-city 'lane' in East London with various shops which provide for the local Bangladeshi community. The warm, sunny day makes this busy area more friendly, even though a predominantly male population is seen frequenting the stores. Nasima and Eve have decided to buy a Qur'ān to add to their collection of materials for their project. Among the various food, clothes and music/book shops, they enter one which displays these holy books and other wares in its windows. On entering, a bearded man wearing a holy cap, nods and looks away. The two visually absorb the goods around them. The shop space is fully utilised, with shelves full of Arabic and Bengali books rising high above their heads. It looked like 'Aladdin's cave' with amulets, rosary beads and prayer mats decorating the walls and tables. The Qur'āns on show are beautifully embossed with gold Arabic lettering, in all shapes and sizes. Their eyes fall on one of the larger ones. 'Shall we take a look at that one?' asks Eve, as she points to a large green one. 'If you like,' replies Nasima. 'You are going to get it if we decide to buy it?' she continues awkwardly. 'What do you mean?' wondered Eve. 'You are going to hold it?' she says more specifically. 'I will if there's a problem, but why?' queries Eve. 'Well I can't hold it!' cries Nasima. 'Why, what's wrong with your hands?!' After which, Nasima explained that the washing of the body is essential before touching the Qur'ān, or one will be damned . . . However, they were able to get the book wrapped before leaving the shop.

(Gregory et al. 1993, p. 1)

The purpose of telling this story is to underline how easy it is wrongly to assume that we share common understandings and interpretations even with colleagues. In this case, the English teacher (myself) had assumed that buying a Qur'ān would be no different from purchasing a Bible. Similarly, Nasima (my colleague) of Bangladeshi origin had assumed that I would be aware of the reverence with which Muslims treat the Holy Book, hence the need to undertake 'wazu' (the washing ritual) before touching it. After all, I had been teaching and working with Muslim families for many years when the shopping incident described above occurred.

When travelling abroad, we tend to accept that expectations of how to go about doing things, words to use in sensitive situations, school learning and teaching and even what constitutes 'right' and 'wrong' are likely to be different. We know that, especially during the early stages of our visit, we need to make a special effort to observe the host culture and we know that mistakes will inevitably be made. Sometimes, we feel helpless and unable to understand what is required of us. At times like this, we may wish that the rules could be made more explicit by our hosts, particularly when a situation is formal and/or has important consequences (visiting a bank manager or even an invitation to a special meal!). Yet it is easy to forget these experiences when we return to our own world as teachers in school. It is easy implicitly to assume that emergent bilinguals share our own understanding of 'reading' and will find school methods and materials meaningful although their families may well have learned to read in a world quite different from our own.

In his influential work *Thought and Language* (written during the 1930s but translated only in 1962), the Soviet psychologist Lev Vygotsky examines the relationship between thought, language and learning and stresses that words need to be interpreted on two levels: their *meaning* (the dictionary definition) and their *sense* (the feeling called up by a word to an individual or a cultural group). He uses the example of the word 'flag' to show how the dictionary definition (or meaning) 'piece of cloth esp. bunting, often attached to a pole or staff decorated with a design and used as an emblem, signal or standard or as a means of signalling' (*Collins English Dictionary* 1992) may be very different from the 'sense' of the word which may conjure up pride and honour or humiliation and shame according to the experiences of an individual within a cultural group. Words which have a high emotional content or those where experiences vary greatly are likely to evoke a very different 'sense' for individuals or cultural groups. 'Reading' is one such word. Its dictionary definition (or meaning) of 'comprehending the meaning of something (written or printed) by looking at and interpreting the written characters' (*Collins English Dictionary* 1992) masks the vast span of 'sense' definitions it will conjure up both for different individuals and for cultural groups. In this chapter, we shall be looking at the 'sense' conjured up by 'reading' for families and teachers from different parts of the world.

The vital point about the 'sense' of words is that they are rooted in experience with others, perhaps caregivers, friends, colleagues at an institution or members of a cultural group. In other words, the individual first has an experience with others, then internalises the experience which will be symbolised in the word. Because of this, the 'sense' of a word can change for us as we have different experiences with it in life. This definition of 'sense' forms part of Vygotsky's central thesis which is this: all mental processes have social origins.

Any function in the child's development appears twice, or on two planes. First it appears on the social *plane, and then on the* psychological *plane. First it appears between people as an* interpsychological *category, and then within the child as an* intrapsychological *category. This is equally true with regard to voluntary attention, logical memory, the formation of concepts, and the development of volition.*

(Vygotsky 1981, p. 163)

In other words, the child's cognitive or thought development (intrapsychological or *intrapersonal* understanding) evolves from interpsychological or *interpersonal* negotiation with others within the culture; first with caregivers and later with the teachers and peers in school. Vygotsky's ideas have had a profound effect on the way we conceive intellectual development. But how do they fit into our topic of learning to read?

In pedagogical discussions, learning to read has long been considered a *mental* or *intrapersonal process* – the ability to perceive and interpret graphic symbols. More recently, however, attention has also turned to the importance of the *interpersonal dimension* – the way in which teacher and child reach a common interpretation of the reading task together. Courtney Cazden (1983) uses a helpful metaphor to explain Vygotsky's two planes more clearly. She refers to the task for beginner readers as learning to '*situate*' themselves in the '*context*' of reading, whereby context is defined as anything that affects the reader's response to the piece of written language that is the immediate focus of attention. 'Context' itself, then, comprises both the inner *mental context*, which she refers to as 'the context in the mind' and the outer or external *social context*. In the next two chapters I try to show how examining reading in terms of dimensions or contexts is particularly useful for teachers of emergent bilinguals for it provides us with a framework for analysing the learning strategies as well as the strengths and weaknesses of individual children. Chapters 4 and 5 show ways in which we can use this information to plan early reading programmes and activities.

This chapter is concerned with the *interpersonal dimension* or the *social context*. Within this frame reading is viewed primarily as a set of 'reading practices' rather than a particular cognitive skill. If the term 'reading practices' appears strange, an analogy with other cultural practices might be helpful. Imagine, for example, eating. It is not difficult to picture various 'eating practices' taking place in different countries and in different contexts. The *purpose* will vary from one country or context to another. In some countries, partaking of food is traditionally a social occasion where the whole family joins for discussion over a meal; in others, eating might consist of a quick solitary snack walking down the road or even sitting in the underground; in yet others, it might have become a sort of ritual, e.g. Sunday afternoon 'Kaffee and Kuchen' (coffee and cakes) in Germany or Austria. The *methods and materials* used for eating are certainly likely to differ greatly. In some cultures, food is eaten by hand, in others with chop-sticks and in others with a knife, fork and spoon. Little needs be said about the food itself, what is eaten and when, e.g. soup before or after the main course, etc. Finally, the patterns of interaction between participants in the meal (I shall sometimes refer to these as '*participation structures*' during reading interactions) are very different from one culture to another; who is allowed to eat with whom, who receives their food first, what should or should not be talked about and how one is (or is not) permitted to show pleasure during or at the end of a meal!

In the same way, each reading practice will have a group of members who follow certain rules which are likely to concern purpose, materials and patterns of interaction or participation structures. One practice is that of story-reading,

another the reading of religious texts, another 'reading' computers or even that
of reading specialist gardening or wrestling magazines. An important practice is
that of school reading which will differ from one country or historical time to the
next. Later in the chapter, we shall see how the young emergent bilinguals who
feature in this book are becoming members of different reading practices both at
home and in up to three different types of school.

The aim of this chapter is to highlight how important it is for teachers to find
out about the reading experiences and practices as well as the expectations which
young emergent bilinguals and their families bring to school. Examples of families living in London, Northampton and France show us just how varied these
experiences may be. The chapter is divided into two sections. The first section
investigates the role of the caregiver as the child's first teacher. The aim here is
to show the importance of the interpersonal dimension in early learning and to
examine briefly the patterns established between child and caregiver from different cultures during early language learning. The second section bridges home
and school. Examples of children from minority cultural and linguistic backgrounds in the UK and France show the variety of experiences brought from
home and illustrate how children begin to 'situate' themselves differently in the
social context of reading in school. Finally, I ask: how can a knowledge of home
and community reading practices help teachers as they introduce emergent bilinguals into reading in school?

This chapter, therefore, addresses the following questions:

- What role do caregivers from different cultures play in fostering their children's early learning and in what ways do they prepare their children for
  learning to read in school?
- If we focus on reading in terms of different *reading practices*, each with its own
  purpose, *materials* and *interaction between participants* (participation structures), what reading practices might our emergent bilinguals already be familiar with as they enter school?
- How might the child's approach to learning to read in school be influenced by
  home and community reading experiences as well as the expectations of the
  home culture?
- What questions will the teacher need to ask to begin to negotiate a joint
  interpretation of the reading task with the child in school?

I. LEARNING HOW TO LEARN: PREPARATION FOR SCHOOL READING IN CROSS-CULTURAL CONTEXT

The first steps: similarities and differences across cultures during pre-speech development

*It is generally accepted that knowledge itself originates within an interactional process
and that children's learning takes place within shared conceptual understandings, structured behaviours and social expectations. The child only achieves a fully articulated*

knowledge of his world in a cognitive sense as he becomes involved in social transactions with human beings.

(Newson and Newson 1975, p. 438)

Research studies across the world point to the origins of knowledge in the interaction between infants and their caregiver(s). A number of studies show us ways in which pre-speech infants and their caregivers participate in 'social dialogues' or 'conversations' with their infants almost from birth. In her study of pre-speech 'conversations', Catherine Snow (1977) emphasises the importance of noting that any utterance of the infant is accepted as a word and an initiator of a vocal exchange during this early stage. Through being prepared to follow up any opening made by the child, a 'real' conversation is set up. In this way, 'conversation' gives the infant a shared frame of reference. The adult realises that the child will interpret her correctly, as her speech is derived from the interaction itself. This reciprocity between caregiver(s) and their children is such that we refer to the child as possessing a linguistic system in terms of being able to express and understand a range of meanings before s/he knows any words at all. These early 'conversations' are often initiated by the child. Bruner (1979) uses the example of the game 'Peek-a-Boo' to illustrate this: the game depends upon the child looking the partner directly in the eye for signals at crucial pauses in the play. During these early interactions, the child is said to learn what developmental psychologists call 'intersubjectivity', which is another way of referring to an 'awareness of others' or an 'interpersonal concept'.

More specific to different cultural groups is both what is actually learned and what 'counts' as learning at all. Judy Dunn (1989) provides a neat metaphor for comparing child-rearing in different cultural groups. She claims that all children are given finely tuned tutoring but that the nature of the 'curriculum' is different according to the family's cultural background. We know that from birth, caregivers begin attributing infants with having definite intentions which will be framed within their own experiences and those of their cultural group. At its simplest, a child's cry might be interpreted as 'she's hungry, she wants . . .' or 'she's sad because she can't see her teddy/the TV/her daddy's gone', 'she's tired', etc. In this way, the adult gives a crucially important 'model' of the conventional interpretation of intentions within the culture. Caregivers introduce children to how others interpret their intentions in using particular words on particular occasions. Eventually, this may mean that children unconsciously adopt the caregivers' interpretation of the context and the activity.

These 'deep' interpretations or those which have been worked out between families within a culture may well remain with us throughout life or until we are forced into change through entering a very different culture with new expectations and different interpretations. In his book *The Silent Language*, Edward Hall (1959) refers to ten *primary message systems* of communication which he terms 'the vocabulary of culture'. These are key areas of communication such as interaction, learning, play, temporality, etc. which are likely to be interpreted very differently from one culture to another. The interpretation of 'learning' is important here. Hall's point is that people reared in different cultures learn to learn differently. Cross-cultural studies on the interaction between caregivers and toddlers give us an insight into important aspects of difference. One international team of researchers from the USA, Guatemala, India and Turkey (Rogoff *et al.* 1993) contrasts the ways in which caregivers assist their toddlers in learning different tasks. They note vital similarities across all circumstances:

1. Caregivers collaborate with children in determining the nature of the activities and their responsibility, i.e. they *create bridges* and *structure children's participation*.
2. They work together and, in the process, the children learn to manage new situations under the collaborative structuring of problem-solving attempts.
3. '*Guided participation*' includes both tacit communication and explicit instruction.
4. Children learn about the activities of their community with the support of a system of social partners including peers and a number of caregivers.

Within this overall common framework, the researchers found striking differences in explicitness, intensity of verbal and non-verbal communication and the interaction status of child and adult. Caregivers and toddlers from Salt Lake City, USA, interacted much more through vocalisations than their Guatemalan Mayan counterparts where caregivers spoke much less, but interacted much more through non-verbal communication such as gaze and guiding children's hands. The status of adult and child also differed considerably in the Mayan and Salt Lake City groups. Salt Lake City caregivers participated in their toddlers' play as equals, negotiating meanings using simplified talk and co-operating with the infants to build propositions. However, the children remained largely excluded from the economic functioning of the household. Mayan caregivers, on the other hand, did not play with their infants nor engage with them in playful talk. But infants were integrated into adult activities and ensured a role in the action, even if only as observers. Their asymmetrical role *vis-à-vis* adults enabled them to 'eavesdrop' on activities outside the mother's circle and become powerful informants at home. What the Salt Lake City child learns through careful talk and play with an adult, the Mayan child learns through observation and passive participation.

A unique opportunity may present itself, however, if we later move to a new culture with different message systems. When no longer able to use old 'recipes' to interpret events, the newcomer is freed from 'of-course' assumptions and may be particularly clear-sighted in analysing a different language and a new 'world'. Schutz (1964) refers to such newcomers as 'strangers' whose position in a new country gives them the unique potential of being able to 'place in question nearly everything that seems unquestionable to the members of the approached group' (p. 96).

Early language development: scaffolding and modelling

Scaffolding

In every culture, caregivers of whatever age support children's early language learning. The type of support they give is often referred to as '*scaffolding*'. This is a useful metaphor as it reveals precisely the way in which assistance can be gradually removed as the child gains competence in a task. 'Scaffolding' is an important term which we shall return to later (Chapters 4 and 5) in relation to the teacher's task in school. The type of 'scaffolding' given will be different across cultures according to how 'learning' and 'interaction' are perceived. The western approach is to *extend* a child's utterance, to *question* and to *model* appropriate speech. At different stages in children's language development, this will look as follows:

Stage 1: the holophrastic (one word) stage

Here the child first understands that meaning can be expressed in a word, e.g. 'doggie' = particular dog > all dogs > dog.

The following incident took place recently on a crowded No. 73 bus in Oxford Street, central London. An infant of about fifteen months sits with obviously adoring parents on the seat nearest the conductor. The child is holding a book open with a picture of a bus which he shows the harrassed conductor, mumbling something which could be 'bus'. The conductor at first ignores him, but when the parents say 'He's showing you his bus. He wants you to talk to him about it', the conductor eventually repeats 'Bus'. Other passengers who get on and stand close by are more forthcoming. 'Yes, it's a big bus,' says one. 'What a lovely bus,' says a second. 'You have got a nice bus,' says a third. The parents and their infant smile contentedly.

Stage 2: the 2-word stage (around 2 years)

vocative (child): Oh, look!
question (adult): What's that?
label (child): Fishy.
confirms (adult): It's a fish. That's right!

The adult's question is embedded in the child's attempts to complete a new task (naming the fish); the question implicitly models an appropriate structure of narrative (What's that?); after the child's response the parent directly models the appropriate form (It's a —). In this way, the adult 'frames' the interaction, keeping the child's attention on the task and finally provides an evaluative feedback. The form and content of the question as well as the nature of the feedback are just about the level the child can understand.

Stage 3: 'telegraphic speech' (usually between 2 and 3 years)

K (child): Mummy sock dirty.
Mummy: Yes. They're all dirty.
K: Mummy sock.
Mummy: There.
K: Mummy sock.
Mummy: That's not mummy's sock. That's your sock. There.
K: Kathryn sock.

Although the adult is said to 'scaffold' unconsciously, the pattern is unchanging and the repetitive tutoring quite explicit. Bruner (1986) refers to this assistance as a 'loan of consciousness' which the adult freely offers and the child has the confidence to 'borrow'.

Modelling

Another type of assistance given by adults is 'modelling' for the child. Alan Luke (1993b) provides us with an example of an Australian middle-class mother talking with her two-year-old child while standing in line in a restaurant:

> *'We're in a long line, Jason, Aren't we? There are lots of people lined up here, waiting for a drink. Look (pointing) they're carrying a Christmas tree with lots of things on it. They're moving it. Do we have a tree like that?'*

The child did not answer during the 20–30 second monologue by the mother. Linguistically, we see how the mother is providing the child with a number of quite complex structures: two different ways of constructing questions (Do we . . .? Aren't we . . .?); the present continuous tense (waiting, carrying, etc.); various prepositions (in, on, up, for). In addition, Luke maintains that the mother is 'situating' the child in the culture through talk, that is, she is naming salient objects (Christmas tree) and foregrounding reasons, norms and ethics for actions (e.g. 'why' we line up, how to move things, what 'we' have). So we see that, with adult help, children learn to 'situate' themselves in different contexts long before learning to read in school.

Cultural variations

These ways of 'tutoring' are probably taken for granted by many of us. Nevertheless, although 'scaffolding' will be carried out by caregivers from all cultures, it will follow a different pattern from one cultural group to another. Longitudinal work by Shirley Brice Heath gives us detailed information on the language tutoring given by the caregivers of different cultural groups living in the USA. In her book *Ways with Words* (1983), she traces the child-rearing practices of three groups (black working-class, white working-class and white middle-class from the larger town whom she refers to as 'mainstream') living within close proximity in the Appalachian mountains. Heath's study shows how even groups speaking the same language socialise their infants into using words differently.

Heath traces the way in which the language learning process is quite different for her 'Trackton' infants (the name given to the black working-class group in her study) and those from Roadville (the white working-class group). Roadville infants receive very explicit tutoring of names. Here is two-year-old Sally being taught by her aunt:

> *When Sally was just a little over two years old . . . Aunt Sue was peeling tomatoes . . . She was trying to get Sally to say* tomato, *but each time Aunt Sue asked 'What is that?' and pointed to the tomato, Sally would answer 'red'. Aunt Sue kept insisting 'Yes, it's red, but it's a* tomato.' *'You like* tomatoes, *don't you?' Repeatedly, parents reject children's descriptions of things by their attributes before they have learned to respond with the name of the item. When adults misunderstand or mishear a child's statement, they ask for clarification most frequently by saying 'A what?' 'You want a what?' requesting a noun*

or a noun phrase rather than a repetition of the entire statement or another part of the sentence. Children are expected to learn through incrementally acquiring knowledge which includes names, attributes, phrases and stories.

(p. 141)

The experiences of a Trackton infant are very different. Rather than participating in topic-centred question/answer routines or direct labelling activities, children between twelve and twenty-four months learn rather through repetition, repetition with variation and finally participation. Lem's progress, therefore, looks like this:

> *Lillie Mae: 'n she be goin' down dere 'bout every week, but I don't believe dey/: got no jobs =*
> *Lem: = got no jobs:/ (Lem at 16 months)*

This pattern of repetition is continued throughout the adults' conversation. By twenty months, Lem participates in the following way:

> *Lem . . . was playing on the porch while his mother and several other women were talking. He had been repeating and varying the ends of her utterances, when suddenly he stopped his play and went to his mother, pulling and tugging at her jeans: 'Wanna pop, wanna pop, bump, bump, bump.' His mother looked at him and said 'Stop it, Lem, you wanna, wanna, wanna, you ain't gettin' nut'n, Darett ain't home. Go ask Miz Lula.'*
> *(p. 94)*

In contrast with the Roadville children, Lem is not the centre of attention, nor is he being explicitly tutored into labelling objects or events. Instead, he enters into the conversation on equal terms; his mother attends to the message itself rather than the language used to express it – even if she does misinterpret it (she overhears the word 'pop' and focuses on the 'bumping' Lem received from Darett the night before). The examples of Lem, Jason, Sally and Kathryn will begin to help the reader understand strategies used by young emergent bilinguals later in this chapter and throughout the book.

We do not yet have such detailed comparative studies on early language socialisation in families from different cultural backgrounds living in Britain, but Heath's work teaches us to observe all our children carefully as they first step into the classroom. Do they find it difficult to ask questions even if we think they know the words to use? If so, why might this be? Do we need to assist emergent bilinguals in 'situating' themselves in a whole new context, of which the language is only a part? Chapter 4 will illustrate one way of doing this with very young children. Heath's own findings led to in-service programmes where teachers first became aware of the resources their children had to offer and then went on to devise early language and literacy programmes which built upon these existing strengths.

Learning appropriate 'recipes': language socialisation in cross-cultural context

'Mamma and daddy just talked to me and made me talk to them. They'd ask me questions; it was then that I began to learn how to talk to other folks. They'd uh, ask me over

and over again, to tell my aunts and uncles things, and I'd know they wanted me to say it right. They taught us children to be polite, too, to talk right when other folks were around. Mamma would always say: "What do you say?" "Did you forget your manners?" If I didn't say something when I was supposed to, they'd fuss at me for not acting *right, not* doing right *by other folks. Saying "I'm sorry," "excuse me" and "thank you" were important, showed the kind of person you were. If you couldn't learn to say the right things, seems like they thought you couldn't do nothing right.'*

(Heath 1983, p. 142)

All children – given normal neurological and physiological functioning, and interaction with other humans – will learn to use oral language appropriately in their own speech community. Before starting school, they will already be able to use many acceptable verbal 'recipes' (more formally referred to as 'speech genres' by Bakhtin 1986) during different cultural routines of typical situations. Examples of such 'recipes' spring to mind from different countries in Europe. Think, again, of meal-times which are preceded by the politeness recipe of *Bon Appetit* in France or *Mahlzeit* in Germany (translated literally 'Good appetite' and 'Mealtime' or more freely as 'I hope you enjoy your meal') for which we have no equivalent in English. These recipes are often the most difficult aspects of language for foreigners to learn, perhaps because they call upon knowledge taught to us at a very young age by our elders which we then share implicitly with members of the same culture.

The sociolinguist Dell Hymes (1974) provides the useful term of 'speech events' into which we can slot both recipes and other different types of oral language use needed for particular cultural practices. At first glance, these may seem spontaneous, like, for example, a telephone conversation, ordering in a restaurant, etc. But we need only imagine our situation as a foreigner in a strange country appearing, perhaps, at a wedding or a funeral to realise that our interpretation of the situation (or our own cultural practices of 'weddings' and 'funerals') are no longer valid and we lack the appropriate words. In cases like this, we are, perhaps, most aware of language as an 'event'. Like any other 'event', language events are not random or arbitrary, but rule-governed and structured, following exact protocols and patterns and with definite boundaries.

Cross-cultural studies show us how caregivers undertake quite explicit and conscious tutoring of their infants to make sure that they participate using appropriate language in important cultural practices. Yet in each culture, what was referred to earlier as the 'curriculum' delivered to the child will be very different. 'Speech events' which are likely to be particularly important for the child to feel at home upon entering school are those linked with politeness and disciplining recipes and narrating or storytelling. But what might 'difference' look like?

Politeness and disciplining recipes

Tapes made of 'mainstream' western caregivers in ordinary interaction with young children at home reveal distinct rules of politeness as well as a variety of language structures used in enforcing politeness or disciplining children. One important rule is that children should listen if the caregiver is reading from a book; another is not to interrupt if adults are talking; another is to say 'please', 'thank you' or 'sorry' at certain times. Requests or 'tellings-off' may be encoded by the adult as questions underlying the adult's statement – 'What do you say?', 'What do you think you're doing?', 'Do you mind?' – or indirect statements – 'I'm waiting', 'I'm speaking', etc. We know that both politeness rules and the formulae used to enforce discipline are likely to be different in different cultural groups. The politeness recipes used by Heath's Roadville group might strike a familiar note to teachers in British classrooms:

> *'We grew up with a lot of shoulds in our house. "You oughta do so and so", "You should say 'thank you', 'I'm sorry'." "You should write a thank you note." Uh, I remember whenever I, uh, when I first learned that 'I'm sorry' could take care of most anything . . . We learned to do that at school, too. Most anything you did, if you talked right afterwards . . . you'd be O.K.'*
>
> *(1983, p. 142)*

In a number of cultural groups such recipes will not be at hand. In many Asian cultures it is not customary constantly to say 'thank you' if the person you are speaking to is considered a friend. In the other extreme, a German-speaking child will be taught to reply 'please' or 'you're welcome' (*Bitte!*) immediately after hearing 'Thank you' (*Danke!*) from a conversation partner. 'Sorry' is not used as widely in many cultures as it is in Britain. We see that it will not automatically be easy for our emergent bilinguals to situate themselves in the 'classroom manners' of reading. Picture Tony who has just started British school. Tony's family originates from Hong Kong. For the first few weeks at school he is so quiet. His teacher constantly tries to get him to play in the home corner with others, to talk, play, make a noise and move about. One day, at story-time, he starts clicking his fingers while she is reading. She stops and says quietly 'We're just waiting for Tony'. It takes Tony some time before he understands that his actions are inappropriate in this context. Should he have known? It seems that politeness is very much a cultural matter.

Narrating and story-telling

Narrating itself is a universal experience, beginning with the human urge to tell about an event, person or feeling. It may be 'the oldest and most basic human-language activity. Someone telling someone else that something happened . . . Basic narrative is preoccupied with holding on to occurrences by telling about them, thus creating sequences of events ordered in time' (Whitehead 1990, p. 97). However, we know from studies in homes and classrooms that the idea of 'story' calls up different meanings for children from different cultural back-grounds. Difference concerns both the *purpose* for which a story is used and the *manner* in which it is told. Roadville (white working-class) children in Heath's study are brought up with the tradition that stories must be factual and must have a moral which highlights the weakness admitted in the tale; stories, then, are similar to testimonials given at their prayer-meetings. Trackton (black working-class) children grow up with quite different traditions. Their stories start with a kernel of truth, but aim then to rivet the interest of their audience, even if this means massaging the facts. Mainstreamers (white middle-class) children see story differently again. They learn that 'telling a story' means relating a story from a book; even indirect story items (for example, pictures of Humpty Dumpty on wallpaper) may well be linked with both the rhyme and the book.

The manner of narrating may also differ according to the type of stories children are accustomed to. In her study of the different participation of white and black American five-year-olds in 'Show-and-Tell' (newstime) classroom sessions, Sarah Michaels (1986) shows how the white children use a 'topic-centred' approach (tightly organised, centred on a single topic and leading quickly to a punch-line) whereas the black children prefer a 'topic-associating' style (series of episodes which are implicitly linked in highlighting a person or theme). Michaels' point is that the teacher implicitly expects all the children to adopt her own 'topic-centred' approach, but never makes her expectations explicit to the black children. The result is that the black children do not understand what is expected of them and simply learn to resent the 'Show-and-Tell' lessons. Like Heath, Michaels shows how the quality of tuition given to young children will depend upon a teacher's knowledge of the resources a child brings to school as well as the ability to make her own expectations explicit. In the second section of this chapter, we shall begin to investigate the variety of resources our emergent bilinguals may bring as they step into the classroom.

Some questions to consider from this section

- How far can we take over the role of 'scaffolding' an emergent bilingual's language in the classroom? Which aspects might be most effective and which will need to be adapted?
- What kinds of strategies for 'peer scaffolding' can we devise?
- How many of our emergent bilinguals already relate to us as responsible caregivers and what might be the implications of this?
- How much do we know of the language 'recipes' in the lives of our pupils and how they might differ from those important in school?
- Which 'recipes' will our emergent bilinguals need to learn in order to be able to 'situate' themselves in the social context of classroom reading?
- How explicit do we make these to all children?

We shall return to these questions in the second part of the book.

II. LITERACY PRACTICES IN HOMES AND COMMUNITIES

We come to every situation with stories; patterns and sequences of childhood experiences which are built into us. Our learning happens within the experience of what important others did.

(Bateson 1979, p. 13)

In this section, I examine the interpretations and experiences of reading in the families of a group of children who are just beginning school. I then ask: how do the children begin to situate themselves in the social context of classroom reading practices? Some of the children talk about reading, others show us how they read outside school. All of the children are emergent bilinguals and all are beginning school in Britain except Nicole who lives in France. In the British classrooms the children have a large variety of attractive books which they may choose to read, both in school and at home. Their teachers encourage the children to enjoy looking at books as soon as they enter school and to take these home to share with their parents. This approach contrasts with the French school, where reading is taught using a single textbook, purchased by everyone. Here the teacher follows a strict order of teaching sounds and blends which the children must then put into words.

As each family talks about home experiences and expectations for school learning, readers might consider the following questions:

- What are the features of the children's reading experiences from home in terms of *purpose*, *material* and *interaction with others* (participation structures)?
- How does each family differ in its interpretation of what 'counts' as reading and what do they share in common?
- In what ways might the teacher benefit from knowing about children's home reading practices and how might she build upon these in the classroom?

Nicole and her family: when you read in French, your lips come out

'Children's books are so expensive. But I think you can always get hold of them cheaply if you want to. When we lived in England, I used to go to the library and get a pile of books they were throwing out. They only cost a few pence each and there was nothing wrong with them.'

(Nicole's mother)

Nicole left England for France with her parents when she was just two. Two years later, they were joined by her grandparents and now they all live together in a comfortable house at the edge of an attractive village in Normandy. Like most French children, Nicole started nursery school at three and at six has now been in the 'real' school for a year. Out of school she plays mostly with a younger girl from a neighbouring English/French family, but she sometimes goes to tea with French children. An only child, most of her time is spent with her family. She watches both English and French TV and videos and is the only child in this group to have access to a computer and a typewriter at home. Her English is excellent, marked by adult turns of expression and vocabulary which sometimes seem strange in a child so young.

Nicole's parents did not benefit from higher education and do not have happy memories of school. Her mother taught herself accountancy skills and was able to gain a good job in England. In France, she runs a 'Bed-and-Breakfast' whenever the custom is there. Nicole's father is partner in a business for medical

Figure 1 Nicole's early reading in her French state school shares much in common with Bengali, Chinese and Arabic community classes in Britain.

journals run from England, but works mostly at home in France. Both are determined to give Nicole the educational opportunities they lacked. Their own French is limited, but they have purchased a variety of dictionaries and grammar books and use them with Nicole. At the same time, they realise that their main role is teaching her skills in English. Nicole has always kept her languages separate. Both parents read Nicole stories almost from birth and then gradually encouraged her to take over the reading. By four she was reading reasonably fluently and by six she happily reads texts appropriate for English ten-year-olds. Both parents and grandparents continue reading with her in English and she benefits from lots of outings and trips abroad.

After a tearful start, Nicole fits happily into her French school. The only native speaker of English in her class, she is 'special' and given extra help to catch up quickly in spoken French. Her mother is invited to give English conversation lessons to small groups of children. Learning to read and write presents no particular problems except the odd occasion when her parents panic that they are unable to help her with her homework.

A somewhat irate voice comes from somewhere under the boiler in the kitchen as Nicole's father tries to complete a repair job: 'No, Nicole, think. It's the future perfect you're supposed to be doing now, not the "imperative".' 'We had to go out and buy a grammar book to learn all these ourselves,' says Nicole's mother. Nevertheless, they know precisely from her exercise-book what her homework will be, that the task will be confined to practice from her reading book and that she will receive regular weekly feedback on her work in French and Maths (which comprise most of the curriculum at the beginning stage).

Nicole herself feels confident in her French reading. She feels that she can 'just read' English but has very definitely been taught to read in French (where she can cite and give examples for most phonic rules as well as use words like 'syllable', 'imperative', 'future continuous', etc. comfortably). Reading in school is very much a 'performance', where children witness what their classmates can achieve. Nicole feels she must 'do well' even when just talking about how she learned to read. In school, everything must be just right or practised until perfect:

'The teacher comes round to us all and you have to go "ü". And if you can't do it she squeezes your cheeks in, like this (demonstrates) until you can.' In a quiet voice, she adds, 'I hate it actually . . .'

Nevertheless, she has already reached a point where she can read thick paper-backs in French bought by her parents, with the aid of a huge Collins dictionary at her side.

The story-reading practice, which has always been part of Nicole's life, has long received attention from a number of researchers. Longitudinal research shows how this is an organised social routine, specifically framed and separated from other events. In their analysis of a story-reading event, Ninio and Bruner (1978) refer to the activity as a 'book-reading cycle' containing systematic rules and patterns of discourse into which caregivers 'tutor' their children. Important-ly, a very early stage of these involves teaching the boundaries between 'literate' and face-to-face encounters through 'lexical labelling'. Snow and Ninio (1986) show how this takes place with a very young infant:

Mother: Look!
R: (Touches picture)
Mother: What are those?
R: (Vocalises a babble string and smiles)
Mother: Yes, they are rabbits
R: (Vocalises, smiles and looks at mother)
Mother: (Laughs) Yes, rabbit.
R: (Vocalises, smiles)
Mother: Yes. (Laughs)

The authors go on to outline how children participating in this practice are taught to subscribe to a 'contract of literacy' which involves: accepting the symbolic nature of books; accepting that books represent an autonomous fictional world; accepting the 'picture reading procedure', i.e. that an appropriate response to a picture is saying the name of the object; accepting the book as leader of the activity and the focus of attention; and accepting that books are to be 'read' not just touched or looked at. Other studies illustrate ways in which the rules of the contract are quite explicitly taught, how the adult 'frames' the event and shows the child what 'belongs' to story-reading and not to conversation.

Gibson (1989) gives the example of a mother with her two-year-old daughter showing how the child (i) echoes phrases, (ii) anticipates and supplies appropriate phrases, especially key words, (iii) listens to the same story over and over again, (iv) 'reads' the pictures as the mother reads the print, and (v) expands the story through the illustrations. Caregivers are shown often to introduce the event by saying 'Let's read' and often refer to the children as 'reading' to emphasise yet further the parameters of the frame. In a study which compares 'mainstream' American early reading behaviour with that of the Athabaskan population they are working with, Scollon and Scollon (1981) describe how their three-year-old daughter marks the boundaries between 'reading' and 'talking' by standing to read and sitting to talk. In addition, she always 'reads' stories from a book rather than 'telling' them. This means 'talking like a book' with a different intonation and style and trying to create language characteristic for written text.

Nicole's parents feel that they are 'doing the right thing' by reading her stories and are satisfied that she has learned to read in English so well. But they are aware that what 'counts' as reading for a five-year-old in a French school is something quite different; namely, knowing sounds, blends, grammar and rules. Nevertheless, they have no worries. Nicole seems happy and they feel informed about what is expected of her and of themselves. Every day Nicole writes down what she must do for homework. The family tackle the tasks together; Nicole often provides expert knowledge of French and her parents the conceptual knowledge of the task. So far, all seem to cope admirably. For our next child, Tony, the situation is a very different one.

Tony and his family: the talismanic value of the book

When Tony does not want to take books home, Mrs G. (his teacher) visits the family taking an attractive dual language picture book which she hopes to leave them to read with Tony. She is surprised by the frosty reception she meets from his grandfather:

'Tony can't have this book yet. You must keep it and give it to him later.'
'But why?'
'Because he can't read the words. First he must learn to read the words, then he can have the book.'

Tony's grandfather pulls out an exercise-book from under the counter and shows it to the teacher. A number of pages have been filled with rows of immaculate ideographs. His grandfather says proudly that Tony has completed these at his Chinese Saturday school.

With a sceptical look at the teacher, he pulls out a screwed-up piece of paper. On one side was a shop advertisement from which it had been recycled. On the other was a drawing of a transformer. Tony's grandfather:

'This is from his English school. This is rubbish.'

Pointing to the corner where 'ToNy' is written, he says,

'Look. He can't even write his name yet!'

(Gregory and Biarnès 1994, p. 21)

Tony's grandparents crossed from China to Hong Kong before they moved with his parents to Northampton, Britain, ten years ago. His family now has a 'Take-Away' above which they live. His mother and grandmother speak little English, but nod agreement as his father and grandfather discuss Tony's progress. Tony's family remember learning to read as a difficult experience involving physical punishment if they failed to recite or repeat a word correctly. They look back to their own schooling in Hong Kong and China which presented them with a definite set of rules. These rules maintained a dichotomy between work and play together with a belief in the authority of the teacher and the strict enforcement of obedience if need be. In practical terms, the rules meant that children sat in rows and learned by recitation. There was no choice of activity and they would receive homework from the very start as results would determine which kind of secondary school could be attended. There would be no talk to other children or to the teacher unless requested. The authority of the teacher also enforced duties on her part. It was seen to be the teacher's duty to 'teach' the children, telling them explicitly what they should or should not do.

Tony's father and grandfather repeat these rules in their expectations as Tony enters school. They are anxious that pressure should be put upon their child to learn to read and write and to be obedient, through force if necessary. The concept of 'wanting to learn' does not enter this frame. To support literacy learning in Mandarin, Tony is to start his Chinese and English schools simultaneously. His parents foresee no difficulty in learning to read and write in both languages and his father appears keen to supervise the homework he assumes he will receive from both schools.

Literacy has traditionally been held in the greatest respect in the Chinese culture and China has been claimed as the first highly literate society in the world where a small group of 'litterati' or literates wielded immeasurable power in society. This tradition of respect is reflected today in the existence of a special 'educated' or 'beautiful' script alongside the everyday script. Mastery of the 'beautiful' script needs years of concentration and hard work. It is so special that children relate it to a folk tale 'The Chicken with Golden Eggs' (The Golden Goose). Attempting to rush the learning of this script will only spoil it. It is so complex that Chinese students will spend the first year of their Language and Literature degree learning to perfect it.

Although only the highly educated will aspire to mastering the 'beautiful' script, it serves as an example of what may finally be achieved through personal application and hard work. This need for application applies equally to the

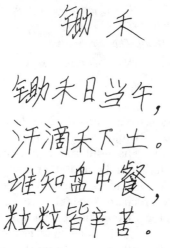

Figure 2　A famous poem learned at home by many young children whose family origins are from China. Tony was six when his grandfather taught him to write this. Translation:

> <u>*Working in the rice-fields*</u>
>
> *Having worked in the rice-fields all morning,*
> *My sweat has fallen onto the fields*
> *Now I have got to know all the rice on my plate*
> *Every grain is the result of my hard work*

essential beginning stages of literacy. Tony's family and his Chinese school teacher explain how Tony has been given an exercise book where he must divide the page into columns and practise ideographs over and over again until they are perfect (see Figure 2). This attention to detail is particularly important, for the misplacing or omission of a single stroke will completely alter the meaning of the symbol. At each lesson, Tony learns to read by reciting individual words after the teacher in chorus with the other children. Examining the appearance of the symbol is particularly important, for a number of ideographs are pictorial. Learning is based on first understanding the meaning of the word and learning how to pronounce it correctly in both Cantonese and Mandarin. This is followed by repetition, memorisation and careful copying. After copying, the child will be taught how to use the word in different sentences. Tasks at school are carefully and clearly delineated and confined in scope.

The completed exercise-book is important to Tony's family, for a number of these bear witness to a child's achievements and proficiency. Only when a child can prove this competence is he or she given a book to read. To have immediate access to books devalues both the book and the principle of hard work. Children must work their way towards knowledge step-by-step and the book is a reward for a child's conscientious achievements. A love of books, therefore, comes after reading is learned and not as a necessary prerequisite to it. For Tony's family, books have a talismanic value and the few family books which the family own are placed well out of the children's reach. In contrast to the high status and respect accorded to the Mandarin script, English literacy is viewed as primarily functional in nature. However, they are very aware of the importance of English literacy for business, which for them means the running of the 'Take-Away' which they hope Tony might later extend. English literacy for Tony's family is seen as a means to opening doors upon which their financial security might depend.

Tony enters school smiling at four years ten months. During his first few weeks in school, he appears the picture of enthusiasm. Every morning, he leaves his father or grandfather eagerly and rushes to the 'name table' where he quickly finds his name. This task accomplished, he often chooses to draw. Tony draws methodically and his drawings are usually immaculate copies of the covers of books. The detail of both the illustration and print are exact to the dot over the 'i'; nothing is omitted. *Meg and Mog* covers appear to be his favourites. During class discussions in the first few weeks, Tony concentrates intensely, watching the other children and always putting his hand up when he hears the words 'Put your hand up' said by the teacher. One morning, Tony comes proudly carrying a plastic bag with Mandarin script on it, which is shown to the class. During this early period he often amuses the teacher by his constant 'What's that?' questions, reminding her of a much younger English child.

Tony is not drawn to the book corner which displays a wide collection of attractive picture books. He is also inattentive during lessons where the teacher reads aloud and asks the children to join in. Only one reading lesson seemed to catch his interest. Children were invited to bring print from home which they then read to the class. As another child's newspaper was held up, he suddenly called from the back 'Princess!' Not understanding at first, the teacher looked and suddenly realised, 'Oh yes, it's the Queen'. To this, Tony replied, 'She in Hong Kong. I see in the television.'

Tony's eye for detail, his disciplined and structured approach to reading learned from his Chinese school, shares much in common with an experimental day nursery in Beijing. The account below is from a group of Swedish Early Years educators who visited the school in the 1980s:

> *The children are four years old. They are learning the symbols for maternal grandfather and grandmother, younger sister, child, elder brother, mother, father. The teacher puts up two of the characters on the flannelgraph and one child at a time goes forward and chooses the pictures which fit with them and puts them beneath the right character. The children are deeply involved and are eager to have a turn. The teacher mixes the characters and makes the task more difficult. She puts up four characters, and the children cope splendidly. The teacher encourages the children to call out 'right' when it is correct . . . Now the teacher removes the pictures and characters, and takes out a character for the colour green. Alongside the character, she puts a piece of green paper. The children are now to say a sentence including the word green . . . The children say long, complicated sentences about the spring greenery and differentiate what they say by using light green and dark green . . . One boy makes a mistake . . . (and) the teacher . . . goes into the difference between dark green and light green.*
>
> *(Liljestrom et al. 1982, p. 77)*

After Tony's initial enthusiasm for school, his teacher feels that she has 'lost' him. Tony does not appear to enjoy speaking English, reading books or school in general. After a few months she sees his continual question 'What's that?' as part of his 'collection fetish' to 'possess words for their own sake'. Tony does not seem able to choose an activity and wanders aimlessly around the classroom. He does not mix with other children and is unable to play. Tony's teacher encourages the children to experiment with writing but he appears to want only to copy print exactly. Nor does he want to take work home to his parents. Tony's behaviour grows increasingly poor. His teacher puts Tony's problems largely down to his family's lack of encouragement or interest in his work.

Nazma and her family: realising how to behave in society

'The children come home and talk about school and show their pictures. The teachers know what they are doing . . . Of course, they will learn to read in English the way they learn in Arabic and Bengali.'

(Nazma's mother)

Nazma's mother was widowed a year ago when her husband went on holiday to Bangladesh and caught an unknown stomach complaint. Nazma was just four and her younger brother a baby at the time. A year later Nazma, her mother and four brothers and sisters live in a large attractive council house in Spitalfields, London.

Nazma's mother speaks almost no English and relies on her children for interpreting on the rare occasion she might need it. She relates with enthusiasm her own memories of school in Sylhet, Bangladesh which she attended until completion of Grade 5 (age eleven). Here she recalls learning to read:

'Of course, I learned the alphabet before going on to read and write. You must do this, otherwise how can you learn? I learned with chalk and a stone slate, practising letters I was unsure of. When we became neater, we were allowed to use a pencil . . . I enjoyed school but I couldn't go on to High School as there wasn't one in the district . . .'

Now she claims to find time only for letter writing and reading the odd leaflet which she finds in her letter box. Her daughter fills out any necessary forms. No children's books or toys are apparent and Nazma's two-year-old brother is playing with a screwdriver on the floor when we arrive. However, upon mentioning reading, she opens a high cupboard (well out of the baby's reach) and reaches down the children's Bengali exercise-books and reading primers and proudly shows their writing (see Figure 3). She explains where each child is up to in the book and speaks confidently about the importance of learning to read:

'Children need to learn to read and write to become good people. With education it's possible to become independent, to become someone, to get a good job anywhere. I pay £7.50 a week for their Arabic and Bengali instruction because they need this to realise how to behave in our society . . . I hope my children will be able to work in an office or maybe as a doctor, but only if they feel like it.'

Nazma attends her Bengali class for two hours on Mondays and Tuesdays and Arabic class for two hours from Wednesday to Saturday. Her Bengali class takes

Figure 3   A writing exercise: one of the first pages of Nazma's Bengali reading book.

place in a neighbour's home with a teacher who has recently arrived from Sylhet. On this occasion, eight children are present, of which Nazma is the youngest. The children sit on the floor, all quietly practising different pages of their book. The lesson lasts two hours without a break but the children make no sign of restlessness. Nazma occasionally glances at the older children but mostly focuses on her own book. She points to each word as she says it, returning to the beginning of each page after reaching the end. Finally, it is her turn to be called up for tuition and testing. The pattern of 'Demonstration/Practice/Test' will be repeated in a number of lessons with different children:

Teacher: 'K, KO, GO.'
Nazma: (repeats)

Teacher: 'Go on, read it.'
Nazma: (mutters quietly)
Teacher: 'Read it loudly.'
Nazma: (quietly says the alphabet)
Teacher: 'Say it again.'
Nazma: (repeats the letters)
Teacher: 'Not like that, like this.' (stresses the different inflections of the letters)
  'What, what did you say?'
Nazma: (quietly repeats)
Teacher: 'Good. What next?'
Nazma: (continues)
Teacher: 'Which one is "Dho"?'
Nazma: 'This one.'
Teacher: 'Then carry on. No, say it like this "Pho".'
Nazma: (repeats)
(Nazma continues reading, receiving an occasional murmur of approval until it is the next child's turn.)

Nazma's entry into the English school is not an easy one. She appears fidgety, tearful and sulky when she is not the centre of attention. During the 'quiet reading' time at the beginning of each day when children choose a book to 'read', she flicks through pages impatiently and changes her book frequently. Like Tony, she finds free writing hard and sometimes writes Arabic script from right to left on her page. She insists upon using a rubber constantly and finds it impossible to sit at her work for longer than two minutes at a time. One approach to reading, however, rivets her attention. Her teacher uses a puppet who introduces separate words on card which the children make into sentences. Nazma has a remarkable memory, reads both words and sentences she has seen only once and manages to extend her concentration until the task is complete. One day, she speaks (in Sylheti) about school reading:

Nasima: Do you like reading in school?
Nazma: Which school?
Nasima: This school. (English)
Nazma: Yes.
Nasima: Why do you like it?
Nazma: Because we do 'work'. (uses the word for manual activity)
Nasima: What work do you do?
Nazma: Um, I don't know.
Nasima: What work do you do in the Bengali school?
Nazma: We read . . . and write.
Nasima: What do you read and write about?
Nazma: Everything, we read all kinds of things.
Nasima: What do you do at mosque class?
Nazma: We read . . . we learn prayers.
Nasima: Which school do you like best?
Nazma: This . . . English school.
Nasima: Why?
Nazma: Because of story.
Nasima: Which story?
Nazma: Anyone . . . I like to hear.
Nasima: How do you like hearing, by reading or listening to teacher?
Nazma: Teacher.

Shabbir and his family: 'You've learned what this country has provided as I have from mine'

'When I receive official letters, like those from the Council, I have to take them to the school because I can't read them. I want my son to be free of all that.'

(Shabbir's father)

Shabbir lives with his parents and a younger brother and sister at the top of a Victorian block of flats in Spitalfields, London. The flat is too small for their growing family. Shabbir's father is a tailor, but is frequently at home owing to a heart complaint which also makes it difficult for him to climb the stairs to the fourth floor. Shabbir's mother left school in Sylhet at the end of Grade 5 (age eleven) as her parents thought that it was only important to know how to write her name and behave well. The High School was also further away and her parents thought that her reputation would be spoiled by walking the two miles daily past a market. She was disappointed not to continue studying:

'Work you can do at any time in your life, but studying is an opportunity that isn't with you for very long. Now is the time when the child's mouth is light (receptive to every-thing). Later, it will become heavy. As the years go on, he will settle down and have a family and then he will have to think of his children.'

Although the parents' own reading is now limited to the occasional newspaper, they pay for Shabbir to attend Bengali classes six times a week. His mother proudly pulls down a new satchel containing carefully covered books and a new pencil-case from a similar high cupboard to that in Nazma's house. By comparison, practice in English is very brief:

'He often brings home his reading book, but when he doesn't know a word, I tell him to ask the teacher . . . Look, he has more sense than I do (said laughing as he corrects an English word his mother has read) . . Let's leave it, leave it to the teacher, who can help the child more, because it's too hard for us.'

Shabbir is quiet and timid at school. Experimenting seems alien to his character and he becomes distressed unless he understands exactly what is expected of him. He likes his writing and drawings to be meticulous; this means that he is extremely slow and rarely manages to finish anything. Like Nazma, he has an excellent memory for recalling individual words. His good behaviour, enthu-siasm and generosity in helping others make him popular yet inconspicuous as he goes about learning to read.

Sabina and Shahina and their family: 'Learning to read is a gradual process, like learning to eat rice'

Father: We taught them the alphabet, then word formation as far as possible. Then they started school, so the teacher will take over.
Nasima: Is that how you think the teacher will teach?
Father: Well, yes, that's how we learned in school, so why should it be any different? And if it is, we have no complaints because we believe the teacher has enough knowledge about the methods used.

At five, the twins are the youngest of five children. The whole family live in a comfortable and immaculate house in Spitalfields. Their parents are loathe to speak of their own education, but keen to stress that some of their relatives in Bangladesh hold degrees. Both parents are at home; the father was a machine operator but is now unable to work owing to chronic ill-health. At present, they regularly buy a Bengali newspaper and Mrs Ali occasionally reads novels. They have no hesitation in stressing the need to learn to read in English:

> 'Our children need to learn to read and write in English to have a good life and obtain a well-paid, professional job. They need skills to be independent and to have a good life once we have departed.'

> (And in Bengali?) 'By becoming educated our children will be able to pass on their knowledge to future generations.'

The children have private tuition for Bengali and Arabic. A qualified Bengali teacher, who also works as a nursery assistant at a local school, comes twice a week from 5.00 p.m. to 7.00 p.m. to teach all the children together. Four other evenings are spent at a larger Arabic class. We meet the children in a typical lesson around a large table in the living-room, while their parents sit on the sofa and listen:

> The lesson begins with a spelling test for all. The older children have about 50 spellings; the twins only 20. While the teacher is correcting the older children's work, the twins practise their reading homework. (See Figure 4.) They recite the text below in unison; their reading swift, precise and fluent. They then learn the next piece (in Bengali it rhymes). Again, we see the same pattern as in Nazma's lesson:

> Teacher: 'In mother's hand there is milky rice pudding.'
> Twins: (repeat the text)
> Teacher: 'Bella, go and put the ducks and chickens in the house.'
> Twins: (repeat)
> Teacher: 'Give grandmother her medicine.'
> Twins: (repeat)

> This continues until the page is finished. The twins then practise the text in unison for the rest of the hour while the older children are questioned on the meaning of the passages they read. The teacher later explains that she will first teach the vowels, then the conso-nants, then word/picture recognition and finally read a continuous text with the children. The twins have only been learning for three months and are progressing extremely well.

After the lesson, the rest of the evening will be spent resting and reading to-gether from the English book they may have taken home.

At school, the twins are stars amongst their 100 per cent emergent bilingual classmates. Like Nazma and Shabbir, they like their work to be immaculate and become upset if they cannot correct an error. Their reading is not as fluent as in Bengali, but it is evident that they have received help at home. If faced with an unknown book, they remain silent until they have been told the words and try to take the book home to practise. Their perfect behaviour and immaculate dress make them into 'model' pupils for their teacher who holds them up to others to emulate.

সন্ধ্যাবেলা কে কি কর ? আব্ আর আন্ কি করছে ? দাদীর কি হয়েছে ?
ছড়াটি সবাই এক সঙ্গে বল।

বেলা গেল।
হাঁস মুরগী ঘরে তোল।
দাদীকে ঔষধ দাও।

মামীর হাতের দুধভাত
খেতে বেজায় মিঠে।
ঘরে আছে ভাপা পুলি
পাটিসাপটা পিঠে।

আমার বই ১৯

Figure 4   The page Shahina and Sabina are reading in their Bengali book.

Louthfur and his family: 'Those who have studied have a separate wisdom'

'The teacher tells me that Louthfur is slow and very naughty. He still has the devil in him, but this will be rectified as he grows older.'

(*Louthfur's mother*)

At five, Louthfur is the eldest of three children. The family live in a cramped flat around the corner from Shabbir. His mother remembers in detail her own school days in Bangladesh.

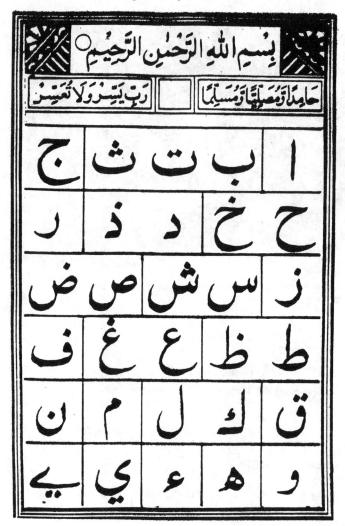

Figure 5 During their first year at mosque school, where reading is in classical Arabic, children are expected to proceed from reading individual symbols to joined up script (as shown at the top of the page).

> *'The teacher would show us how to write letters and make sounds. We also had a private tutor and he would guide our hand with his to help our handwriting. In Class 1, we learned the alphabet and the sounds and then we were tested. In Class 2, we learned to make words and memorised them. Then we started writing independently. After learning the basic principles, you can learn things easily.'*

She finished school at sixteen in order to come to England as a bride. Louthfur's father was already in England, where he was educated. He now deals with filling out all the necessary forms, etc., although as a mini-cab driver he is mostly away from home. She, herself, finds time only to read the occasional newspaper. Louthfur occasionally brings home English books, but she feels unable to help him. In contrast, she sits correcting him as he practises from his Bengali primer. Her ideas on the need to learn to read are very definite:

> '*If you can't read, you can't interact with society and you will have no respect for yourself because others can't respect you. Those who have studied have a separate wisdom; you can see the difference between those who have and those who haven't.*' '*What do you mean by "a separate widsom"?*' '*To have a separate wisdom means you aren't tied to the kitchen sink!*'

Louthfur attends both Bengali and Arabic school, but started Bengali school at six, a year later than most of his class-mates. Below is a typical Arabic lesson after he has been learning for seven to eight months (see also Figure 5):

> *The class takes place in a neighbour's front room. About thirty children of all ages including Louthfur line the walls like a human square, seated with their* raiel *(a beautifully carved wooden stand upon which to place the Qur'ān or the initial primers) in front of them. There is a loud hum as they all chant their individual practice piece. Their elderly teacher whom the children affectionately call 'nanna' (grandfather) holds a bamboo cane which he uses only lightly as if symbolically. 'These children need discipline, or they will climb the sky!' Occasionally, Louthfur also receives a tap for talking. Nevertheless, he has already covered the basic sounds of Arabic and will have been tested on them. Like many of the children, he rocks to and fro to the sound of the voices. Children do this because they are encouraged to develop a harmonious voice; they are told Allah listens to His servants and is pleased if time it taken to make the verse sound meaningful. The old man's wife takes children who have already started the Qur'ān into a separate room, so she can hear the recitations clearly. She comments, 'English is very important for this life. But Arabic is required for the life hereafter which is eternal! Therefore, it must be given greatest importance . . Or else, how can our children know?'*

Louthfur has always had considerable difficulties in his English classroom. He appears hyperactive and has great difficulty in concentrating. He displays no interest in books or reading and, after two years in school, his English is extremely limited. The only object which holds his attention for a few minutes is the computer, where he appears momentarily spellbound. However, even this interest disappears after about five minutes and he gets up with the words 'Me no want play computer!'

THE SENSE AND MEANING OF READING: TEACHERS' AND FAMILIES' LEARNING

> *One of the most effective ways to learn about oneself is by taking seriously the culture of others.*
>
> (Hall 1959, p. 54)

At a recent in-service course on reading in the multilingual classroom, a group of teachers were asked quickly to jot down an answer to the question 'What is reading?' When the responses were shared out amongst the group for discussion, it was found that almost every definition contained the word 'meaning'. When questioned about what they meant exactly by writing 'gaining meaning', most teachers said 'having pleasure', 'enjoyment' or 'fun'. Interestingly, teachers found it impossible to separate what reading *is* from what reading *does* for the reader and what is *needed* to begin to learn to read. Within our Vygotskian framework, their own 'sense' of reading involved the notion of pleasure from the very start of learning to read. If we return to the Qur'ān story opening this chapter, it is easy to see how it is but one step away to assume that 'gaining meaning from reading' must necessarily equate with 'fun' or 'pleasure' for everyone and from the very start of learning to read.

If we return to examine the *purpose* of reading in the lives of our families above, we find that *immediate* fun does not figure highly. Only Nicole's family wants her to read simply for fun. She has a variety of annuals and other story books in French and English and having a new story read by her parents or grandparents is a treat. Of course, it is important to remember that the fun accompanies quite explicit tuition from her parents (constantly reading to her, then asking her to recognise the words). But reading also serves other important purposes in the life of her family. Her father sits for most of the day at his computer, he sends and receives faxes, they have important mail, etc. Nicole's mother studies recipe books in English and specialist magazines for buying and selling in French. Nicole has been bathed in print since she was born.

The concept of reading simply for fun is unfamiliar to our other families. Indeed, they have little time for leisure. Tony's family works all hours in the 'Take-Away'. The other women spend most of their time cleaning, cooking and looking after young children. A sewing machine often has a prominent place in their home. The men spend time at the mosque and are often responsible for shopping. If leisure time is found, it is often spent watching a Hindi video. Nevertheless, all live in a print-filled environment. Like Nicole's parents, the other families see reading in the new language largely as functional in purpose. Visiting the bank or post office, reading tax or benefit forms or bills, etc. are all vital for everyday survival. The families speak of 'getting a good job', 'gaining independence' or 'becoming someone'. In contrast, reading in the first language is seen as important in terms of membership of a culture of origin, of belonging. When Nicole's mother is asked which language she thinks Nicole prefers to read in, she replies 'English, I should think. Well, its *her* language, isn't it?' Nicole sees it differently: 'I suppose I prefer French, because it's easier.' Learning to read in Arabic has yet a different purpose, summed up by Louthfur's teachers as 'Arabic is required for the life hereafter which is eternal.'

All of the families view reading as a future investment. Pleasure and satisfaction are seen as the result of hard work and do not belong to the beginning stage of learning to read. This is particularly strong in Tony's family whose reaction against the picture-books sent home was so difficult for his English teacher to understand. All the parents are aware of the important role likely to be played by their children as '*brokers*' or mediators of the new language and culture and so far are happy for this to take place. Nicole's French has already outstripped that of her parents in terms of vocabulary and accent. She is able to explain words to her parents before they can help with her homework and put labels to (what seem to her parents) weird and wonderful dishes served up for lunch at school. Shabbir is also able to correct his mother as she helps him. Tony's family may be upset precisely because they would like Tony to help them and fear that he cannot.

All the children are introduced to very different reading *materials* at home and in school. Only the English schools possess a wealth of attractive picture books. At Chinese school, Tony learns largely from the blackboard or flash cards, although in some schools children have a thick textbook; at Bengali and mosque school, the children have flimsy 'primers' often in black and white and on poor paper; in France, Nicole has a thick textbook containing short texts followed by exercises. It is important to realise that the purpose of these is only as a preliminary for the investment of the 'real' book. The Qur'ān itself is a beautifully embossed book and Bangladesh is famous for its poetry sold in hardbacks in the numerous bookshops in the Spitalfields area. In the French, Bengali and Chinese schools writing is practised from the start in lined exercise-books and never on blank sheets of paper.

In her longitudinal study of a group of parents reading school books at home with their children in Coventry, Britain, Hilary Minns (1990) comments on the *pattern of interaction* between five-year-old Gurpreet and her father, whose family origins are in the Punjab. Her father reads the text word-for-word with his child. She contrasts this approach with that of the child's teacher in school who encourages the child to discuss the meaning of the text rather than read each word accurately. Minns questions why the father goes about reading in this way. She suggests that he is interpreting the task required of him by the teacher in terms of a formal reading practice he is familiar with; that of listening to the reading of the Holy Book in the temple.

This may be the case. But we have examples from cross-cultural studies to show that a similar pattern of interaction is by no means unusual. Notice how this ten-year-old Athabaskan child sits with her two-year-old sister 'teaching' her to read:

Older sister: 'because'
Younger sister: 'because'

This single word method continues throughout the book. The Scollons (1981) describe the ten-year-old's amazement as she tries to tutor their own daughter who is accustomed to story-reading with her parents:

Older sister: 'because'
Rachel: 'because a goat might eat it for supper'
Older sister: 'the whole thing!'

The teaching in Nicole's school is very similar to that in the Bengali, mosque and Chinese classes. The pattern is explicit and comprises: 'Demonstration, Repetition, Practice, Test'. In contrast to the Bengali and mosque classes where teaching mostly takes place individually, Nicole's teacher has the whole class together and the atmosphere is very competitive. But it is important to remember that understanding plays an important role in learning to read in all these classes. The children in the French, Bengali and Chinese schools are first taught to understand the meaning of the word before they learn to pronounce it accurately and then read it. Meaning, then, proceeds from the word to the text. After they have practised writing the word accurately, they will go on to use it appropriately in sentences. Questions on the task in hand are encouraged and, although discipline is strict, a friendly atmosphere prevails. Learning the Arabic script is different. Children learn the rules of decoding the sounds of the language without first understanding the meaning of the words which will first be mediated through the priest and only attained on an individual level through lengthy study. Questioning the content of study by young children would obviously be inappropriate.

Of all the children in the group, Nicole finds it easiest to 'situate' herself in the social context of reading during her first formal year in school. Undoubtedly, she has many advantages from which the other children cannot possibly benefit. She is a white European child from a neighbouring country where both language and cultural 'recipes' share much in common; both languages use a Roman script which means that reading a new language is much easier for her parents; she is entering school with a high status language which everyone wants to learn; she is the only non-native speaker in her class; her parents can afford to spend a considerable amount of time in supporting her work. But are there lessons to be learned from her case?

Other factors may be important in contributing to her ease and the confidence of her family. First, she was able to start nursery school at three. Here she was in a small class where the development of spoken language played an important role for all children. From the very start, the teacher sent home weekly short reports on her progress. Second, the teacher in her 'real' school presents Nicole and all the class with structured, confined exercises which do not demand a fluent knowledge of the language. She treats all the children equally as 'beginners' and each task is explicit (often a new page in a book). Third, Nicole's parents always know what she needs to do at home and are constantly kept informed of both her strengths and what needs further practice. Even if they initially have difficulty in helping Nicole to learn parts of speech and conjugate verbs, they know what they have to do and have the textbook to help them. Both the parents and Nicole are treated as important learners in the eyes of the school. There is no doubt that the other children in the group are seen as important in their community classes. Whether the parents are present or not, the children know that their financial investment in community class lessons is considerable. However, the parents' link with the English school is much more tenuous. We see that they still have no real idea as to how reading is taught. Nor are expectations of their own role in the process made explicit. All the parents are waiting for homework where they can help their children step-by-step. In most cases, the books they receive are too hard, contain no direct instructions and leave them floundering.

We do not yet know the extent of the influence a home culture might have on children's learning. However, it is difficult to believe that the neatness and love of accuracy of our Chinese and Bangladeshi origin children is totally unrelated to their learning experiences outside the English school. Nicole, on the other hand, seems now to be deliberately calling upon strategies taught in her French class to help her English reading at home. Whether the direction in which strategies are transferred relates to the way in which expectations for the children are clearly delineated in the Chinese, Bengali and French classes or whether other factors come more into play, we simply do not yet know.

With her example of Gurdeep's father and his 'word-for-word' reading strategies quoted above, Hilary Minns (1990) sums up the challenge ahead for many British Early Years teachers:

> *although his responses may seem repressive to some infant teachers, they are, in fact, a gift of cultural inheritance to Gurdeep and his sister.*
>
> *(p. 15)*

In other words, it seems that the father's 'sense' or interpretation of learning to read is different from that called up by the teacher in school. But need this present a dilemma? The metaphor of an 'inheritance' is useful because it conjures up an image of a resource or wealth which the inheritor brings to school and which can be used wisely or squandered according to advice given. Like the other children in this chapter, Gurdeep is formally learning to read in English within the culture of the British school with all the rules and 'recipes' this entails. Yet we cannot assume that these are superior to those in any other culture in which children are successfully learning to read. The families we have met in this chapter show us that terms such as 'gaining meaning' or 'taking pleasure' from reading will mean different things for different people. For some, it may be individual or an immediate feeling of satisfaction. For others, pleasure and meaning in reading may be intimately linked with becoming a member of a cultural group. In other words, we cannot assume that teachers, children and their families enter school with the same 'sense' of reading. Recognising the wealth of knowledge and reading practices brought by children from home at the same time as introducing them explicitly to our cultural rules will be important first steps towards enabling children to 'situate' themselves in the social context of reading in the classroom.

Some questions to consider:

- How can teachers learn of the reading practices taking place in their pupils' lives outside school?
- What particular strengths does each of the children in the group bring to school?
- Which strategies could be devised to build upon the children's strengths?
- In what ways can we make our own interpretation of reading explicit to children and their families?

IN SUMMARY

This chapter focused on the social context in which beginner bilinguals learn to read. Within this framework, reading was viewed not as a particular cognitive

Summary of children's out-of-school reading activities

Child	Type of activity	Language	Materials	Length of time per week	Participation structures
Tony	Reading ideographs from the blackboard and copying them into exercise-book until perfect at Chinese class; reciting and writing traditional poems at home	Learns to read in standard Mandarin; spoken language of classes and home is Cantonese	Lined exercise-book, biro, pen, pencil, brush	3 hours Saturday class; most evenings with father	Teacher demonstrates, child repeats, practises and is tested
Nazma	Reading Bengali book and practising spellings at Bengali class; reading kaida (preparatory book for Qur'an) at Arabic class; reading storybooks at home from English class	Learns to read in standard Bengali; spoken language of Bengali class is Sylheti dialect; learns to read kaida in classical Arabic; school storybooks are in English	Bengali primer, kaida, lined exercise-book, biro, English storybook	8 hours Arabic; 4 hours Bengali	(as above)
Shabbir, Shahina and Sabina Louthfur	All share Nazma's reading experiences		(see Nazma above)	Shabbir has 7½ hours Bengali and has not yet started Arabic; Louthfur has 4 hours Arabic and 4 hours Bengali; Shahina and Sabina have 4 hours Bengali and 8 hours Arabic	(as above)
Nicole	Reading storybooks and old reading scheme books 'anything her mother can lay her hands on'; practising sounds, pronouncing syllables, matching phonemes to graphemes, learning grammar for her French homework	English and French	Storybooks, scheme books, computer, video, typewriter, comics, puzzle books, magazines, school textbook	Approx. 10 hours (1 hour per day for homework)	Caregiver demonstrates, child joins in and 'echoes' words and phrases; sometimes caregiver 'sounds words out' for child

skill but as a set of reading practices. Different cultural groups were shown to value and regard as valid very different reading practices. This applied equally to schools in different countries. Britain and France were shown to lay emphasis on different knowledge as children begin reading in school. The first section of the chapter examined ways in which infants are initiated from the time they are born into the learning practices of their cultural group. Examples showed how all infants are given 'finely tuned' tutoring from caregivers who scaffold and model important language recipes and interpretations of events. Nevertheless, examples from cross-cultural studies showed how the 'curriculum' and what counts as learning itself would be different according to the cultural background of the family.

The second section linked home and school. Case studies of a group of children beginning school in Britain and France showed how children enter classrooms already familiar with a whole variety of reading practices. We saw how some children would be able to recognise certain practices as part of the teacher's repertoire in school; others would find their existing knowledge to be very alien to the classroom. It was clear that most emergent bilinguals would need not only to step into new reading practices themselves in school but also to be responsible for introducing these to their families at home. Throughout the chapter, the focus was on the need to question our assumptions on what reading is and how it is best learned. As the families in this chapter clearly show us: reading is a cultural matter.

Further reading

Dombey, H. and Meek-Spencer, M. (eds.) (1994) *First Steps Together. Home–School Early Literacy in European Contexts*, Stoke-on-Trent: Trentham Publishers/IEDPE.

Heath, S. B. (1983) *Ways with Words: Language, Life and Work in Communities and Classrooms*, Cambridge University Press.

Liljestrom, R. *et al.* (1982) *Young Children in China*, Clevedon: Multilingual Matters.

Minns, H. (1990) *Read it to Me Now*, London: Virago Press.

3

The Context of the Mind

'Can you remember how you learned to read, Nicole?'
(Nicole) 'I learned to read in English first. When I was five, I picked up a book and just read it out.'
'Can you tell me what you do when you read?'
'Well, you look at it, and when you finish reading one line, your eyes go down to the next.'
'What about when you read in French?'
'When you're reading French, your lips come out.' (demonstrates)
'Which language is easier?'
'French is easier to pronounce. In English, you have to break it into syllables, like this "ti-r-ed" (claps to each syllable), but there are some syllables I can't read.'

Asking any young fluent reader about learning to read is a frustrating business, for it is so difficult to ask the right questions. We learn much more from observing children's strategies as they go about the task. As they read, we find that even when children learning two or more languages do not mix them at all in speech, they will often transfer reading strategies learned in one language to another. When shown a difficult English word in isolation, six-year-old Nicole will always try the 'clapping out in syllables' approach learned in her French school. If she sees an English word in a sentence, she first reads ahead, leaving it out to see if she can come back to it. If not, she tries the syllable approach again. Because she first learned the importance of syllables and sound blends in French, e.g. 'ou' (mouton, double, loup, etc.), her first instinct is to pronounce 'double' as it is in French if she sees the word separately. However, she has no problem at all in seeing it as the English 'double' (as in 'double your money'). Her eye goes to the central sounds in English words too; she, herself, points out the different sounds of 'ea' (as in 'heaven', 'read', and 'lead' as in 'lead paint' or 'the dog's lead').

Five-year-old monolingual children who are just beginning reading are scarcely more specific when asked what they believe reading to be and how they go about the task:

> Joan: 'You say one word and then the next . . . You say "m-a-t" . . . Some people know
> them . . .'
> Andrew: 'You spell it. You say the letters that make the words . . .' (demonstrates by
> sounding out 'come' and 'have' letter by letter and then pronouncing them correctly)
> (Reid 1966, p. 59)

Nevertheless, young children seem to be of one opinion that learning to read has to do with the brain or mind ('knowing', 'spelling') and language ('saying', 'pronouncing'). Teachers and researchers agree with them but are more precise in seeing an inextricable link between word recognition and understanding; both are required if reading is to take place. This chapter focuses on reading as a mental and linguistic process. We examine the way children learn to 'situate' themselves in what Cazden refers to as the inner context or 'the context of the mind' (Vygotsky's 'intrapsychological plane') as they set about making sense of reading.

This chapter, therefore, addresses the following questions:

- What is the nature of the mental process of learning to read for mono- and young emergent bilinguals?
- Do emergent bilinguals have special strengths and weaknesses which the teacher should consider as she prepares a reading programme?

The chapter is divided into two sections: the first briefly outlines the nature of the reading process for all children and summarises important *cues* (clues) which help them learn. The second section focuses on each cue in turn and analyses the different ways emergent bilinguals use them to make sense of text. Our group of children from Chapter 2 are joined by others who speak a variety of languages and are learning in British schools. Finally, I ask: What use can teachers make of a detailed insight into the reading strategies of emergent bilinguals as they introduce reading during the first years of school?

I. LOOKING FOR SENSE: THE VITAL CLUES

Symbolisation: the very first steps

Four-year-old Tajul, who speaks Sylheti and just a few words of English, and seven-year-old John, a monolingual English child, help us understand the very first steps of reading:

> The teacher is sitting with Tajul who has recently started his reception class with no
> nursery experience. She is reading Joseph's Other Red Sock (Daly 1983) and Tajul is
> joining in:
>
> Tajul: There's dog. (points to illustration)
> Teacher: Is it a dog? Or is it a tiger?

Tajul: Tiger.

Teacher: It's a tiger. There's Joseph with one sock on (points). He's lost a sock. (Reads) 'Did you look in your toy-box?' asked his mum. 'Yes,' said Joseph, 'but I could only find Harold . . .'

Tajul: Question mark! (points to it)

Teacher: (continues reading) '. . . and a rabbit there' There's another question mark, that's right. (Reads) 'Did you look in your cupboards? . . .'

Tajul: Question mark! (points to it)

Teacher: Yes, and here's another one, look! (points) (continues reading) '. . . asked mum'

Compare Tajul's experience with that of seven-year-old John who is a monolingual English speaking child:

John is not yet able to read. A teacher has come to his school to work with him individually. She considers the words of his class teacher who says 'John seems to be up against a brick wall' and decides to begin by using a picture-book with no words. John is to make his own text for the book which she will tape and transcribe to make into his own book. When she leaves, he will have this book and tape from which to practise until her next visit. She explains to John that he is to make the story for the book and he enthusiastically and fluently weaves his own tale around the illustrations. Pleased with this practice-run, the teacher says, 'Now we'll put it on tape. When I turn the tape on, you start reading. OK?' She turns on the tape and waits. John blushes and looks confused. 'Can you start reading your story, John?' John looks upset and eventually stutters the sound 'p'. 'Pardon?' says the teacher, herself confused. Hesitantly, John repeats 'p'. 'P?' the teacher repeats astonished and, at that moment, realises what has happened . . .

John thinks 'reading' means 'saying the correct sound' and attempts to do this even though there are no words printed on the page. After two years in school, he still has no definition which makes sense for him. When a task is defined as 'telling a story' he is competent and able to co-operate. When the same task is defined as 'reading', he is at a loss and tries to do what he feels is right which is saying a sound.

Fortunately, children like John are rare. However, Tajul and John illustrate clearly the very first steps in becoming literate as well as the gulf which already exists between them. Step 1, then, is the realisation that an object can stand for or symbolise another object and, consequently, that a 'label' or word can be separated from the object it represents. Step 2 is understanding that the 'label' or word can be represented not just by another word or object but by a written mark on a page or a screen which, if one wishes, can be permanent. Vygotsky (1978) views these steps as part of the unique development of humankind. He uses the example of a broom handle to illustrate how early symbolisation takes place. For the young infant, a broom handle is simply the object it stands for. A giant step is taken on the day the child picks up the broom and makes it become a horse. In other words, the broom is no longer a broom; it symbolises or represents something else. Written language, says Vygotsky, can be called 'second order symbolisation' as the object is represented not just by another object or a 'label' but by a written symbol on the page.

Tajul's incipient bilingualism already enables him to realise that objects can be 'labelled' differently in speech according to which language you happen to be using. For example, he realises that something we know as 'an object to play with' can be labelled 'khelna' if you are speaking Sylheti but will be 'toy' when you switch into English. He also realises that when you are speaking one language you try not to use another if your partner cannot understand – even if this means swallowing what you would really like to say. In other words, from the very start, learning another language means learning that labels cannot be 'stuck' to objects. It is but a short step for Tajul to realise that the new label 'full stop' can be represented on paper too. But what about John? From John's point of view, taking these initial steps would mean understanding that his story can be 'removed' (as it were) from his mouth, represented on paper and then reread by him. These are steps John as yet is unable to take. John and Tajul pinpoint how complex and yet how simple these first steps into reading can be. Tajul begins to show us the potential advantages of bilingualism even from the first day of entering another language. Does this mean that it is potentially easier for beginner bilinguals to 'situate' themselves in the mental context of learning to read? By the end of the chapter, readers may be able to make up their own minds. But first we need to consider the nature of the task ahead for all children.

The process of learning to read

The setting is an inner-city classroom of five- to six-year-olds. Husna and Naseema are reading Each, Peach, Pear, Plum *by Janet and Allen Ahlberg, together. Despite the attractions of the illustrations, their eyes are drawn to the print and they read quickly and fluently. Husna points carefully to each word to help Naseema who is more hesitant. 'Each, Peach, Pear, Plum, I spy Tom Thumb. Tom Thumb in the cupboard, I spy Mother Hubbard. Mother Hubbard down the cellar, I spy Cinderella. Cinderella on the stairs, I spy the Three Bears . . .' Husna breaks off with 'I can count to ten in Bengali: Ek, dui, teen, chaar, panch, chhoy, shaat, aat, noy, dosh.' 'Gosh?' asks the teacher. 'Mmm. But this is ten/dosh, not like gosh in "Oh, my gosh, my golly".' The teacher laughs, knowing she is referring to one of the 'Storychest Big Books' with which she is very familiar. The children continue with the text glancing only occasionally at the illustrations which complement this nursery rhyme world. As they reach the page featuring a magnificent plum pie, the teacher interrupts and asks 'Can you show me the plum pie in that picture?' The children stare blankly at the teacher and the page. Eventually, Husna points quickly to something nondescript in the background. The teacher shows them the pie and allows the children to get back to their reading. They finish the text and are impatient to change the book for another.*

(Gregory and Kelly 1992, p. 144)

How do research studies help us in understanding how these children are tackling learning to read and how teachers can best assist them? Briefly, there is no consensus of opinion. The relationship between reading, language and the mind has long been a question of debate. In his revolutionary book *The Psychology and Pedagogy of Reading* published in New York in 1908, Edward Huey claims reading to be 'a highly complex task which involves very many of the most intimate workings of the mind' (p. 6). Since then, there have been contradictory ideas on exactly how these 'workings of the mind' take place.

The 'great debate': 'bottom-up' *v.* 'top-down' theories

The traditional debate (sometimes referred to as 'the great debate', Chall 1979) which has taken place throughout the twentieth century is between those supporting *'bottom-up'* and those upholding *'top-down'* processes as children learn to read. Such specialist jargon can be confusing, but it is important to understand these terms for they reflect contrasting theories which have been influential in informing beginning reading tuition throughout the twentieth century. So what do they mean and how do they explain what Husna and Naseema need to do as they learn to read?

At its simplest, the 'bottom-up' theory claims that learning to read proceeds from the particular to the general; from the smallest unit of meaning (individual sound or *phoneme*) to the largest – knowledge of the world (*semantic knowledge*) and knowledge of the structure of language (*syntactic knowledge*). Those supporting the 'bottom-up' process of reading maintain that learning involves 'a reconstruction of the sound forms of a word on the basis of its graphic representation, whereby understanding arises as a result of correct recreation of the sound form of words' (Elkonin 1963 in Melnik and Merritt 1973, p. 38). In other words, decoding sounds and pronouncing words is seen as a *means* to gaining understanding. Early reading tuition based entirely on the 'bottom-up' theory will stress the need to teach children first to match *phonemes* (sounds) to *graphemes* (symbols) which are gradually built up into words (*lexis*) and larger units of meaning. This is sometimes referred to simply as taking a *'phonic approach'* to beginning reading. How does this view relate to the task ahead for Husna and Naseema? We see that Husna is already very aware of word units. On other occasions, she shows that she is able to use sounds to form words. Nevertheless, it is clear that we cannot surmise that understanding will automatically arise from being able to say the word. Indeed, it is evident that she can read words fluently without any idea of their meaning.

The 'top-down' theory is a reversal of the 'bottom-up' view. It states simply that understanding proceeds from the general to the particular; from general experience of life and a knowledge of the language of the text to predicting and reading individual words and letters. Those supporting the 'top-down' process believe that the recognition of printed or written symbols serves only as 'stimuli for the recall of meanings built up through past experience and the reconstruction of new meanings through the manipulation of concepts already possessed by the reader' (Tinker and McCullough 1962 in Melnik and Merritt 1973, p. 38). Early reading tuition influenced entirely by this view will stress the importance of teaching beginner readers to use existing semantic and syntactic knowledge in order to be able to select from alternatives and predict the written word. This is sometimes referred to simply as taking a *'top-down'* approach. How does this view relate to our beginner bilinguals above? Clearly, we cannot surmise that recognising the word 'plum' will set off a chain of memories linked with the English language which will enable the children successfully to predict the text. Neither 'bottom-up' nor 'top-down' views alone will suffice in explaining the reading task for Husna and Naseema. Pronouncing words will not necessarily lead to understanding them; nor will children be able to switch into the English words linked to a past memory if it was experienced in another language.

Interactive approaches

The example of Husna and Naseema begins to show that a different framework will be needed to explain the reading process for emergent bilinguals. From the mid 1970s onwards, an alternative way of viewing learning to read has gained credence with teachers of both mono- and bilingual young children. Known as the *'interactive' model*, this approach is concerned with how information

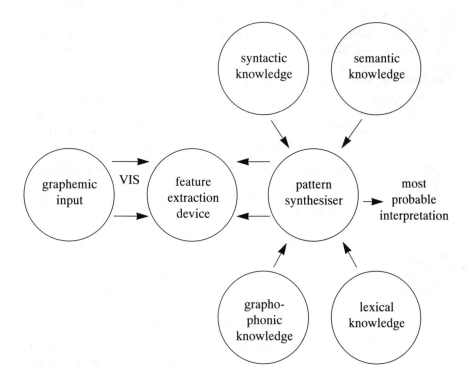

VIS = Visual Information Store

(*Source*: an adaption of Rummelhart 1977 and Verhoeven's model 1987, p. 31)

contained in the higher stages of processing (the syntactic or structure of language and semantic or wider meaning) influences the analysis occurring at lower stages (the *grapho-phonemic* or letter-sound correspondence and lexical or word recognition) and how information from all four sources (*grapho-phonic, lexical, syntactic* and *semantic*) are synthesised and influence perceptions. The model on page 53 attempts to show how both types of information must be drawn upon before the reader comes to an interpretation of the text.

Each of the four sources of information converging on the pattern synthesiser can be seen as a *knowledge centre* providing different sets of clues or *'cues'* which children draw upon as they learn to read:

- **The grapho-phonic knowledge centre** comprises *orthographic* and *phonological* knowledge which sends out clues concerning the patterns of letters in words and the sounds they make, e.g. 'splash' which is acceptable in English rather than 'sjcit' which is not.
- **The lexical knowledge centre** sends out clues concerning the word and the company it keeps, e.g. 'knife and fork' rather than 'knife and powder puff'.
- **The syntactic knowledge centre** sends out clues concerning the structure of the language, e.g. 'Catching rats is as easy for ratcatchers as catching toves is for — —'.
- **The semantic knowledge centre** sends out clues concerning the meaning behind the words (within the culture or within the text), e.g. John tried hard to persuade his father that, far from being the — report in the class, his was, in fact, the —. (Readers know from their experience of life in our particular culture that 'worst' and 'best' could never be the opposite way round!)

Of course, information from different knowledge centres constantly interacts. Interaction might look like this:

Lexical/orthographic

- More letters can be remembered in a given unit if they spell a word rather than a non-word, e.g. alligator rather than rllaagtio.
- More letters can be remembered in a nonsense string which conforms to the rules of English spelling than one which does not, e.g. vernalit rather than nrveiatl.

Syntactic/semantic/lexical/orthographic

- Semantic knowledge influences word perception. It is easier to read a word if presented with one which is related, e.g. bread/butter; doctor/nurse rather than doctor/butter.
- Our perception of syntax depends upon the context in which a word is embedded, e.g. 'They are eating apples' where our comprehension depends upon whether the question was 'What kind of apples are they?' or 'What are the children eating?'
- Our interpretation depends upon the context in which the text is embedded, e.g. 'The shooting of the hunters was terrible' where our understanding

depends upon whether the prior text indicates that 'Their markmanship was terrible . . .' or 'Their cruelty was awful . . .'

All these knowledge sources provide simultaneous input into our *'pattern synthesiser'*. This can be viewed as a general message centre which accepts them, holds the information and redirects it as needed. The message centre, then, keeps a runing list of hypotheses or hunches about the nature of the input; each hypothesis is evaluated by the knowledge source and confirmed or disconfirmed. The procedure is continued until a decision is reached and the hypothesis is deemed to be correct.

Different metaphors have been used to illustrate the nature of this process. One uses that of wheels on a car (Hynds 1984, p. 23). Hynds' image is helpful because it indicates the vital importance of each wheel (or cue) as well as the way all must move together to ensure smooth advancement in learning to read.

Hynds adds to Rumelhart's set the bibliographic knowledge centre providing clues on how books work (that, in English, we turn the pages from right to left, read from left to right, top to bottom, etc.) as well as the type of language used in books. However, he omits the 'lexical' or 'word' clue.

The interactive view of reading and emergent bilinguals

How useful is the interactive model in explaining the mental process of learning to read in an unfamiliar language? Let us try to understand Husna and Naseema's strategies using the framework provided by Hynds and Rumelhart. Using Hynds' image, we have evidence indicating that the children's bibliographic 'wheel' seems strong (they are familiar with the book and its layout and can draw upon knowledge of other texts); their syntactic 'wheel' is on (because they are familiar with the language of this particular text); their grapho-phonic wheel looks wobbly (the inability to distinguish 'g' and 'd') and their semantic 'wheel' is very definitely detached – leaving them unfortunately but unavoidably broken down on the wayside! Here we see also the weakness of Hynds' image. It omits the children's greatest strength which is their lexical knowledge (awareness of words as complete entities as well as an ability to remember and compare English and Sylheti words) and allows no possibility of one 'wheel' compensating for another. Rumelhart's notion of knowledge centres sending out different clues to assist a child in making sense of a text is helpful, as it highlights the strength of individual clues (in this case, clues from the children's strong lexical knowledge) feeding into the pattern synthesiser. Nevertheless, Rumelhart's model omits bibliographic knowledge which also supports the children. The interactive model of reading is, therefore, valuable but neither Hynds nor Rumelhart makes adequate allowance for the way in which one knowledge centre may compensate for another.

Husna and Naseema suggest that we may need a different framework to explain the reading process for emergent bilinguals; one which accounts for all five 'knowledge centres' or 'clues', but which highlights the way in which one may compensate for another during the early stages. One way of representing this framework is through the mnemonic of a hand, where each of the five fingers represents a different clue.

Obviously, all fingers will be needed for certain difficult jobs. Nevertheless, unlike the wheels on a car, fingers can compensate for others that are lacking and thus manage to cope with most tasks. In the next section, we shall consider the special strengths and weaknesses of emergent bilinguals as they draw upon all the clues they can from each 'knowledge centre' to 'situate' themselves in the mental context of reading.

Some questions to consider from this section:

- What helps emergent bilinguals to have an early understanding of the symbolic nature of language?
- In what ways can teachers build upon this skill?
- How far does the use of 'knowledge centres' demand a fluency in the language in which reading is taking place?
- Which 'knowledge centres' are emergent bilinguals most and least likely to call upon as they begin reading?
- How can certain clues overcompensate for others which are lacking during the early stages of learning to read?

II. USING THE SAME CLUES DIFFERENTLY

Gillian, Fozia and Kalchuma are just five when they enter school together in North-ampton, Britain. Gillian is a monolingual English speaker. Fozia speaks Panjabi *and Kalchuma speaks* Sylheti *at home and both appear to understand little English. None of the children has been in a nursery and neither Fozia nor Kalchuma has yet started learning to read in their first language. Here they are a few weeks after starting school with the same 'Mr Men' books by Roger Hargreaves which they have chosen to 'read'.*

Gillian: (turning the pages and 'reading' in a sing-song way) Mr Jelly man. Mr Jelly bast sweet shop. Ah, Mr Jelly, nice Jelly. He picked the jelly up, he did. He picked the jelly up. He was laughing at pie. Oh you warp up. Oh, a new lot of pie. And now he's in a shed. Good.

Fozia: (turning the pages and 'reading' fast and fluently) There's some writing. Mr (?) (Funny) have a sleep in bed. Now a mummy wake up. It's home time. Mummy sleeping now it's home time. Daddy wanna sleep at. He close his mouth. You better . . . you better choose . . . you better choose any colour that you want books . . . (picks up 'Mr Messy')

Fozia: (turning the pages and 'reading' in the same way as above) One time two men see what they do . . . sleeping a bed . . . knocking at door. (there is a real knock outside)

Teacher: Naughty children.

Fozia: Yes. (returns to book) Now they're saying 'Good-bye' and in the sun . . . and dinner-ladies (pointing to a picture of Mr Messy and Mr Tidy together) come out. Now finish it.

Kalchuma: (turning the pages and 'reading' each word very definitely) Bump.
Mr Bump is go to gone bump.
Mr Bump is go to gone.
Mr Bump is to all down.
He went there to bump.
Mr Bump to . . . what's in there missing?

Mr Bump go stick . . . his stick, there, stick. (means a 'sticking plaster')
(continues using similar English constructions 'go to go/go sitting/go he go to his steps,
etc.' throughout a number of books)

Observing young children as they 'pretend read' opens a window onto both how they view the task and the different strategies and clues they call upon. Gillian, Fozia and Kalchuma all realise that book reading is something 'special', in that the words and pictures hold a meaning which is different from ordinary conversation and they treat it as a performance. They do not yet know what that meaning might comprise, but they are drawing upon all the clues at their disposal which they hold to be appropriate. However, they go about doing this very differently. Gillian is unfamiliar with books at home, but in school she listens to stories and nursery rhymes. With its repetitions and sing-song intonation, her 'reading' has much in common with reciting a rhyme like 'Here we go round the mulberry bush'. Fozia seems to be trying to imitate her teacher. She plunges in, 'reading' fast and fluently and using all the clues picked up in class 'dinner-ladies, home time, you better choose, etc.' Both Gillian and Fozia seem to prefer fluency to any attempt at focusing on individual words. Kalchuma's approach is very different. She is already aware that the new language comprises distinct words and structures and she is very particular about saying each word individually. She wants to be accurate, too. Later in the text she points to the plaster/bandage and says 'What's this? Not stick?'

In the second section of this chapter, emergent bilinguals from various language backgrounds provide an insight into their strengths and weaknesses in 'situating' themselves in the mental context of learning to read. A framework is provided by presenting each knowledge centre or set of clues (each 'finger' in our hand image used in the last section) in turn and focusing on three issues: its strengths, weaknesses and a brief summary of questions for pedagogy. These questions will be the springboard for constructing classroom reading programmes which is the focus for Part Two of this book.

As the clues provided by each knowledge centre are unpicked, readers might consider the following questions:

- Which clues appear most useful to different children?
- Can we see a pattern linking the mental and the social context of reading?
- How do children use some clues to compensate for others which are still lacking?

Lexical knowledge (the knowledge of words)

Here is a snippet from Tony, our Cantonese speaker, whom readers already know well:

('reading' Mr Fussy by Roger Hargreaves a few weeks after starting English school)
Tony: What's his name?
Teacher: Mr Fussy.
Tony: Mr Fussy. (repeats four times with different intonation)
Mr Fussy is in the house. (turns page)
Mr Fussy . . . What's that?

Teacher: It's a glass . . . Oh no, it's a jar of marmalade.
Tony: Jar marmalade?
Teacher: Yes . . . to put on your bread . . . you know, in the morning.
Tony: Here's . . . (mumbles)
  What's his name?
Teacher: It's Mr Fussy's hand, I think.
Tony: That's Mr Fussy's hand. What's he touch . . . his hand?
Teacher: It's an iron.

Just like Kalchuma and many other emergent bilinguals, Tony is storing up a bank of words. Their insistence on hearing words correctly, asking for repetition and then repeating them after the teacher show how important lexical clues are in the reading process. A practical example makes this more explicit. Readers might like to imagine looking at a picture-book in an almost unknown language and being expected to make some sense of it. The eye is drawn to important

Figure 6   The importance of lexical and visual clues.

nouns (naming words) in the illustrations. In this case, the eye goes to the beautiful lady on the cover (see Figure 6). Even without being able to say 'What (or who) is it? it is easy enough to point to it and look questioningly. The teacher replies 'La Ventafocs' and points also to the words. Both the oral and visual label give the beginner something to hang on to and to pick out in a stream of sounds. As the teacher reads, it will probably sound something like this: 'La Ventafocs blah blah blah La Ventafocs blah blah, etc.' It makes sense for the beginner to point to every other illustration which looks as if it might be 'La Ventafocs' and to keep repeating it until certain it is correct and stored away in the memory. This process is exactly what Tajul is doing as he focuses on the question marks earlier in this chapter. His eye is drawn to the written symbol, but the teacher then links sound to symbol and includes the word in her reading, pointing to it every time. In this way, Tajul will gain an automaticity of important sight words both individually and in context. We shall return to 'La Ventafocs' as other clues are examined later in the chapter.

Tony and Tajul show how actively they are building on this strength. Yet, paradoxically, what is potentially their strongest set of clues as emergent bilinguals begin reading is also in danger of being their weakest. This is epitomised by Husna and Naseema reading *Each, Peach, Pear, Plum* as they sadly fail to understand the meaning of 'plum pie'. Examples of early 'reading' help us analyse more precisely the nature of both the strengths and weaknesses of lexical clues.

The power of words: the strength of lexical clues

I scream	*Fuzzy Wuzzy was a bear*
You scream	*Fuzzy Wuzzy had no hair*
We all scream	*Fuzzy Wuzzy wasn't fuzzy*
For ice cream	*Was he?*

Many children's rhymes and songs contain *oronyms* like those above, highlighting how strings of sound can be carved into words in two different ways. Steven Pinker (1994) neatly summarises the place of words in speech:

> *All speech is an illusion. We hear speech as a string of separate words but unlike the tree falling in the forest with no one to hear it, a word boundary with no one to hear it has no sound. In the speech sound wave, one word runs into the next seamlessly; there are no little silences between spoken words the way there are white spaces between written words. We simply hallucinate word boundaries when we reach the edge of a stretch of sound that matches some entry in our mental dictionary. This becomes apparent when we listen to speech in a foreign language. It is impossible to tell where one word ends and the next begins . . .*
>
> *(pp. 159–60)*

Many young children enter school aware of speech only as a seamless string of sounds. Learning to read will show them how this flow can be divided up into words, phrases and sentences. At seven, John, whom we met earlier in the chapter, is still unaware of this. But in what ways might becoming bilingual help children to put in the 'seams' needed for beginning reading?

In *Thought and Language* (1962), Vygotsky claims that becoming bilingual enables a child 'to see his language as one particular system among many, to view its phenomena under more general categories . . . (which) leads to awareness of his linguistic operations' (p. 110). How does this awareness come about? An example from the classroom may help to illustrate the process. When young monolingual children hear the teacher say 'Go and get your writing-book, a pencil and a ruler and get on with your work' they may wonder whether they actually want to do as they have been asked or even try not to do it, but they focus on the message itself and are able to ignore or overlook individual words. For children unfamiliar with the language the task set is a different one. They need first to sort out the words 'writing-book', 'pencil', 'ruler', 'work', etc. Often the teacher helps them do this by holding up the object in question and labelling it. In this way, children are forced to focus on the words themselves as necessary means of communication from the very first word learned in the new language world of the school. This process itself forces children to become more conscious of language as a grammatical system with words to name and describe objects and actions, etc.

The excerpt from Husna and Naseema reading *Each, Peach, Pear, Plum* earlier in this chapter shows us how aware they are of language as a system and the way words fit into this. This is sometimes referred to as a *metalinguistic awareness* which means they are able to focus on the forms and properties of the words themselves in a way that is often not yet possible for monolingual children. In what ways do we see this taking place? First, they have completely separated their two languages and are able to use appropriate *linguistic sets* (sets of rules) in different situations. They know the names of their two languages and refer to them. Then, they have an interest and excitement in the words themselves, shown by wanting to pick out separate words and compare them. Third, the children already realise the *arbitrary nature of language*. This means that simply by realising the word 'dosh' can mean different things in different languages, they are able to 'detach' a word (sometimes referred to as a *'signifier'*) from the object it signifies (sometimes referred to as the *'signified'*). This realisation is vital in learning to read, for children will need not just to 'detach' the word from the object but understand that it can be expressed symbolically as a mark on a page or screen.

We witness another aspect of metalinguistic awareness in the children's interest in ascertaining the boundaries of both words and their meanings. 'Is "dosh" the same as "gosh" although in such different languages?' It makes sense that choosing the appropriate language in a given situation will be vital for a young emergent bilingual and knowing where a word begins and ends is part of this. Early Years teachers know that emergent bilinguals master one-to-one correspondence easily and at a very early stage. Husna and Naseema carefully point to each word in turn as they read. Kalchuma and Tony both know that it is one label they require as they point and ask 'What is it?' Nicole is always aware that a word which looks the same (e.g. double) will be pronounced differently according to whether she is 'in' French or English. Here is Tajul 'reading' with his teacher after a few weeks in school:

Teacher: (reads from Meg at Sea*) That's the magnifying glass . . . There's the fire. Can you see?*
Tajul: Yes. There?
Teacher: Yes.
Tajul: There's the window. (points to the magnifying glass)
Teacher: That's the magnifying glass. It's nearly the same as a window, isn't it?

Is Tajul trying out the boundaries of words as he learns to distinguish 'window' and 'magnifying glass'? Similar examples with emergent bilinguals indicate this may be so. A second task in boundary demarcation will be to realise that the boundaries of words and their meanings will differ according to the language spoken. A single word 'cousin' in English needs many different words in most Asian languages (according to whether on the mother's or father's side, etc.). In reverse, the strict demarcation of gender (he/she, his/her, etc.) in European languages will be covered by one word in most Asian languages. With all this to consider, emergent bilinguals learn from the start that reality can be divided up differently according to the language spoken and that they must operate within a double set of rules.

The awareness that language is arbitrary, together with a lack of knowledge of the conventional word in the target language, may enable children to play with words and experiment with them. Teachers of emergent bilinguals can provide lists of imaginative experiments with words, such as 'necklace man' (a mayor), 'a kissing lady' (a bride), 'Happy Wu Year', 'a ghonster' (ghost/monster), 'a polly' (kettle), 'a bzzz' (a bee). Lacking the word used unconsciously by their monolingual peers may force children into a conscious search for the real meaning behind a concept in order to find an appropriate synonym. Tajul uses a number of strategies to get the appropriate English word out of his teacher. For example, he points to a lion in an illustration and says 'That tiger?' to which his teacher replies 'No, it's a lion'; or he points to an illustration and uses a negative 'That's not Daddy' to which his teacher replies 'No, it's the milkman'. At six, Shabbir's English has developed enough simply to ask 'What's the opposite of "up"?'.

These examples reinforce results from more formal tests conducted mostly with older children which show how slick they become at attending selectively to words and their boundaries. Working with four- to nine-year-old bilingual English/Afrikaans children, Ianco-Worrall (1972) found that bilinguals excelled in ability to state the principle that words are arbitrarily assigned to things. For example, they understood symbol substitution games such as the following two to three years earlier than their monolingual peers:

Researcher: This is named 'plane', right?
Well, in the game, it's 'turtle'.
Can the turtle fly?

Cummins (1979) extended this in a test of 53 monolingual English and an equal number of bilingual English/Irish eight- to nine-year-olds, matched on verbal IQ, socio-economic group, gender and age. Here, children were not only asked whether words could be interchanged, but required to justify their answers. A significantly higher number of bilingual children gave answers such as 'You could change the names because it doesn't matter what they're called', whereas a large majority of monolinguals replied 'They are their right names, so you can't change them'. Similar tests led the authors to conclude that bilingual children were better able to detect contradictions, ambiguities and *tautologies* (repetitions) and generally possess more flexibility and emancipation in separating words and their meanings. Ben-Zeev (1977) found that bilingual English/ Hebrew children between five and eight were able not only to substitute nouns but to analyse *linguistic stems* (structures) by ignoring both word meaning and sentence framing, for example:

> Researcher: If 'they' means 'spaghetti, how do we say 'They are good children'?

In being able simultaneously to reply 'spaghetti are good children', the children had grasped the basic idea that the structure of language is different from the *phonological* (sound) representations and meaningful words in which it is embodied.

A double-edged sword: the weakness of lexical clues

The teacher is reading Rosie's Walk *to Kalchuma, Fozia and Tony. As she comes to the page with the bumble bee, she makes the sound 'bzzz' in order to try to make the meaning of the word 'bee' clear. After she has finished, the children turn over the pages of the book, looking at the pictures. Suddenly, Kalchuma points to the bee and says, 'Bangla say "bumbla", English say "bzzz"!'. Realising her mistake and anxious to avoid misunderstandings, the teacher quickly says, 'No. English say "bumble bee", too, but it makes the sound "bzzz"!'*

This example highlights the complexity involved in matching the right word to the appropriate object as emergent bilinguals set about learning the new language. Teachers can add their own examples to the 'bee' story and may become paranoid about their language use when they hear certain of their own 'key words' appearing in the most inappropriate places in the mouths of the children! One story, told by an older teacher, comes from the days when a single reading scheme ('The Happy Venture') was often used in British schools, featuring Dick and Jane and Fluff the cat. An important indication that her reading programme was somewhat limiting was made clear by the insistence of some children on referring to all cats as 'fluffs'!

During the early stages of second language learning, a major task is to sort out 'real' from 'nonsense' words. In Holland, Verhoeven (1987) conducted an in-depth study of 63 young Turkish speakers beginning ordinary state schools using both 'whole-word' and phonic approaches to reading and compared their progress with monolingual Dutch speakers. Although the monolingual children performed better at reading words in context, the Turkish children were better at reading a list of nonsense words. Such tests highlight differences between mono- and emergent bilinguals. The emergent bilinguals relied on their superior memories whereas monolingual children were able to draw upon the meaning of the text. It is clear that prediction of a word will be very difficult if its meaning is not understood and the syntax (grammatical structure) of the language is not at the command of the child. As Tajul reads with his teacher, he pinpoints this difficulty and shows how he is trying to work it out for himself:

> *(Tajul's teacher is reading* The Tiger who Came to Tea *(Kerr 1968) and Tajul is joining in wherever he can)*
> *Teacher: (reads) 'And tiger started eating all the sandwiches.'*
> *Tajul: You know, lion . . .*
> *Teacher: They're* like *tigers, aren't they?*
> *Tajul: Yes.*
> *Teacher: But tigers have got stripes.*
> *Tajul: Yes.*
> *Teacher: Lions haven't got stripes.*
> *Tajul: And tiger . . . And lion is tiger's friend.*
> *Teacher: Yes, that's right. (reads) 'And ate all the buns.'*

Tajul is showing remarkable dexterity for a beginner in trying to work out the double meaning of the word 'like'. In the hubbub of the classroom, it is impossible for the teacher to pick up on this. Nevertheless, we see how he manages to make sense out of the situation and continue the discussion.

Lexical clues are also weakened for emergent bilinguals by the sheer abundance of words. When children read in a familiar language many non-content words such as *prepositions* (on, off, up, down, under, etc.), *conjunctions* (and, but, etc.) and *possessive pronouns* (his, her, etc.) are *redundant* as they can be predicted in the context of the sentence; for example:

> He fell (down) flat (on his) face.

Other lexical clues also help words become almost redundant for young children reading in a language they are familiar with. Words often restrict the company they keep. A few examples make this clear:

> A knife and (plate or fork)?
> A cup and (spoon or saucer)?
> A handsome or a pretty prince?
> A wicked or a bad witch?
> To wipe or to clean your nose?

This mutual expectancy is known as *collocation* and it will be important when we study bibliographic clues. Knowledge of these 'partner words' comes easily when speaking a first language. Nevertheless, anyone speaking another language knows only too well that words differ in the company they keep. In German, the term *putzen* can be used for cleaning shoes, brushing teeth or wiping your nose. In Mandarin, the same word is used for 'seeing' a film, 'watching' TV and 'reading' to oneself (or a newspaper). 'Reading out loud', on the other hand, needs a different word. One theory on beginning reading, 'the verbal efficiency theory' (Perfetti 1984), proposes that there is something akin to a cake for all the clues needed for beginning reading. In other words, the more taken up by one slice (in this case, word identification), the less there is left for others (phonic, syntactic, semantic). Although we have no evidence to prove this, it would make sense that the huge demand made on memory if every word must be read equally is likely to make beginning reading more difficult.

But the most important lexical clue for children and adults as they read in any language must be the extent to which the word carries deep personal meaning (its 'sense', using Vygotsky's definition). Readers can probably draw upon their own experiences as illustrations. Perhaps there springs to mind the name of a station in Cyrillic script (in this case Russian) which is memorised out of fear that one will disappear forever into the depths of the Moscow underground system or even the name of a delicious Greek cake in order to buy it again. We cannot underestimate the value of 'one-sight-words' in early reading. This term was coined by Sylvia Ashton-Warner (1963) to mean words which are close to children's hearts or deep in their personal experience, sometimes referred to as their 'organic' vocabulary. Ashton-Warner worked as an Early Years teacher during the 1950s with Maori children in New Zealand. Realising that the 'Janet and John' reading scheme in use in school bore no resemblance to the children's lives, she devised an approach whereby children thought of personal words they wanted to learn to read, which then became their first reading material. Ashton-Warner's work will be presented in greater detail in Chapter 4 of this book where we focus on her practical approach for the classroom. What is important here is the role of 'one-sight' or important words as vital lexical clues in early reading.

It is not too difficult for teachers to predict some of these words for mono-lingual children. 'Mum, dad, television (and favourite programmes), McDonalds' as well as emotive terms, such as 'kiss, cry, scream, terrified, hate, etc.' are likely to figure high on children's lists. These words will call up an experience or *schema* (abstract knowledge structure) which may trigger off a whole web of words. We see this clearly from Jessica's reading in the introduction of this book. Her schema is that of 'getting up in the morning' (see diagram below).

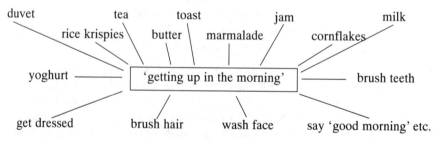

But what about children for whom *schemata* follow a different pattern and 'one-sight' words are in other languages? In her book *The Woman Warrior* Hong-Kingston (1977), whose family emigrated from China to the USA, describes poignantly ways in which the new language (English) 'does not fit on my skin' (p. 53). As monolingual teachers (or teachers unable to speak our children's first languages) it is obvious that important emotional words in the lives of our emergent bilinguals outside school will remain inaccessible to us. The question, then, must be: In what ways can we create together 'one-sight' words in English for children in the classroom?

Lexical clues: in summary

This section shows us that young emergent bilinguals are potentially able to call upon a wealth of lexical clues, but that these are of a different nature from those at the fingertips of children learning to read in their first language. They have an advanced metalinguistic and analytic awareness in that they are able to see the arbitrary nature of words as labels and can detect and compare the boundaries of words in their different languages, and, usually, they have excellent memories. At the same time, they cannot call upon experiences or schemata to call up a network of words in the new language nor can they depend upon the redundancy of words to assist prediction. To make the most of the children's lexical clues as they plan a reading programme, teachers will need to ask:

- How important is lexical knowledge in learning to read for emergent bilinguals?
- What approach to lexical knowledge might children bring from home or their Community classes?
- In what ways can this be accommodated in a home reading programme?
- How can we build upon children's metalinguistic skills in classroom practice?
- In what ways can we both ensure automaticity of certain key words and expand children's knowledge of collocational expressions in English?
- If 'one-sight' words are intimately linked with important experiences, how can we provide such experiences and the language belonging to them in the classroom?

Grapho-phonic knowledge (the knowledge of letters and sounds)

Nine-year-old Saida has recently come to Britain from Bangladesh. She speaks and understands only a few words of English. However, it is obvious that she has attended school regularly in Bangladesh as she is literate in Bengali and quickly completes mathematical tasks once they have been explained to her in Sylheti. Her teacher is at a loss to know how best to help her. So that she should not appear different from the other children, she gives her an easy reading scheme book, which depicts children at the fairground. To her amazement, Saida says almost every word correctly. She stumbles only over the word 'dived' which she pronounces 'deeved' and 'climbed' which she says as 'climb-ed'. Upon questioning, it is obvious that she has understood virtually nothing of the text, yet she has successfully decoded comparatively difficult and very culture-specific words, such as 'roller-coaster'.

Later, Saida explains in Sylheti how she is able to do this. She has already successfully completed Class 5 (the final primary school year) in Bangladesh and has learned to read in Bengali and English. 'But how did she learn to read in English if she couldn't understand it?' asks her teacher. Saida explains that she learned all the sounds, then how to put the sounds together into syllables which she then practised. She explains earnestly that she only got as far as learning to say the words and that understanding was to follow, but at that point, she had left

for England. Saida's approach does not seem unusual to her. After all, it parallels the way she is learning to read the Qur'ān in Arabic where she is already on
her second reading of the Holy Book and is progressing towards understanding.
Her teacher is now able to use Saida's decoding skills as a means towards
learning English. She makes picture sequences for each story and discusses
appropriate sentences for each. Saida is also making her own dictionary and her
lists of objects, each written in a sentence, are increasing rapidly.

Saida's experience reflects the debate on how proficient we have to be in a
language before learning to read in it. Some researchers claim that acquiring
literacy in a language needs a basic threshold level of both receptive (understanding) and productive (speaking) skills (Hatch 1974, Carroll 1977). Others
refute this with examples of children learning written and oral language together
(Goodman, Goodman and Flores 1979). Children like Saida provide a window
onto how the two processes interact and show how reading itself can be used as a
medium for learning to speak a language. Her 'reading' highlights both the
strengths and weaknesses of grapho-phonic clues as emergent bilinguals make
sense of the reading task. Both are outlined further below.

Looking and listening carefully: the strengths of grapho-phonic clues

Nicole's use of phonics when she reads French in some ways mirrors that of
Saida. She is now confident in knowing how to 'sound words out' in French and
her success leads to her claim that French is easy to read. The power of her
French tuition is strong. When shown a word which can be either French or
English (e.g. double), she will first try the French [du:bla], saying that 'ou' always
says 'u' in French. 'French is always like that . . . Only there are some "secret"
letters, like 'souris', but I know the rules for them.' When asked, 'But what if it
were an English word?', she immediately pronounces it correctly. 'But it's not
always like that,' she adds and cites 'cloud' and 'ouch' – 'that's why French is
easier than English'. She illustrates her point by citing 'read, lead and heaven'
and stresses 'that's why it's hard!' She prefers to transfer another strategy from
her French school to her English reading: that of dividing words into syllables.
'Like if I see "tired",' she says, 'I divide it into "ti-r-ed".' She demonstrates with
a previously unknown word, clapping at the same time: 'gua-ran-tee'.

Both Saida and Nicole show how grapho-phonic clues can assist the emergent
bilingual to read and even speak a new language. First, learning to match symbols to sounds is a confined task. It does not demand the sophistication of
needing fluent or colloquial English and consequently gives children confidence.
Both Nicole and Saida are already in the habit of consulting dictionaries and
very quickly look words up independently. Second, many emergent bilinguals
are familiar with phonic clues from reading tuition in their first language or from
learning the Qur'ān in Arabic. Although both sounds and symbols will obviously
be very different, children will understand the function of these clues in learning
to read and will be in a strong position to transfer learning into a new context.

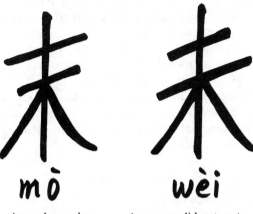

mò

tip; end; powder;
non-essentials

wèi

have not; did not; not;
the 8th of the 12th earthly branches

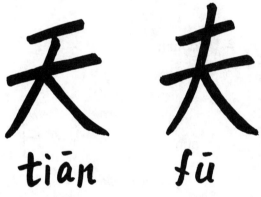

tiān

sky; heaven; day; season;
God; heaven

fū

husband; man

Figure 7   Chinese classes emphasise the importance of accuracy. It is important not to confuse characters which look similar but have very different meanings.

The case studies in Chapter 2 show that the use of phonic clues in learning to read is also very familiar to many parents. Even parents with little English feel confident in completing tasks based on sounds and spelling with their children. As one Bangladeshi origin family explained, 'We understand "a, b, c", but this "wishy-washy" (referring to an English book which had been sent home) is too hard for us. It's for the English teachers.'

Nicole shows how carefully she dissects words and focuses on individual or groups of letters. Of course, she is at an advantage because French uses the same *orthography* (alphabet system) as English. Some researchers argue that learning to read in two different orthographies simultaneously is likely to put children at a disadvantage (Barnitz 1978). Nevertheless, Saida and other emergent bilinguals show that their home or Community class tuition gives them both an eye and an ear for detail. This is particularly true of children learning to read in Mandarin where there is a symbol/meaning rather than a symbol/sound association. As soon as he enters his English school at just under five, Tony is able to copy writing and drawings meticulously. His eye for detail is not surprising when we consider the work that he and many other Hong Kong origin children are engaged in at their Saturday schools (see Figure 2 in Chapter 2 and Figure 7). The Mandarin script contains six sub-groups, three of which are of particular importance to the early reader:

1. Pictographs

(Derived from pictures of the object)

= mouth

= sun   = moon

2. Ideographs

(Representing ideas like 'up' and 'down')

= up   = down

3. Compound ideographs

(Based on metaphorical extensions or associations of constituent parts; 'bright' is derived from the combination of 'sun' and 'moon')

= bright

The child, therefore, needs to focus very carefully on both the constituent parts of *characters* as well as how they can be used as parts to create a new character which holds a different meaning.

Problems of pronunciation: the weakness of grapho-phonic clues

The mishearing of 'gosh' and 'dosh' by Husna and Naseema and their teacher as they read *Each, Peach, Pear, Plum* symbolises the difficulties had by emergent bilinguals in utilising phonic clues. Emergent bilinguals are likely to have considerable difficulty in distinguishing and pronouncing certain sounds or combinations of sounds which do not exist in the same way in their first language. The combination '-sps' is particularly difficult for children speaking most Asian languages. Many teachers recall searching desperately for 'crips' which have disappeared or even more desperately for 'wops' which refuse to disappear from their classrooms. Similarly, it is often difficult for speakers of Asian languages to distinguish between the sounds of 'v' and 'w' as they begin English. The difficulties of other sounds are more subtle, for example:

walked	jogged
slapped	sobbed
passed	fizzed

Saida's mispronunciation of 'climb-ed' illustrates the first rule (do not stress the '-ed'). In addition, she must learn that '-ed' after *voiceless* consonants (e.g. 'k', 'p' and 's') will be pronounced as 't' and after *voiced* consonants (e.g. 'b', 'g' and 'm') will be pronounced as 'd'. In his study comparing the early reading progress of 63 Turkish and a similar number of first language Dutch speakers during their first two years of school in Holland, Verhoeven (1987) found that even where phonics were the main medium of tuition, the Turkish speakers made many more mistakes on basic phonic tests.

But pronunciation difficulties are only one aspect weakening phonic clues. Consider the following words:

ptak	thole	hlad
plast	sram	mgla
vlas	flitch	dnom
rtut	toasp	nyip

All of these phonemes are found in English, but it is not difficult for a first language speaker to recognise that 'thole', 'plast' and 'flitch' could actually be English words, whereas the others could not. Speakers of a language learn at a very early stage that certain sounds can occur together (for example, in English, thr-, cr-, spl-, etc.) whereas others cannot. Similarly, they learn about the position of certain sounds (for example, in English, -ng must come at the end although it can occur initially in some African languages).

These examples highlight how important it is for understanding the meaning of words to parallel the learning of phonic clues. Without this understanding, it is very difficult to know where sounds end and words begin. When is a 'pea' a 'p' for example? Is a 'bzzz' an object or a sound? Even Nicole, whose phonic tuition is now proving extremely effective, recalls her early problems at school:

> '*Learning to read in French was a bit hard at first – like, if you have the word "chantais"*
> *(where the "-ais" is pronounced) and "chantent" (where the "-ent" is silent). I wanted to*
> *pronounce the "-ent" and say the whole word!*'
> '*Why was that, do you think?*'
> '*Because I couldn't understand it.*'
> '*Does that ever happen in English?*'
> '*No.*'

In any case, 'sounding out' a word is likely to be a meaningless activity unless a word is understood. Nicole epitomises this as she attempts to read an adult book *A to Z Gastronomique* which mixes the names of dishes written in French with descriptions written in English. She comes to the recipe for 'colin' (hake) and pronounces it in the French way (kɔlɛ̄). When asked if she knows what it is, she shakes her head. Then she reads the brief description of the fish in English. A flash of recognition comes, 'Oh, I know now. It's Colin (pronounced in English) the cod, isn't it!' A neat summary, perhaps, of the advantages of reading in a language you can understand.

Grapho-phonic clues: in summary

Like lexical clues, phonic and orthographic clues are likely to be different for children during the first stages of second language learning. There is no doubt that children who are using a phonic approach to learn to read in another language are more able to capitalise on these clues in English. In Arabic, for example, learning to *read the Qur'ān* involves learning complex phonic rules where the use of accents changes the pronunciation of a symbol. A whole set of these will need to be learned before a child is ready to begin the Qur'ān. Although the sounds will be learned using different orthographies in different languages, it is clear that the principle itself of sound/symbol association will make sense to both children and families who will support them. Even writing systems using symbol/meaning rather than sound/symbol associations, such as Mandarin, equip the child with the skill of focusing precisely on parts of words and noticing the way a tiny alteration will change the meaning.

Nevertheless, there are two distinct hurdles to be overcome before beginner biliterates can benefit from their headstart; the problems of pronunciation and the 'feel' for what sounds are 'allowed' in a language. The first is a relatively confined task to work upon. In both France and Catalonia (where Catalan is the language of instruction although a majority will speak Castilian (Spanish) at home), the teachers spend a considerable amount of time focusing on correct pronunciation by children. As Nicole says, 'I have to pinch my cheeks in to say it right.' Although there is an obvious danger in over-emphasising this, we shall not be thanked by children if they suffer prejudice owing to poor pronunciation later in life. The second hurdle involves understanding words and their contexts and is much more difficult. It is the topic for Part Two of this book. To make the most of children's phonic and orthographic clues, teachers will need to ask:

- Are children familiar with phonic approaches through learning to read in their first language or in Arabic or are they learning a different writing system such as Mandarin? If so, how can their knowledge best be utilised?
- How can the use of phonics be incorporated into a family reading programme where parents read only in other scripts?
- In what ways can pronunciation be practised using interesting and imaginative approaches?
- Can we ensure that the teaching of phonics always includes teaching the meanings of words? If so, how?

Syntactic knowledge (the knowledge of the structure of a language)

We return to Husna and Naseema whose analogy of 'gosh' (as in the English 'Oh, my gosh, my golly') with 'dosh' (as in the Bengali 'ten') summarises neatly the strengths and weaknesses of syntactic clues for young emergent bilinguals. The children are aware not only that the two words have a different meaning, but also that they are used differently in sentences, in other words, that they are different *parts of speech*. What the English 'gosh' actually means is almost certainly unclear to them. Nevertheless, they are able to use it accurately and in context when referring to the book. No one has heard them use the term in any other context. Their strength, then, lies in their early awareness that the new language has structural rules which they will need to master. Some children go about this systematically, even when very young. Notice how Tajul breaks off to practise in the middle of reading *Meg's Car*:

> *Tajul: You know, milk . . .*
> *Teacher: Milk? Mmm. What?*
> *Tajul: Do you eat milk?*
> *Teacher: Drink?*
> *Tajul: No. Milk.*
> *Teacher: Do I drink milk? Yes. Sometimes. Do you?*
> *Tajul: Yes.*
> *Teacher: Do you like milk?*
> *Tajul: Do you like . . . (teacher understands 'driving')*
> *Teacher: Driving? . . . a car?*
> *Tajul: No. Ribena.*
> *Teacher: Yes. I like Ribena. Do you?*
> *Tajul: I like. Do you like coca-cola?*
> *Teacher: Yes. I like coca-cola. Do you?*
> *Tajul: Yes. Do you like sweets?*
> *Teacher: Sweets? Do you?*
> *Tajul: Do you like big sweets?*
> *Teacher: Mmm. Do you?*
> *Tajul: Do you like that big (shows huge) sweets?*
> *Teacher: Big, big sweets! Yes. And cakes.*
> *Tajul: You can't eat big, big sweets!*

Teacher: Well, perhaps if my mouth were bigger, I could!
Tajul: And long.

We are left uncertain as to how far Tajul is really interested in finding out about the likes and dislikes of his teacher and how far he is simply trying out and practising a grammatical structure. Whichever may be the case, he is very success- fully doing both. His teacher notes that this type of repetition is a well-used strategy by Tajul and some of his peers who seem to be more concerned with the structure of the language than collecting words like Tony or using phonics like Saida. Kalchuma, whose 'reading' opened this part of the chapter, is another child who constantly 'practises' a few structures: 'Mr Bump is go to gone, etc.' Never- theless, both children reveal how limited their knowledge of the grammar of the target language is and how much they have to learn in order to benefit from the sort of interactions engaged in by monolingual children and their teachers. Here is monolingual Jessica 'reading' from *If You Were a Bird . . .* (Duncan (1983):

Jessica: Look! They're scared. (points to illustration) Look! Her hair's gone on end.
Teacher: Mmm. The cat's terrified, too.
Jessica: He didn't know, did he, that there was a lion around.
(Teacher and Jessica read together: 'The park would be a jungle and you could be king')
Jessica: What does that say? (points to notice in illustration)
Teacher: It says, 'Keep off the grass'.
Jessica: Why does it say 'Keep off the grass'?
Teacher: Well, because people aren't supposed to walk on it, because if they do, it might make the grass die. If people walk on that grass all the time, their feet might stop it growing, you see.
Jessica: So he's obviously stopping it from growing.
Teacher: Mmm.
Jessica: But he's gonna walk off it sometime, isn't he? (turns page) Look, there he is, walking off!

Emergent bilinguals have simply not yet had enough experience in the new language to be familiar with the grammatical structures likely to appear in many early reading books. The dilemma for the teacher is in trying to provide a high quality of dialogue for children like Tajul yet in a language simple enough for them to understand.

Copying others: the strength of syntactic clues

When Tajul uses the word 'window' to refer to the magnifying glass in an illustration, he is using the same strategy of over-generalising employed by much younger monolingual children. Teachers of emergent bilinguals have a store of examples similar to our 'cats = fluffs' one cited earlier as well as evidence of over- generalisations of past tense verb forms such as 'he hitted me', etc. Many re- searchers bring evidence showing that reading miscues made by young second language learners tend to be predominantly *intralingual* (arising from the struc- ture of the target language) rather than *interlingual* (arising from interference from mother tongue influence). Catherine Wallace's (1986) detailed miscue analyses of the speech and reading of a variety of second language learners from age ten to adult in West London shows them searching for appropriate new rules rather than transferring from their first language.

However, how individuals go about learning the syntax of a second language is a complex issue. Goodman and Goodman's (1978) work shows that a number of factors influence the type of strategies used by emergent bilinguals. They conducted miscue analyses on Spanish, Arabic, Navajo and Samoan children's reading at different stages during primary level and found that the Spanish group (who were highly proficient in English) had miscues of exactly the same nature as native English speakers; Arabic children (who were at an early stage of English learning) made miscues showing both inter- and intralingual characteristics: Samoan children's miscues had an intralingual pattern and Navajo children's reading was generally characterised by few responses and long silences. They claim that inter-lingual (interference) errors are more common if (i) the first language is very different from the target language and (ii) children are at a very early stage of second language learning. These conclusions receive some support from other studies which compare the relative ease with which French or Spanish children learn to read English as opposed to those speaking Persian at home (Barnitz 1978). Their findings also highlight the importance of cultural aspects in influencing second language learning strategies which will be discussed in the next section.

Children who are able to take over first language learning strategies have obvious advantages. In Chapter 2, we saw how very young children can internalise and use whole expressions in appropriate contexts in their first language long before they are able to understand them word-for-word. Close observation of young emergent bilinguals who learn a second language rapidly reveals that they also take over 'chunks' of speech during interaction with first language speakers. The important thing about this strategy (referred to by Hatch (1974) as 'chunking') is that the chunks of language do not need to be understood by the child. They are attached to a specific context and can be called up whenever the same context recurs. This often happens in play situations: 'I'm gonna beat you up . . .', 'Oh no, you're not', etc. They can also happen between child and teacher, particularly during book-reading sessions. Tajul is expert at this. Notice the way he models his reply on the structure used by the teacher:

> (*A few months after practising 'Do you like' in the Meg and Mog story, Tajul and his teacher are looking at a Ladybird book* The Fireman)
>
> Tajul: *Look, they're gonna find gold!* (*pointing to the picture of firemen entering a burning house*)
> Teacher: (*laughs*) *Do you think so?*
> Tajul: *Yes.*
> Teacher: (*laughs*) *I don't know. They* might be.
> Tajul: *And there* might be *fish and water.*
> Teacher: *Do you think so?* Might be.
> Tajul: *In there, there's water.* (*points to bubbles under the fire-hose*)
> Teacher: *Underneath, you mean? Under the bubbles?*
> Tajul: *Yes.*
> Teacher: *Could be.*

The same pattern occurs on numerous occasions: the teacher 'models' a certain structure; the child copies it immediately afterwards and then goes on to practise it repeatedly. Tajul continues using '. . . and there might be' throughout the book in the same way as 'Do you like . . .?' a few months earlier.

A year older, six-year-old Shabbir, Nazma and the twins Shahina and Sabina illustrate well Ben-Zeev's (1977) point that learning a second language promotes an early analytic awareness of language. The children are acting out the story and experiencing considerable difficulty with *prepositions* (over/under the bridge, on, into, down, across, etc.). Their teacher plays a game of 'guessing the opposite' which includes nouns and adjectives as well as prepositions. Very quickly, the children use the idea for expressing what they want to say: 'It's the opposite of enormous, Miss . . .' (meaning 'tiny') or 'It's like "down" . . .' (meaning 'under'). Children learning to read in their first language, like Shabbir, Nazma and the twins, will, in any case, be accustomed to focusing carefully on how they express themselves during beginning reading lessons. The first pages of their primers consist of illustrations of different fruit and vegetables which they will be expected to talk about before they begin learning the Bengali sounds and letters.

Wugs or wüge: the weakness of syntactic clues

Nevertheless, grammatical clues are unquestionably weak during the early stages of second language learning. Syntactic clues are probably the most useful and the most reliable for children learning to read in their first language. Children have a 'feel' for the syntax or structure of their language from a very early stage. A much cited example by linguists is the two-year-old English speaker who is told an object is a 'wug', then shown two of the same object and asked to label them. Invariably, the children will refer to them immediately as 'two wugs', not only applying the correct rule for forming plurals, but using the appropriate *voiced* 'zz' rather than *unvoiced* 's' sound. Speakers of other languages would react differently. A German infant might correlate the word with 'Zug' (train) and form the plural in a similar way 'Züge' or 'Wüge'. We see, then, that learning to read in a familiar language aids prediction of a text enormously.

Research tells us (Adams 1990) that reading demands much more syntactic sophistication than listening as the syntactic structure of the written text must be discovered by the reader whereas it is largely given to the listener by the speaker through the context, e.g. 'Haven't I — you somewhere before?' at a party or 'Pick it — — the floor' in a classroom. Young first language readers have a range of syntactic clues as they approach a text. They are able to call upon many *cohesive devices* (devices which link one sentence or part of a sentence to another). Some of these are: *pronominal reference*, e.g. 'I saw John yesterday. *He* was ill'; *synonyms*, e.g. 'sick/ill'; *superordinates*, e.g. 'apples, oranges = fruit'; *collocational expressions*, e.g. 'toast with butter and jam'. Teachers in multi-lingual classes know how easily young children who are confident in a language can predict a word to complete sentences in popular, yet structurally difficult, texts, e.g. *Would You Rather . . .* by John Burningham or *If You Were a Bird . . .* by Joan Duncan. Syntactic clues also facilitate automaticity and enable some words to become redundant (see back also to the section on lexical clues). Until a sufficient supply of chunks have been built up, emergent bilinguals will need to compensate by reading every word, posing great demands on both memory and concentration.

How important are weak syntactic clues for emergent bilinguals? Common sense tells us that prediction of a text must be difficult if we cannot speak the language. Tony shows how difficult book-reading can be if children cannot 'chunk' language:

> *Tony: What's his name?*
> *Teacher: That one's called Mr Impossible.*
> *Tony: Mr Inpossible. (looks at cover and repeats four times) What's his name?*
> *Teacher: Mr Impossible.*
> *Tony: (turns page saying nothing)*
> *Mr Inpossible talking a boy.*
> *Mr Inpossible. He fall down shes hat. There's a girl and a boy . . . that's girl and boy.*

'Shes' is undoubtedly an interlingual error (interference) from Cantonese where gender is not marked by *possessive pronouns* as in European languages. A few months later, Tony and his teacher are reading a counting-book *Over in the Meadow* (Wadsworth 1986) together:

> *Teacher: (reads) 'Over in the meadow where the stream runs blue . . .'*
> *Tont: Blue.*
> *Teacher: 'Lived an old mother fish . . .'*
> *Tony: Fish.*
> *Teacher: 'And her little fishes two . . .'*
> *Tony: Two.*

This continues except where Tony interrupts, e.g.:

> *Teacher: '. . . lived an old mother cat and her little catties four . . .'*
> *Tony: What she eating?*
> *Teacher: I think they look like strawberries to me.*
> *Tony: I like strawberries.*
> *Teacher: So do I.*
> *Tony: I like, I like . . . strawberries.*
> *(this is obviously not the word he wants)*
> *Teacher: Do you?*
> *Tony: Mmm.*

The important question for teachers is: what enables some children, like Tajul, to learn 'chunks' of the new language very quickly while others, like Tony, seem to find this so difficult?

Syntactic clues: in summary

Syntactic clues are undoubtedly weak as emergent bilinguals learn to read in a new language. In contrast with monolingual or fluent speakers, these children are unable to narrow down the choice and predict words through a knowledge of the structure of the language. They also find it difficult to draw on discourse devices for cohesion, e.g. 'it' referring back to 'the dog', etc. On the other hand, they often have a strong and early analytic awareness and know that a structure actually *exists*. We can trace ways in which successful young second language learners go about practising both specific structures and 'chunks' of language during play and book interactions with their teachers and more fluent peers. To assist children in making the most of syntactic clues, we shall need to consider:

- What types of 'chunks' of language will be particularly helpful for the early reader to practise and which activities will help them do this?
- What cohesive devices seem to present particular difficulties? Are there ways they can be practised?
- How can automaticity be acquired?
- In what ways can children practise the syntax of a new language at home if their parents have limited English?
- What pattern of errors (if any) can be detected in the learning strategies of successful and less successful beginner readers? Does the child who is less successful in learning the target language generally make more errors of an interlingual nature?

Semantic knowledge (knowledge of the meaning of a text)

Tony and Jessica illustrate well the nature and importance of semantic clues in early reading. Even at the moment in which Tony's teacher explains that the stylised illustration in his 'Mr Men' book is 'toast and marmalade . . . you know, like you have for breakfast in the morning', she realises that her words may be senseless for Tony. Later, she learns that Tong's family usually has soup for breakfast. When Jessica confidently refers to 'snuggling under the duvet' and having Rice Krispies which go 'Snap, Crackle and Pop!', we know that it is a world she shares with her teacher. As members of the same cultural group and speakers of the same language, we automatically rely on shared understandings. In his work *Language, Culture and Personality* (1970), the anthropologist Edward Sapir puts this succinctly when he says that language 'does not . . . stand apart from or run parallel to direct experience but completely interpenetrates with it' (p. 8). Later, he illustrates the importance of a shared language as groups interact and where 'He talks like one of us' is equivalent to saying 'He is one of us' (p. 17). Learning to speak a language and consequently to predict that language when reading a text, therefore, is intimately linked with the experiences gained in the language.

In her book *Purity and Danger* (1970), Mary Douglas uses examples from many cultures to illustrate the importance of different rituals in each society and how expectations of these will be different across cultures. Examples from Chapter 2 show us how cultural alliances and language use may be different even within short distances in the same country (Heath 1983). Nevertheless, we know that cultural routines within Europe, the USA and Australia are likely to share much more in common with each other than with those in Asia or Africa. In France, Nicole and her family have few difficulties in this respect. Although she also finds comprehension texts linked with specific cultural practices (particularly those linked with eating and food!) difficult to understand, her family's lifestyle and expectations are largely similar to those of her French peers. She knows the same traditional folk and fairy stories, watches the same TV programmes and listens to the same music. But what if children's cultural routines are very different from those in the host community? With apparently all the odds against them, in what ways might emergent bilinguals benefit from semantic clues as they learn to read in the classroom?

The strength of semantic clues: the potential advantages of being a 'stranger'

At first, it seems sad that Husna and Naseema read the words of *Each, Peach, Pear, Plum* without knowledge of the experience of the magnificent plum pie. They have not yet assisted in the long ritual of making it, smelling it as it cooks and eventually having the pleasure of eating it with their family and friends. If they had, they would most certainly have been able to remember its English name. Yet as we saw from their analogy of 'gosh' with 'dosh', they have a flexibility regarding words and are prepared for adventure as they use them. Lambert (1967) refers to this as a 'cognitive flexibility' where children are learning double sets of lexical and syntactic rules. It may be that this extends to a 'cultural flexibility', an openness towards learning the new routines of the host culture.

It is obvious that children such as Husna and Naseema who enter school from a very different cultural orientation are faced with a different learning task from those like Jessica who share the culture of the teacher. As we saw in Chapter 2, these 'strangers' may be able consciously to inquire into the 'what' and the 'why' of every situation. Tajul seems to be doing this as he shares stories with his teacher:

> *Teacher: (reading from* Meg at Sea*)*
>   *That's the fish.*
> *Tajul: And that?*
> *Teacher: That's the octopus. That's an octopus.*
> *Tajul: (points) That's the fish.*
> *Teacher: (reads) 'A present for you . . .' (out of text) Yes, there's the fish. (reads again)*
>   *Meg cooked the fish . . .*
> *Tajul: And, do you like?*
> *Teacher: Mmm. And they like to eat octopus, too, I think. Do you like octopus?*
> *Tajul: (hesitantly) No. Do you?*
> *Teacher: No. Some people do. (Reads) 'Meg and Mog had a rest.'*
> *Tajul: English do?*
> *Teacher: Well, some English do. Not many . . . (reads) 'Chopper ahoy! They saw a*
>   *helicopter . . .'*

Like Kalchuma establishing 'Bangla say bumbla, English say bzzz', Tajul is eager to learn about the new language and culture he is entering. The enthusiasm and inquisitiveness shown by these children give us reason to believe that attitudes and social experiences in the new culture will be a major influence on the speed with which they learn the target language and are able to utilise semantic and syntactic clues. Similar findings have been made by Wong-Fillmore (1982) who argues that sociable, out-going children tend to learn the target language more efficiently because they quickly learn appropriate language 'formulae' for different events. 'Formulae' are similar to Hatch's 'chunks' discussed in the last section. We saw in Chapter 2 how young children go about mastering these formulae in their first language. Tajul and Kalchuma show us that successful emergent bilinguals do something similar, but, unlike monolingual infants, they are aware of what they are doing.

In his detailed study of 63 young Turkish children learning to read in Dutch, Verhoeven (1987) found that the degree with which children were able to identify with both their language and culture of origin and with the new culture paralleled their reading progress. He cites Lambert's (1967) notion of four patterns of identification with a new culture: (i) identification with both cultures; (ii) identification with the majority culture and rejection of the culture of origin; (iii) identification with the culture of origin and rejection of the majority culture; (iv) failure to identify with either culture. Lambert argues that learning a new language will, of course, be possible, simply by living in the country and using it entirely for instrumental purposes. Nevertheless, learning is likely to be much more successful if the new group is taken as a reference point and if new life-styles and values are grafted onto old. Where families have recently arrived in Britain, it may be the children's responsibility to mediate the new language and culture to their parents. The task for the teacher, then, will be both to initiate the child into the host culture of the country and jointly to negotiate a classroom culture of reading.

Strawberries or strawberries? The weakness of semantic clues

Tony's positive responses as he read *Over in the Meadow* with his teacher in the last section were to count carefully from one to ten, pointing to the numbers as he did so and to pick on a detail in one illustration, saying 'I like strawberries'. But he does not manage to get his meaning across to the teacher. He wanted to add something else that he liked, but realised he did not know the name and, rather than risk complications, he simply repeated dejectedly 'strawberries'. Does he want to tell his teacher but does not know the English word and is loathe to risk saying something that might be wrong? Or does he feel that what he wants to refer to will be outside the experience of his teacher and he would rather keep it to himself? The teacher's experiences when meeting his family lead her to suspect the latter.

Undoubtedly, emergent bilinguals will be at a disadvantage when calling upon semantic clues to predict words and texts. Their difficulties are likely to be on two levels. First, children may have difficulty in predicting a text because it describes something outside their experience. Many teachers recall tackling an explanation of 'plum pies' or even simpler fare with children to whom such dishes are inconceivable. Of course, we all meet unknown or culturally strange items in texts. Nevertheless, if it happens frequently enough and is combined with the whole text being in a new language, learning to read will obviously be made more difficult. Teachers, themselves, recall how much more difficult it is at first to remember the names of bilingual pupils in comparison with familiar ones. In a study with fluent adult biliterates, Steffensen, Joag-dev and Anderson (1980) show how familiarity with an experience makes a difference to reading. They gave American and Indian readers two letters about a wedding in each culture and found that each group read the passage relating to their own culture faster and more accurately. The familiar occasion made sense to them and consequently they could predict what was likely to happen. Looking back to the section on lexical clues, we saw how a network of words is linked to a particular schema (in this case 'getting up in the morning'). The schema itself enables us to call up a range of experiences and corresponding lexis and expressions. Tony obviously gets up in the morning too, but parts of the experience are very different from those of children like Jessica.

The second level is wider. In Chapter 2, we saw how Tony's family interprets 'work', 'play', 'reading' and 'learning' very differently from his teacher. For Tony's teacher, learning to read involves experimentation and pleasure and the attractive storybook is an essential tool in fostering these. For Tony's family, literacy is seen as mediated through obedience and training and 'the book' is the reward rather than the medium for learning to read. Tony is learning these ideas too when he attends his Saturday school. Scollon and Scollon (1981) showed us in Chapter 2 how different the 'word-for-word' reading of the Athabaskan child is from the 'whole-text' approach of their own western mainstream daughter. They go on to suggest that particular discourse patterns and forms of literacy are related to personal and social identity. Important questions for teachers are: How are 'learning' and the role of the learner conceived by families? Are experimenting and risk-taking part of their understanding of formal education or do they view learning as taking place initially through copying and repeating? If views of home and school are very different, how will home/school reading programmes take account of this?

Semantic clues: in summary

During detailed observations of monolingual children in an East London nursery class, Valerie Walkerdine (1981) noticed how effectively monolingual children used dialogue in certain role-play situations in the dramatic play area. Particularly, she identified the context of 'watching TV' and recorded how children seemed able to interact together, calling upon 'chunks' of speech which were quite specific to that context but would otherwise have been inaccessible to them. In some ways, the children were re-enacting the 'modelling' and 'scaffolding' we saw taking place between the caregiver and young child in Chapter 2. Rather than relying on adults, they were using a familiar context to support each other. Where young first and second language learners are in classes together, fluent speakers will be able to help emergent bilinguals 'situate themselves in contexts and the pre-packaged routines of the target language at the same time. Hatch, Peck and Wagner-Gough (1979) give examples comparing how effective this sort of language can be for children at a very early stage in second language learning. They describe a five-year-old Taiwanese child playing with a first language speaker during the first two months of beginning English:

> *First language child: I got a real gun.*
> *Second language child: I got a real gun.*
> *L.1: You gotta parachute?*
> *L.2: Yeh. Gotta parachute.*
> *Adult: What's a parachute?*
> *L.1: It has a man go down.*
> *L.2: Yeh? go down, down, down.*

Using semantic clues effectively will inevitably involve a blending of new ways of life onto the home culture. Young emergent bilinguals will often be in a stronger position to do this than their parents. They are surrounded by all types of exciting oral and written language initiating them into the new culture. Even in classes where almost all children are second language learners, they are unlikely to escape a variety of crisp, chocolate and biscuit wrappings, street and bus-signs and probably (though not inevitably) TV programmes. Children's cultural flexibility will be a strength upon which to build in the classroom. Grosjean (1982) develops this idea and stresses an integrated or holistic view of the bilingual whereby we realise that children combine a unique blend of two cultures and languages rather than being two monolinguals with separate languages and cultures. To assist children in making the most of semantic clues, we shall need to consider:

- How can teachers provide emergent bilinguals with opportunities for developing experiences and corresponding language routines in the target language?
- How and in what ways can teachers themselves develop cultural flexibility?
- In what ways might the 'scaffolding' and modelling given by the teacher differ from that offered by the first language child? How might both complement each other?

Bibliographic knowledge (the knowledge of books)

Until then, I had thought each book spoke of the things . . . that lie outside books. Now I realised that not infrequently books speak of books; it is as if they spoke among themselves. It (the library) was, then, the place of a long . . . murmuring, an imperceptible dialogue between one parchment and another, a living thing, a receptacle of powers not to be ruled by human mind, a treasure of secrets emanated by many minds.

(Eco 1980, p. 286)

When Jessica confidently predicts that the little elves finished the shoemaker's work although they have not yet appeared in the story of 'The Elves and the Shoemaker', she is calling upon her knowledge of the story from her home repertoire. Her comment 'and they (the shoemaker and his wife) have hard beds' fits into her fairytale picture of 'Long ago, there lived a poor shoemaker and his wife . . .'. Husna and Naseema are also beginning to call upon chunks of language from English storybooks when they have at their fingertips 'Oh, my gosh, my golly!'

Ways in which a knowledge of written stories helps children situate themselves in both the social and mental context of reading have been documented at length in studies by Dombey 1983, Wells 1987 and Gibson 1989. Through a detailed analysis of a three-year-old, Dombey (1983) shows us how a child involved in story-reading with her mother is able to 'switch into' complex language structures involving appropriate story lexis and *story collocations*, e.g. *grinding* the corn, etc., and *ellipsis*, e.g. omission of words – 'John walked over to the table and (he) put the cheese on (it)' – which would have been too complex during normal conversations. In her study of a nursery class of 'school-oriented' monolingual children in the USA, Cochran-Smith (1984) claims that children of three and four already bring what she terms 'readerlike behaviour' from home. By this, she means that they already act like readers although as yet unable to read at all. She details two strategies the children are able to use in order to situate themselves in the social context of reading: (i) 'life-to-text' strategies – they are able to bring their own life experiences to help them work out the meaning of the text; (ii) 'text-to-life' strategies – they use happenings in the story to refer to what happens in their own lives. In other words, there is a constant interplay between what they know from life and the events of the story; they use their own experience to understand the text and at the same time, the story is related to their lives and enables the children to reflect upon life experiences.

In his longitudinal study set up in 1972 of 128 monolingual families from different socio-economic backgrounds, of whom 32 were followed up in depth between the ages of one and eleven, Wells (1987) maintains that, of all the factors in pre-school literacy investigated, only listening to written stories at home has a strong correlation with school literacy success at seven. A lack of familiarity with stories, claims Wells, means that children are likely to enter school with a very limited understanding of the purposes of literacy and how to gain meaning from print. Wells refers to this as a cycle of disadvantage and goes on to say that these children 'urgently need the experience of books and the pleasure of being read to' (1987, p. 146).

Wells' conclusions give a dismal forecast for emergent bilinguals who enter school unfamiliar with the story-reading practice. But must this really put them at such a disadvantage? Nicole enters her French school with an excellent grounding in story-book reading in English. Yet this is not called upon at all during her early French reading lessons which require a detailed matching of sounds to graphemes, etc. That Nicole manages this with relative ease would seem to have more to do with her confidence in herself and her parents as 'readers' rather than a familiarity with story-reading itself. Nicole's classroom experiences bring home to us the danger of assuming that educational practices and beliefs will be the same everywhere. It would be a mistake to believe that children who have no experience with written stories cannot offer bibliographic knowledge of a different sort.

Written language as a code: the strength of bibliographic knowledge

Alif has been sent to the headteacher accused of hitting someone in the playground. The expression on his face is very serious as he denies the offence. Asked why his opponent should be crying if he has not been injured, Alif replies: 'I was just looking and then the tears came into his eyes . . .'

Alif has taken a chunk of literary language from his reading and is using it in speech. Books are important teachers of the target language to emergent bilinguals and may enable them to step straight into academic 'school' language. An immersion programme in Canada whereby native English speaking children completed their first two years' schooling in French (Lambert and Tucker 1972) revealed that the children achieved almost as well on English reading tests and better on mathematical tests than their monolingual peers. The researchers proposed that the new language was being used as a sort of 'code' attached directly to new concepts. There are a number of reasons why emergent bilinguals may be able to learn the language of books easily. First, as in the Canadian experiment, these children learn 'chunks' of book language from listening to the stories where they are used. There is no problem that they might mix features of spoken and written language as first language speakers, for their two languages will be totally different. Then, we know that emergent bilinguals are particularly sensitive to the language used by the teacher, who acts as a role model. Together with their usually excellent memories, children may well take 'book' or academic language on board simply as the new 'school language'.

To recognise the bibliographic strengths of emergent bilinguals, we cannot restrict our definition of 'book knowledge' to 'story-book knowledge'. All the children in Chapter 2 possess books, but not 'story-books', at home. That these contain the alphabet, exercises, short reading texts, etc., and are sometimes of flimsy material or in black and white does not diminish their validity or value for the children and their families. Quite the contrary; for most families, these books are seen as preparation for reaching important texts (in some cases the Qur'ān or, for Tony, the book itself). In addition, the children are aware that books can be written in different scripts and can be read from right to left if they are in Urdu or sometimes from top to bottom in Mandarin. All this sort of knowledge is not of the traditional story-book variety but is important book knowledge just the same. In her study of dual language books, Edwards (1995) shows how easy it is to become 'culture-bound' when defining a 'good book'. She contrasts the views of children and their teachers when choosing dual language books. Teachers preferred glossy 'western' looking dual language dictionaries whereas some children preferred the rather faded Indian dictionaries with traditional illustrations on the grounds that they were more 'adult' and 'serious looking'.

The descriptions in Chapter 2 of children's Community schools and Nicole's state school in France show us that even the term 'book knowledge' is not sufficient and that we need to include knowledge of all types of written materials. Research studies on both indigenous and immigrant origin families who do not share the reading practices of the school show that they participate in a whole variety of literacy activities, albeit not linked with children's story-books or books themselves. One study taking place with groups of Hispanic, white and black lower-class parents in the USA (Anderson and Stokes 1984) points to the importance of journals, newspapers, games and religious texts in people's lives. Shabbir's and Louthfur's homes contain a whole variety of dual language calendars. In their study of a Vietnamese child in the USA, Schieffelin and Cochran-Smith (1984) show how letter writing is likely to hold an important place in the lives of families who have recently immigrated. When Tony links the Queen's appearance on TV with her photo in the newspaper – 'Princess . . . She in Hong Kong. I see in the television' – he shows us the important step he has made in realising the purpose of both in conveying information through image or print.

'Sticking doors' and 'Winning hands in marriage': the weakness of bibliographic clues

Jessica, Gillian, Scott, Fozia, Tony and Kalchuma sit down to listen to The Elves and the Shoemaker *together. The teacher asks the children to predict who might have made up the shoes while the shoemaker and his wife were sleeping. Scott argues strongly that 'the man in the picture' (a customer the following morning) must have made them. There was no reason to suppose it should have been anyone else, as no elves had yet appeared on the scene. Nevertheless, Jessica says confidently 'It was the little elves.'*

Emergent bilinguals are likely to have three main weaknesses when calling upon bibliographic clues: (i) they will probably be unfamiliar with traditional and well-known European stories in the same way as Scott, a monolingual child, illustrates above; (ii) the language used in many books will be even more complex than spoken language and, therefore, very difficult to understand; (iii) the use of story-books for beginning reading may not correspond to their families' interpretation of what 'counts' as valid material for learning to read.

(i) Reading the words of a story is much easier if the plot is familiar

Nicole's parents buy her traditional European fairy-tales in French. The whole family laugh together over 'Cendrillon' which they are already so familiar with as 'Cinderella'. Just a few pictures from *La Ventafocs* is enough to tell her that it is the same story and she is able confidently to learn a few key words. Other emergent bilinguals receive the same clues when they listen to traditional stories with their families in their first language before tackling them in English in school. Of course, the stories need not necessarily be from the families' country

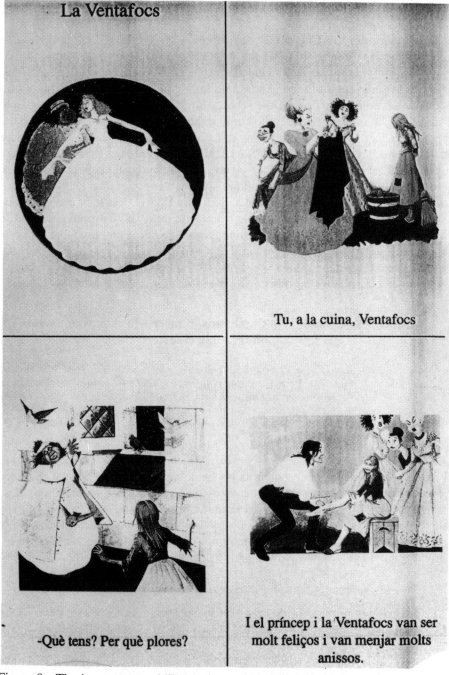

Figure 8 The importance of illustrations, simplicity and context when reading in a new language. What differences does it make that the story and the script are familiar and the language is of European origin?

of origin. Nevertheless, a familiarity with names, items of clothes, food and other cultural practices represented will all assist prediction and remembering the relevant words to attach to items. A good way to test the importance of familiarity is to try learning to read the text in Figure 8. How much easier is it than learning the text of unfamiliar and unrelated pictures?

(ii) The language of stories and books can be very difficult

A glance through children's story-books reveals just how complex structures and decontextualised language can be for the emergent bilingual. Here are just a few examples from well-used books:

Your daughter is indeed clever if she can do as you say.
(Rumpelstiltskin, *Ladybird Grade II Easy Reader*)

The wood-cutter, who had a kind heart, agreed, and the little man in green was so grateful that he promised to grant the first three wishes the woodcutter might make, whatever they were.
(The Tall Book of Nursery Tales, *pub. by Edmund Ward*)

Captain Crab rushed out, ranting and roaring, and STREAK went the brush, right through Jethro's work. Down came Jethro to give Captain Crab a piece of his mind.
(Don't Blame Me!, *Rogers 1990*)

Would you rather . . .
(In the book by John Burningham; an excellent book but not until you understand what 'Would you rather . . .?' actually means . . .)

Inversion of language may add to difficulties:

In came two little elves.
(The Elves and the Shoemaker, *Ladybird*)

Headfirst into the well he fell.
(Tell me a story, *E. Colwell*)

Idiomatic language can be hard, too:

'He picked it (the golden apple) *up in a flash and rode away like the wind.*
(A Second Story-Teller's Choice, *E. Colwell*)

There are many similar examples. It is important that children hear and learn the language of books and Alif above shows how he has taken this into his spoken repertoire. Part of the magic of books is the sound of words and not understanding them all (abracadabra, open sesame, Rumpelstiltskin). Nevertheless, children will need time, repetition and practice before some book language makes sense to them and becomes a useful clue as they set about learning to read.

(iii) Not all cultures or educational systems view the story-book as essential in learning to read

Tony's Chinese class and his grandfather for whom the book is seen as the reward for learning to read show how the story-reading practice cannot be seen as 'natural'. Nicole's French school does not use story-books for teaching

Different use of clues by mono- and emergent bilingual children

L1	L2	Action
Graphophonic clues		
Know certain sounds occur together: 'spl–', 'cr–', etc.	May have difficulty in distinguishing or pronouncing certain sounds and blends and recognising constraints	Build upon analytic awareness and knowledge of metalanguage
Know some sounds start or end words; 'ng' to end but not start a word	If meaning unknown 'sounding it out' can be meaningless	Practise pronunciation
Have no difficulties with pronunciation, e.g. 'nose' (voiced 's') or same sound, different pronunciation (read (ee), read (e), etc.)	May be familiar with and understand concepts such as 1 to 1 correspondence earlier than monolinguals	Achieve automaticity upon which to build
	May be familiar with approach from community class	
Lexical clues		
Easy to build up bank of high frequency words; attractive 'one-sight words' can be built up	Difficulty in accessing high frequency words if unknown; 'one-sight words' not available in English	Build upon good memory and analytical awareness; provide experiences to gain 'one-sight words'
Redundancy facilitates learning	No redundancy	Automaticity important; words must be in context
Collocation ('grind' 'corn', etc.)	Difficult to use collocation	Introduce words in lexical sets (groups on same theme) and opposites; mimes; elicit words on certain theme (words about 'witches', etc.)

Different use of clues by mono- and emergent bilingual children (*continued*)

L1	L2	Action
Syntactic clues		
Can narrow choice through awareness of structure of language, e.g. 'Haven't I – met you somewhere before?'	Slows child down as child must rely more on memory and sight recognition through limited understanding	Draw on analytic ability and ability to rephrase
Can 'chunk' phrases	Less ability to 'chunk' language	Build upon ability to repeat chunks after teacher; focus on play and role-play for 'chunking' language and linking language and experience
Easy to use discourse devices for cohesion, e.g. 'it', etc. to refer back in text	More difficult to draw on discourse devices	Provide lots of repetition of exact words, e.g. in stories to practise anaphoric reference
Semantic clues		
Can draw on experience of life and culture to predict text	TV helps but shared cultural knowledge missing, e.g. Husna and Naseema reading *Each, Peach, Pear, Plum*	Experience in English play and role-play; many stories
Bibliophonic clues		
Possible to draw on knowledge of way books work in English, e.g. open right-left; print left-right; top-bottom, etc.	Not always same as in English, e.g. Arabic, Mandarin, etc.	Explicit modelling of reading

reading in the early stages; neither do the Community classes visited by Shabbir, Nazma, Louthfur and Sabina and Shahina, the twins. The children will go on to read stories in their Bengali and Chinese classes, but only after they have completed an apprenticeship of learning the alphabet, describing the pictures, etc. The story of Tony's family underlines the danger in assuming that parents will automatically understand school teaching methods and highlights the importance of dialogue between home and school.

Bibliographic clues: in summary

Gemma: Porridge was too hot and they set off in the woods. Long time ago. Her name was Goldilocks . . . Too sweet, said Goldilocks, Daddy bear . . . too hot. Tries mummy bear. Too lumpy . . . Tries mummy bear . . . tries baby bear . . . the best, so baby bear now just right. So she ate it all up . . . Tries baby bear's bed. Just right.

(Minns 1990, p. 104)

This excerpt highlights the importance of bibliographic clues as emergent bilinguals learn to read. Gemma has already grasped the narrative in that her story has a beginning 'Long time ago . . .', a middle and an end 'Just right'. Although still at the early stages of learning English, the book has provided her with complex 'chunks' of language. She is comfortable with the past tense of the verbs 'to be', 'to eat' and 'to say'; she can say that something is 'too sweet, too hot, too lumpy' and she has mastered the superlative 'the best'; she knows the conventional opening 'Long time ago . . .' and she can use the complex verb 'they set off'. Margaret Meek (1988) points out the importance of illustrations in explaining a story and assisting prediction for young readers by using the example of the chicken followed by the fox in *Rosie's Walk* (Hutchins 1968) to show how excitement, fear and anxiety can be awakened in children in spite of a very simple text. Books such as this will be especially important in enabling emergent bilinguals to make sense of texts. Story-books may act as a catalyst in developing emergent bilinguals' other clues as they set about learning to speak and read a new language together. In Chapter 5, we shall trace how this can take place in the classroom. As they assist children in developing bibliographic clues, teachers will need to ask themselves:

- Why types of 'written knowledge' do children bring to school from home?
- Which story-books best enable children both to make sense of text easily and 'chunk' important pieces of book or story language?
- Which stories are likely to present emergent bilinguals with difficulties and why?
- Is there a dialogue between family and school on the place and use of different types of materials in early reading programmes?

IN SUMMARY

This chapter focused on reading as a mental and linguistic activity. The first section explained different views of reading in terms of the 'bottom-up' (from the smallest unit of sound to the most general context) and the 'top-down' (from the most general to the particular) approaches. An adaptation of the 'interactive' view of reading was then presented, whereby children are seen to draw upon clues sent out by five knowledge centres (orthographic/phonic; lexical; syntactic; semantic; bibliographic) in order to make sense of a text.

The second section examined how emergent bilinguals draw upon the same clues as their monolingual peers, but use them in different ways, reflecting different strengths and weaknesses. Examples of children's early reading teach us a number of lessons. First, we see clearly how some children are able to transfer strategies learned in one context and in one language to another. This view is sometimes referred to as a common underlying cognitive proficiency and is supported in various research studies (Vygotsky 1962, Cummins 1979). Second, we see that children can learn to read before they have oral competence in the target language. Indeed, it is clear that these young children are learning English *through* their reading. Reading, then, can lead oral language development. Third, we see how one set of clues (particularly strong lexical clues) can compensate for others during the early stages of learning to read. Fourth, it becomes clear that the social and mental contexts of reading constantly interact: the children's home and community class experiences are likely to influence their view on what counts as valid approaches to beginning reading as well as the strength of particular clues; the strength or weakness of syntactic, semantic and bibliographic clues will depend upon children's knowledge and acceptance of the host culture and the sharing of new cultural practices. Finally, we see clearly how both spoken language and reading development are inextricably linked with experiences gained in the language itself.

These lessons provoke key questions for work in the classroom: If words are only useful in the context of enabling us to predict a sentence, how can children's lexical strengths best be developed without becoming simply strings of individual words? If syntactic and semantic clues depend upon 'welding' language onto experiences so that phrases become automatic, how can the teacher provide such experiences within the confines of the classroom? If children learn English through reading itself, what sort of texts do we need for this? How clear do 'chunks' of text need to be and how can they be transferred into real life? How might bibliographic knowledge inform all the other clues? These are topics for the second part of this book.

Further reading

Donaldson, M. (1978) *Children's Minds*, Glasgow: Fontana.
Goelman, H., Oberg, A. and Smith, F. (eds.) (1984) *Awakening to Literacy*, London: Heinemann Education.
Meek, M. (1991) *On Being Literate*, London: The Bodley Head.
Scollon, R. and Scollon, B. K. (1981) *Narrative, Literacy and Face in Interethnic Communication*, Norwood, NJ: Ablex.

Part Two
Emergent Bilinguals in the Classroom

4

Starting From the Known: the 'Inside-Out' Approach to Reading

Tony, our Cantonese speaking child, is looking at a book with his teacher shortly after starting school at five.

Tony: What's in that book?
Teacher: That one's called Mr Impossible.
Tony: Mr Inpossible. (looks at cover)
  Mr Inpossible. (repeats four times with different intonation)
  Mr Inpossible is in . . . is (points) the house. (turns page)
  What's his name?
Teacher: Mr Impossible.
Tony: Mr Inpossible talking a boy. (turns page)
  Mr Inpossible. He fall down she's hat. (turns page)
  He's talking.
  And girl and boy. What's that? (points at Mr Impossible)
Teacher: Mr Impossible.
Tony: There's a girl and a boy . . . that's girl and boy.

We have met Tony before and noted that he is particularly drawn to what his teacher calls 'collecting words'. Tajul does the same as he begins a new language. At first, he is keen to participate in the only way he can with 'full-stop' or 'question mark' as his teacher reads; later he guesses 'window?' as he points to the magnifying-glass in a 'Meg and Mog' book. Later still, he tries to get information from his teacher by his deliberate use of negatives. He will point to a picture of a milkman or a fireman and say 'That's not Daddy' and receive the appropriate label 'No. That's the milkman (fireman).' Kalchuma does it too as she is concerned to find out which words she can transfer from Sylheti and which ones she needs to learn in English: 'Bangla say bumbla, English say bzzz.' Most of us use a similar strategy as we learn a new language. Returning to our Catalan story

La Ventafocs, we see how much easier it is for a beginner to label objects or people, like '*Ventafocs*' or '*dama*' rather than master whole sentences like '*Mira, aqui teniu la Ventafocs!*' or '*Si haguessis vist quin vestit duia aquella dama!*'.

In Chapter 3, we saw that the lexical (word) knowledge centre is likely to be emergent bilinguals' greatest resource as they begin reading in a new language. Different research studies showed us that the children have an early understanding of one-to-one correspondence as well as an excellent memory and a sensitivity for words should they slip into the wrong language. At the same time, we saw that children are likely to be held back particularly by two factors: (i) they lack personal 'key' or meaningful words in the target language, and (ii) they are forced to remember every individual word until they have enough 'chunks' of language at their fingertips. This chapter suggests a programme based on emergent bilinguals' strengths while structuring activities to recognise their particular weaknesses. It starts from the child's own knowledge and experience and gradually moves outwards into the new world; it starts from the smallest units of meaning, the letters and words, and gradually links these into complete texts. The approach outlined in this chapter shares a number of common features with 'Language-Experience' approaches to beginning reading. But its crucial feature is not to tie children into known experiences. Rather, it has in mind the countless experiences of the new world to come. I call it an 'Inside-Out' approach. It is but one half of the programme, complemented by the global or 'Outside-In' approach based on the life and language of the book which we shall meet in Chapter 5.

The chapter is divided into three sections: the first examines the theory behind the approach and explains the principles upon which it is based. The second section shows ways in which these principles are illustrated in different practices taking place at different times and in different countries. The third section presents practical ideas for a programme in classes of emergent bilinguals today. In Chapter 2, we asked how far teachers can 'scaffold' the learning of young emergent bilinguals in the classroom. This chapter outlines ways in which explicit 'scaffolding' may take place when working with very young children in the classroom context.

I. WHAT DOES AN 'INSIDE-OUT' APPROACH TO READING MEAN?

During the 1950s and 1960s important parallel developments were taking place in psychology and linguistics. In psychology, the work of Piaget (1959) and in linguistics the work of Chomsky (1964) were influential in providing evidence to show that children do not learn simply by copying the actions and language of adults. Instead, they actively construct their own view of the world and use language both to represent and extend experiences made. In his book *A Theory of Personality* the American psychologist George Kelly (1955) outlined a view of 'personal constructs' which conveys vividly the active nature of human learning. He uses the metaphor of humans constantly working as 'scientists'. Like scientists, we are constantly making hypotheses in order to predict what awaits us. If our hypothesis proves to be correct, the experience is stored within our 'construction' of reality to be used as a template for generalising and predicting in similar circumstances. If wrong, it is discarded and a new hypothesis tried out. A simple example to illustrate this is 'waiting at the bus-stop'. We soon learn to predict that a bus will stop, especially if we hail it. However, it is essential to realise that our learning is specific to our cultural group. Although the bus-stop might be common to many cultures, knowing whether or not to queue, whether to get on at the front or back or whether to pay the driver or a conductor, is not.

Our language learning takes place in a similar way. We know that an infant learning the word 'dog' will generalise and predict that all four-legged animals are dogs until the prediction proves inadequate and a new word is learned. Young monolingual children are often still over-generalising the past tense in nursery school when they tell us they have 'sticked their picture on', etc. Language prediction can be extremely useful. In Chapter 3, we saw how even very young children were able to predict 'two wug-s' from their knowledge of English syntax. Imagine being at a party where loud music blocks out much of the conversation. If the talk is in a language we understand, we have little difficulty in predicting the sentence 'Haven't I – you – before?' We are able to do this first by understanding the context of the situation. Our conversation partner was hardly likely to be presenting complex medical findings. If this had been the case, and if we had been unfamiliar with the world of medicine, prediction would probably not have been possible. Then, our knowledge of syntax or the structure of the language enables us to complete what we cannot hear. Assuming our partner knows the language, he or she is hardly likely to be saying 'Haven't I mix you sun before?'

It takes little imagination to draw parallels between predicting life experiences and language structures and predicting words as we learn to read. The key question is: What enables learners to take the step from speaking to understanding writing on a page or screen, to realise that knowledge of life and language can help them make sense of words and texts?

II. LANGUAGE-EXPERIENCE APPROACHES ACROSS THE WORLD

It was two inspired teachers working in very different circumstances during the 1950s and 1960s who showed how ideas from psychology and linguistics could be translated into practical reading programmes for both adults and children. Both shared a common approach, yet their interpretation was very different, for their learners were worlds apart. Their common starting-point was that traditional learning materials simply did not make sense for their pupils. The teachers were Paolo Freire and Sylvia Ashton-Warner. Their approach teaches us much about a way into reading based upon personal and group experiences and their ideas are still inspirational to work now taking place in many parts of the world. How and why they abandoned traditional methods of teaching and chose radical alternatives is explained in more detail below.

'Generative words': adults learning to read in Brazil

Paolo Freire was a literacy teacher in Brazil where, during the 1950s and 1960s, few rural workers had been able to attend school. His innovatory literacy programme (translated into English in *Education: The Practice of Freedom* in 1973) was based on two interlocking principles:

(i) Learning is not simply a passive memorising of letters and words but a creation on the part of the learner who is involved in self-transformation. Learners must actively take learning into their own hands and become agents of their learning. This means that learning becomes a dialogue between teacher and learner, symbolised by the words of the teacher who refers always to 'we' rather than 'you' as tasks are undertaken.

(ii) Learning does not, therefore, successfully take place where texts are meaningless for the life of the learner (Freire quotes the first sentence of a traditional reading primer 'Grace eats the grapes' where his learners have neither known anyone called Grace nor eaten a grape in their lives). Instead, learning must take place through 'generative words' or words which enable communication between the pupil and the world so that the content is identified with the learning process.

The programme takes place in five phases:

Phase 1: The teacher researches the vocabulary of the group of learners to find out which words are most weighted with meaning. These might be words linked with work, emotions or even colloquial phrases.

Phase 2: These generative words are sorted and ordered according to (i) their phonemic richness and phonetic difficulty (the simplest first – this becomes clearer below); (ii) their semantic flexibility (some words can be used more frequently and flexibly than others); (iii) the importance of the emotional content of a word (how far it triggers common emotions in the group).

Phase 3: The teacher builds 'codifications' around the generative words (stories or typical situations into which these words can be set).

Phase 4: A time-table or sequence of reading activities or lessons is designed which must be flexible.

Phase 5: The reading sessions take the following form: first, the situation involving the generative word is discussed and only after this is the word shown; the word is then broken down into 'phonemic families', e.g.:

'tijolo' (brick): ti – jo – lo

The family of the first syllable or 'piece' is shown:

ta – te – ti – to – tu

This is followed by the others:

ja – je – ji – jo – ju

la – le – li – lo – lu

A problem is posed by the teacher: do the pieces have something that is the same and something different? The students point out very quickly what is the same and what is different. The teacher then asks: can they therefore all be 'ti'? Again, the answer is not difficult. The same question is asked of the other syllables. Freire stresses that since it is preceded by a problem, the information is not a gift. The most important moment comes when the three families are presented together:

ta – te – ti – to – tu
ja – je – ji – jo – ju   (the discovery card)
la – le – li – lo – lu

At this moment, the group all begin to make words with the combinations available, e.g. tatu (armadillo); luta (struggle); jato (jet); juta (jute); lula (squid); tela (screen), etc. On the same first evening, the participants write the words. On the following day, they bring with them from home as many words as they were able to make with the combination of phonemes they have learned. Mistakes are unimportant at this early stage; what matters is the discovery of phonemic combinations. Finally, the group discuss which of these words are 'thinking' and which are 'dead' words.

Freire asks: 'How can one explain the fact that a man who was illiterate several days earlier could write words with complex phonemes before he had even studied them?' He offers an explanation: the use of 'thinking' or generative words plus learning the mechanism of phonemic combinations or being able to express himself graphically in the way he spoke. A simple example illustrates this clearly: on the fifth day of discussion in which simple phonemes were being shown, one of the participants went to the blackboard to write (as he said) a 'thinking' word: '*o povo vai resouver os problemas do Brasil votando conciente*' (the people will solve the problems of Brazil by informed voting). As with other sentences, the group discussed the text, debating its significance in the context of their reality.

'Key vocabulary': Maori children reading in New Zealand

At about the same time, yet on the other side of the world in New Zealand, Sylvia Ashton-Warner was making similar discoveries about the reading of the young Maori children in her infant class. Frustrated by their lack of progress using the 'Janet and John' readers from England, she realised that the texts these books were offering were as meaningless as 'Grace eats her grapes' to Brazilian illiterates. Within the framework offered in Part One of this book, we can explain the children's difficulties as follows: they were unable to 'situate' themselves in the social context of the classroom since their home language and culture and in particular their highly developed oral and musical culture from home were not recognised as relevant to school learning; nor could they 'situate' themselves in the mental context of the reading task, since they were not able to draw upon appropriate clues in a new language. In terms of our clues presented in Chapter 3, this looks as follows:

- Lexical clues: words such as 'Janet', 'John', 'boat', 'car', 'dog', 'come', 'and', etc. had a very limited meaning in the children's lives.
- Syntactic clues: the children could speak little English, but sentences like 'Look John look' in any case did not encourage prediction.
- Semantic clues: the lives of the middle-class British children portrayed were very strange and their activities were not shared by Maori children.
- Bibliographic clues: book reading was not practised in most of the families' lives.
- Learning the sound or spelling patterns of meaningless words was very difficult for the children.

In the same way as for Freire's Brazilian adults, 'reading' using traditional primers did not make sense for Maori children in the New Zealand classroom. Ashton-Warner's action was radical for her time. She abandoned the textbooks and devised what she termed an 'organic approach' to learning to read. The principle of her approach was simple: children will immediately learn to read their own personal 'key words', words that have great personal meaning to them. Like Freire's 'generative words', she found that a bank of these special 'one-sight words' provided a stepping-stone into reading. In her classic book *Teacher* (1963), she explains how and why she developed her approach:

> *Back to these first words. To these first books. They must be made out of the stuff of the child itself . . .*
>
> > *First words must have an intense meaning.*
> > *First words must already be part of the dynamic life.*
> > *First books must be made of the stuff of the child*
> > *himself, whatever and wherever the child.*
>
> *The words, which I write on large tough cards and give to the children to read, prove to be one-look words if they are accurately enough chosen. And they are plain enough in conversation. It's the conversation that has to be got. However, if it can't be, I find that whatever a child chooses to make in the creative period may quite likely be such a word. But if the vocabulary of a child is still inaccessible, one can always begin him on the general Key Vocabulary common to any child in any race, a set of words bound up with security that experiments, and later on their creative writing, show to be organically associated with the inner world: 'Mummy', 'Daddy', 'kiss', 'frightened', 'ghost'.*
>
> *(pp. 28–9)*

She explains in detail the mechanics of working with the Key Vocabulary approach. Its focus is at the beginning of the school day when children's energy is at its highest. The teacher needs just a supply of cards, about a foot long and five inches wide and a big black felt-tip pen. The cards which are already written on are kept in a plastic folder or cardboard container. Each morning, they are held up and claimed by their owners (names are written in small letters in a corner). While the children work in pairs reading to each other, the teacher calls one pair to read to her and to tell the new word each wants to learn. Any words unread are discarded for the moment. In this way children realise the importance of choosing only important words. After the morning break, the new words are taken out to see which ones are remembered. Those forgotten are immediately discarded. Later in the day, the children use their words as a bank as they go about their writing. Only when children have about forty words in their collection do they start reading 'transitional books' which are the texts of older primary children who have written books on traditional Maori life and customs.

'Language-experience': breaking through to reading in British children's lives

From 1964 to 1970, a major Schools Council research and development project in Britain known as the Programme in Linguistics and English Teaching, directed by Michael Halliday, set out to draw upon relevant findings from linguistics and other fields in developing materials for the teaching of English. Within this project, a smaller initial literacy team was created and led by David Mackay which became known as the 'Breakthrough' unit. Although the approach promoted by the team has its roots in theories of language development, ultimately it shares much with the instinctive notions of Paolo Freire and Sylvia Ashton-Warner that reading must above all make sense for the child and that the reader must take control of the learning.

In a similar way to the 'Organic Reading' approach, children draw individually upon past experiences to compose their first written texts and join together to share these with others in a group or the whole class (Mackay, Thompson and Schaub 1978). But there are differences between Breakthrough and both Ashton-Warner's and Freire's approach. The focus of Breakthrough is upon the structure of language, on syntax rather than lexis. The starting-point for the child is the composition of experience sentences rather than recognising personal key words. For example, instead of simply 'possessing' a personal Key Word like 'tigers', Ashton-Warner's Maori child would learn to put the 'tiger' in a sentence from the start, e.g. I stick my knife in the tiger (from Ashton-Warner's own example) and to go on and refer to the individual words, the sentence and, probably, the full-stop at the end of the sentence. The aim, therefore, is to build upon a child's knowledge and awareness of language and metalanguage (e.g. by understanding and using terms like 'full-stop', 'question mark', 'sentence', etc.).

A second difference is the view of the Breakthrough team of reading as part of the general language development process involving speaking, listening, reading and writing. Although an essential part of Freire's work was discussion and Ashton-Warner's Key Words were used in the children's writing, their focus was very definitely upon the skill of reading itself. Finally, perhaps the major factor separating Breakthrough from Freire and Ashton-Warner is Breakthrough's scope as an international set of published materials. Ironically, in spite of the aim that the child should be in control of learning, this is made difficult by the lack of 'ownership' of the materials by both teacher and child. Where Freire and Ashton-Warner made their own materials, teachers using Breakthrough may rely upon packages. Although the authors stress that the materials should be used as an aid only, there is a tendancy for the 'official' words to take control away from the user. Nevertheless, Breakthrough is now recognised in many parts of the world as an invaluable tool in introducing young children to literacy in both their first and an additional language.

Common features

Although originating in very different communities and taking place with very different age-groups, the above approaches share a number of common features:

- A dissatisfaction with traditional reading materials when used with cultural or linguistic minority groups or with adult illiterates.
- An aim to link the content of reading materials with the reader's life (either important cultural practices or emotions).
- The belief that the learner should be active and in control of his/her own learning.
- The notion of the child learning within a family network which is rich in knowledge and experience.
- An aim to draw upon the language, knowledge and experiences of the learner as the basis for initial reading materials (which explains the term 'Language-Experience approach').
- Ultimately, a belief in the vital role played by the teacher as a mediator of new knowledge and as a bridge between home and school.

III. THE 'INSIDE-OUT' APPROACH AND CLASSROOM LEARNING

The 'Inside-Out' approach to beginning reading draws principally upon theories of learning which the reader has already met in Part One of this book:

- That language and experience are inextricably linked (Sapir 1970). Effective use of semantic clues in reading a text will depend upon understanding or 'feeling' for the experiences described in the language in which they are described.
- That learning to read and write promotes a greater consciousness of language structure and that bilinguals already have a headstart in this (Vygotsky 1962).
- That the teacher's awareness of the child's home culture and an explicit introduction to the new culture of school are prerequisites for the 'joint culture creation' (Bruner 1986) important for successful classroom learning.

Although the 'Inside-Out' approach builds upon children's existing knowledge and experiences, it looks firmly towards the new language and culture which the child is about to enter in school. The child's cultural knowledge is used rather as a springboard for comparing differences and similarities between languages and cultural practices, for showing children that stepping into a new world provides access to exciting experiences but need not mean abandoning the language and culture of home. Within this framework, the teacher plays a vital role as mediator, understanding as much about family funds of knowledge and the children's home reading practices as possible, while providing a bridge to the new culture, knowing that the children in turn may well act as mediator for parents and later for younger siblings.

In classes where additional language learners are a small minority, we know that fluent target language peers do a much more efficient job than teachers at helping young children relive experiences in a new language through play. Later in this chapter we shall see in what contexts this 'teaching' most successfully occurs. In classes where the teacher may be the only (or almost only) target language speaker, she will need to be constantly alive to her role as language model, carefully considering vital 'chunks' of language needed, initiating and practising them in a variety of spoken and written contexts. For this reason, more whole-class or teacher-directed discussions are likely to take place than in either a mixed monolingual/bilingual or a monolingual classroom. The 'Inside-Out' approach differs from Language-Experiences programmes in that the teacher aims to recognise reading experiences brought from home by the children but explicitly to model and discuss different types of reading in different contexts. In other words, the teacher introduces children to the host culture and language by comparisons with others or making it 'strange'. The approach is also only one half of a programme which depends upon the 'Outside-In' approach outlined in Chapter 5. Examples of classroom sessions combining the approaches can be found in Appendix 3.

Working from the Inside-Out: an overall plan

By its nature, any approach based upon the knowledge, experiences and emotions of individual or groups of children cannot be contained within a rigid programme. Each classroom culture will reflect different adventures, different classroom stories. Ashton-Warner and Freire both illustrate clearly how 'generative words' or 'key vocabularies' will be specific to the cultural group. Some words are likely to be tied to the language in which they are experienced. In the Maori culture, for example, certain words awakened deep emotions in the child's first language; to have translated them would have rendered them meaningless. 'Pa', the name given to a Maori village, was one such word and it remained as 'pa' on the children's cards. These key words can be discussed with children and parents and form an excellent basis for discussion which draws upon the knowledge of emergent bilinguals: 'How can we say "mummy" in

Gujarati?'; 'How many different words can we find for "mummy"?'; 'Do they all sound nearly the same or are some very different?' 'Can we write "mummy" using different scripts?' 'Can we make a collage using them?' The only Chinese child in a multilingual class becomes a source of wonder as she writes what sounds very similar to the English 'mum' ('ma') but looks very different in print.

What follows below are some classroom suggestions on beginning an 'Inside-Out' approach with young emergent bilinguals entering school. The framework is divided into three headings and illustrated through examples for individual reading sessions in Appendix 3:

- First things first: starting with questions
- Resourcing the 'Inside-Out' approach in the classroom
- Working from the 'Inside-Out': A simple procedure

First things first: starting with questions

An essential first step in the 'Inside-Out' approach is to find out about the knowledge and strengths of the children, families and communities represented in the classroom. Here are some questions to ask:

- Was the child born in the host country?
  What is the country of origin/religion of the family?
  What is the child's mother-tongue?
  Is this the language the child uses at home?
  To whom and in what contexts?
  Does the child use the target language at home?
  To whom and in what contexts?
  Does the child watch English television/videos?
  Does the child watch videos in any other language?
  Can the child speak/understand any other languages?
- Is the child (or older siblings) learning to read/write the mother-tongue in community language/other private class?
  Are any other community classes being attended (e.g. Mosque class) and do they involve reading and/or writing in additional languages?
  If so, how often do children attend and for how long?
  What standard has the child reached?
  What materials does the child use in these classes?
  What approach does the teacher use?
  Is there a pattern of tuition the children are accustomed to?
  If so, what form does it take?
  Can community class teachers be invited to talk with the staff?
  What other reading materials are available in children's homes?
- What skills/funds of knowledge are available in the community and in families?

In what ways can they be utilised?
- Do parents understand how reading is taught at school?
  How does the school explain its approach to parents?
  Are community class teachers involved in parents' meetings?
- What type of reading activities do children take home?
  How are these explained to parents?
  Is there a dialogue with parents on the nature of tasks given?
  What efforts are made to ensure that parents with limited English understand tasks?
  How is the help of siblings enlisted?

Finally, but most importantly:

- How can the school go about finding out all of this?
  Will it need reorganisation of time-tables, duties of ancillary staff, etc?
  Can the assistance of education departments at universities or colleges of education be called upon?
  Can the work link with teacher in-service or advanced degree work where teachers adopt the role of teacher/researcher in the classroom?

Resourcing the 'Inside-Out' approach in the classroom

Ideas for resourcing the classroom are not difficult if we remember the aims of this approach. The questions to ask are: How far do resources chosen both build upon children's home and community knowledge and enable them to enter a new world? Do they foster children's awareness of what they already know, skills they already have? Do they show children that 'reading' means different things to different people in different contexts, takes place in different languages and can be used for different purposes?

The resources suggested below differ very little from those used in every good Early Years classroom. After all, to a certain degree, every child enters a new world and a new 'language' when walking for the first time through the school gates. In their book *And So To School* (1982), Shirley Cleave and her colleagues show the devastating effect of the crowded school hall on Celia, a child from a middle-class family from the culturally dominant group. Margaret Donaldson opens *Children's Minds* (1978) with the memorable quote from Laurie Lee which tells us how upset a five-year-old was on his first school day, waiting for the 'present' which never came (his teacher told him to sit where he was 'for the present').

Nevertheless, the differences will be quite different in nature and scope for Jessica and Tony, children already familiar to the reader. Jessica may feel shy and anxious about joining in socio-dramatic play in the home corner, participating in cookery or playing with lego, etc., but she understands the rules for participation and she has appropriate language formulae at her fingertips; for example, talking about a favourite TV programme, discussing how to make fairy cakes or constructing a Big Dipper at the fairground. These provide her with semantic, syntactic and lexical clues as she begins reading. Consequently, although the resources themselves may present few surprises, in predominantly multilingual or bilingual classes there will be more teacher-direction in their use. This is because teachers will need to provide carefully planned experiences tied to the spoken and written language currently in focus.

Below are the most essential resources for the 'Inside-Out' approach.

The basics

For 'Inside-Out' class and group reading sessions, the teacher sits in a literacy area which houses permanently the materials needed on a daily basis. These are: card (preferably white) cut into strips, somewhere on which to display recent sentences and words of the children so that they can be seen clearly (the blank part of the Breakthrough teacher's sentence maker produced by Longman is suitable or a large magnet-board), hessian bags to store familiar words cards and sentence strips from past weeks, a thick black pen, a sentence stand into which the words can be inserted or magnets to display them on the magnet-board, scissors, and word banks (either teacher or child produced; for example, a large card picture of a face with words slotted into appropriate places – nose on nose, etc.). These take their place beside old and current Big Books made by the class, a tape recorder with tapes where the texts of Big Books are recorded, alphabet books and a second word maker from Breakthrough for the children to practise spelling individual words. Aside, but close to hand, is a camera and an adequate supply of film to record drama or other experiences for the class Big Books. This area will be in addition to the book and story area attached to 'Outside-In' sessions which are outlined in Chapter 5.

The puppets

We have only to reflect back to the examples in Chapter 2 which introduced the British toddler demanding comments on the pictures in his book on a London bus, the Australian three-year-old learning about queuing and Christmas customs from his mother and Jason in the USA figuring out how to initiate conversations, to remind ourselves of the myriad of experiences and corresponding complexity of language gained in the years at home before a child enters formal school. The magnitude of the task for emergent bilinguals is suddenly clear to teachers when they meet these children in their classes for the first time. It is obvious that no one during a short space of time each day in school can quickly 'make up' these years of daily language 'tuition' given by caregivers in the child's first language. Consequently, teachers are going to need to structure their time carefully to maximise children's experiences and to tie these experiences to essential chunks of the target language needed. It may be a relief to teachers to discover that they have extra 'magic' teacher-assistants waiting to be called upon. The only criterion is that teachers, themselves, must believe in them.

The assistants are small, may be scruffy and cheap and rely for life upon the teacher. Yet, used well, they will teach far more than the teacher within her own skin. Glove puppets are an integral part of an 'Inside-Out' approach in early literacy tuition for emergent bilinguals. At least two puppets are needed; one girl and one boy who also represent children new to the language and culture of the school. Preferably, a collection should be built up of boys and girls from the different linguistic backgrounds of all the children in the class. Different members of their families may also be added. Gradually, puppets from well-loved traditional tales (see also Chapter 5) will also become part of a collection. However, a kernel of these, perhaps two or at the most six, are likely to become the key figures in every class reading session. The puppets become 'real' people, have names which are meaningful to the children, have their own voices and their own personalities which are constant over time. Importantly, they are not available for the children to play with – otherwise their magic disappears. They live separately, hidden from view but easily accessible for the teacher (their dwelling may be as humble as a plastic bag) and need to be awakened or called by the children in a particular way (practising a particular point – perhaps a song a child sings or a greeting given). They are excellent language teachers; they use simple language which is carefully structured to practise the known and extend the child's repertoire to new expressions and they model a particular chunk of language or a language structure which the children unselfconsciously repeat over and over again.

Like the teacher, the puppets serve as mediators, introducing children to the new language and culture, while familiar with those which the children bring from home. Shy children are able to empathise with a quiet and timid puppet, while gaining courage to speak for the first time in a new language themselves. At the same time, a naughtier, more extrovert puppet enables children to practise well-known reprimands. Through their incipient bilingualism, the puppets reflect the children's own position and encourage them to tackle the learning of a new language and culture. Their role as members of a culture with which children identify together with their adventurousness in entering a new world allow children 'a security which experiments' (Meek 1979); the love of being scared as they enter dangerous situations, yet the comfort of knowing that they, themselves, remain safe and sound. Of all the resources needed for the 'Inside-Out' reading classroom, the puppets are the most important. Later in this chapter and in Appendix 3, we see how they come to life and animate beginning reading sessions.

The socio-dramatic play area

The socio-dramatic play area is a focal point of the 'Inside-Out' approach to early literacy. As in every Early Years classroom, the area must be imaginatively planned and well-resourced according to the experiences the teacher aims the children to enact. Where there are a number of native speakers in the class, much can be left to their teaching skills. In a study of a five-year-old Taiwanese child's first two months of English learning in a linguistically mixed pre-school environment in the USA, Hatch and her colleagues (1979) made some interesting observations. They found that 46 per cent of the child's comments were imperatives, 40 per cent 'Wh-' questions and only 14 per cent statements. What the child seemed to be doing was 'chunking' formulae contained in the input from other children, e.g. 'What's that?' often became 'What is this aeroplane?' In other words, the child was able to derive rules combined from the question/ answer patterns of conversations. A little later, the child began memorising large chunks of the target language which he used appropriately in conversations regardless of whether he understood it or not. Hatch and her colleagues trace ways in which the Taiwanese child does this:

> First language child: *I can beat your brother up. I can beat him up.*
> Second language child: *You can beat him up, huh. I can beat him to my party 'n you can beat him 'n you can beat my brother. He beat you up. You xxx it.*

Very early first language learning also takes place in this way. In his study of a child's language between the ages of one and two, Ron Scollon (1979) describes how much is learned in the form of 'pre-packaged routines', language which is incorporated from adults' speech without being internally analysed. This type of approach in second language learning appears to take place only during early childhood, since older children and adults are constrained by the fear of having to make a relevant reply in conversations. Play, then, provides an ideal opportunity for young children to learn formulae which can be used as 'chunks' of appropriate language. The language during play is predictable, repetitious and well contextualised which contrasts sharply with the 'Wh-' questions children are likely to meet from an adult.

Nevertheless, socio-dramatic play areas in classes where the large majority of children have a limited understanding of the target language need particular planning which recognises that the teacher provides the only or one of very few role models for the target language. In some countries, this situation occurs frequently. In Spain, since the death of General Franco in 1975, the Catalan language has gained enormously in importance until now all children in Catalonia receive their early years schooling and early literacy tuition in the heritage language. However, many children enter school speaking only Castilian (Spanish); a small but increasing number of immigrant children largely speak Moroccan. Early Years classrooms are geared to 'immersing' these children in the Catalan language and role-play in the socio-dramatic area plays an important part in this. The teacher works with native language speakers or more fluent children if they are available (or herself and the puppets if they are not) 'modelling' the language of specific situations or practices in the new language and culture, such as making a paella, etc.

Our socio-dramatic play area will, therefore, be resourced for children to enact situations which will often be geared to the 'adventure' of the lesson. The area will be equipped with resources reflecting the theme of the moment. For example, if the theme is 'Food' and the 'Inside-Out' sentences 'I love—' (crisps, etc. – see Appendix 3), one half of the socio-dramatic area may represent a traditional sweet/tobacconist shop while the other becomes a Turkish/Indian, etc. sweet shop/bakery. In this way, use of an appropriate language in each situation becomes clear to the children. Dressing-up clothes will also be geared to the theme or specific reading sessions within it. For example, if the theme is 'My family' and the 'Inside-Out' sentences 'My — is sick', clothes and resources might be geared towards the doctor, patient and 'parent' in the song 'Poor little — (the name of a puppet – see Appendix 3) is sick' (to the tune of 'Miss Polly has a dolly who is sick, sick, sick'). Separate dressing-up clothes for drama will be related to specific stories focused on during 'structured stories' (see Chapter 5).

Cooking

We saw in Part One of this book that eating and drinking habits are very particular to different cultural groups. Understanding the rituals and language surrounding food is a big step forward for the novice to a new culture. The 'Rice Krispies' example with which Jessica felt so comfortable showed us how predicting a text will be so much easier if children can relate what is happening to their own experience. Living within a Hong Kong kitchen at home in Northampton, Tony was probably as dumbfounded by toast and marmalade for breakfast as Europeans might be by eating soup first thing in the morning or by finishing off a later meal with soup instead of ice cream. It is impossible to glance along a row of children's books, traditional tales, songs and rhymes, etc. without seeing how often different items of food figure (plum and cherry pies, jam tarts, bacon, porridge, gingerbread men, turnips, pasta, dumplings, ice cream, pickles, cheese, salami, etc.). Food is an excellent medium to show how language is intimately linked with experience. We may all recall how effortless it is to remember even difficult names of exotic foods when abroad in comparison with other lexis which cannot be related to such pleasant experiences.

Cooking and eating are also an excellent means of drawing children's awareness to words in different languages and showing how the name of a dish in one language simply cannot be translated and allowing children to use 'key words' in their first language meaningfully in sentences in the new language. Language used while cooking is purposeful and can easily be linked with songs and rhymes (either existing ones or with texts invented by the teacher, e.g. 'This is the way we roll our dough . . .', etc. to the tune of 'Here we go round the mulberry bush'). Although not as essential as the puppets or socio-dramatic play, easy and frequent access to cooking facilities is a great advantage for a teacher working to an 'Inside-Out' beginning reading approach. Preparation of food or having tea parties does not have to entail actual cooking; rituals can also be learned through sandwiches, biscuits and squash. Nevertheless, all these activities will mean engaging the assistance of extra adults in the classroom – an excellent way of accessing the different funds of knowledge held by members in the community.

'Playing school'

In monolingual classrooms, a 'playing school' area is often viewed as part of socio-dramatic play provision. In multilingual classes following an 'Inside-Out' approach, however, it receives a special status. Like the puppets, 'playing school' provides a bridge for children from their home and community to the new culture because it recognises that 'school', 'the classroom' and 'classroom learning' may be interpreted very differently by children regularly attending very different classrooms (for example, community classes to learn the mother-tongue and the state school). This is where the teacher as researcher is important. The 'playing school' resources should provide utensils to which the children may be accustomed from both worlds (perhaps lined exercise books, pens, simple primers, a blackboard or slate and chalk for handwriting practice which belong to the community school as well as alphabet books and simple dictionaries, the sentence and key word cards, simple word banks for themes covered in reading sessions, rough paper for practice writing, different thicknesses of pencils and the computer which represent the host classroom). Different 'teaching' methods will be played out by the children in formal and informal situations. When a drama is enacted before the class, it provides an excellent opportunity for fostering children's awareness of 'reading' in different contexts, and signals that both approaches are valid, simply different.

Songs, poems and rhymes

A collection of songs, poems and rhymes relating to the theme of each reading session is essential to assist children in 'chunking' the target language. Children who are at the very earliest stages of language learning will often be able to sing perfectly songs containing difficult language structures. These are important for a number of reasons: they enable emergent bilinguals to practise with others the pronunciation of difficult sounds which means that they do not have to 'perform' alone (the difficulty of pronunciation for emergent bilinguals can often be underestimated); they give children large chunks of language which can gradually be used in conversations. For example, 'Pussy cat, pussy cat where have you been? I've been to London to see the Queen' can be used as a song to question a puppet or a child 'Shahina, Shahina, where have you been . . .?', or as a game to practise spoken and written language, whereby one child either picks a card with a place name (London, Bangladesh, India, home, school, hospital, park, etc.) hides it and asks the others to guess 'Where have I been?' From these large units, children learn to abstract sets of rules for the new language (from our 'Pussy cat' example 'Wh-' question + form of present perfect for the verb 'to be' + to + place name + to + infinitive). Obviously, the child masters all of this unconsciously. Nevertheless, automaticity will facilitate the use of both syntactic and lexical clues during early reading.

Songs are an integral part of the 'Inside-Out' approach where they are used in purposeful situations. For example, the class sings 'Good morning' to the puppets in order to wake them, to sequence the day's routines with corresponding times: 'This is the way we wake up . . .' (sung to the tune of 'Here we go round the mulberry bush'), or to act out a drama where a puppet is sick: 'Poor little Dina is sick, sick, sick . . .' (sung to the tune of 'Miss Polly had a dolly who was sick, sick, sick' – see Appendix 3). These songs are written out in large print so that a child, teacher or puppet can point to each word as the texts are sung.

Classroom rhymes also provide a meaningful context for the class to chant together, practise pronunciation and gain confidence (for example, 'Who put the cookie in the cookie jar?' 'We're going on a bear hunt' or 'Pop!' by Michael Rosen). The teacher must innovate freely inventing new texts for well-loved tunes. These often become the most popular songs as the melody is well-known and easily learned. Again, the puppets are always at hand to encourage children in their singing.

Linking home and school: taking the school culture home and bringing community cultures into school

Considerable evidence is available from numerous projects in English speaking countries (summarised in Topping and Wolfendale 1985, and Wolfendale and Topping 1995) which points to the increased progress made by children when they are able to read at home with caregivers. Yet a dilemma has always existed: how can parents who cannot read the target language themselves go about helping their children? Below are ideas for beginner readers to use with caregivers who do not write the target language but are literate (as almost all are) in their mother-tongue. A main principle is to recognise both the knowledge held by caregivers as mediators of the home language and culture to the child and the incipient knowledge of the child in mediating the host language and culture to the parents. A dynamic two-way process is, therefore, set in action. Parents will be 'expert' in the home language; children in the target language. A second principle is that children take home reading which the parents *understand* and with which they *can* assist as well as learn from the child. They are not 'deskilled' by a lack of understanding of what is expected of them. Even if the child needs to translate the word, the caregiver can discuss the home language translation and, at the same time, learn the target language word.

How does this take place? Each school will devise its own programme in the light of findings from 'initial questions' rather than adopting a programme which may have been devised for fluent target language speakers. Ideas are explained at a parents' meeting which is likely to be well-attended if parents know exactly what is on the agenda. A possible programme for the very first stages is as follows: children take home 'key words' from classroom reading sessions, practise 'matching' them to words and pictures on a card and spelling them (the alphabet is usually familiar to all). If possible, the caregiver writes the word in the child's mother-tongue on the back and discusses the word with the child, encouraging him/her to use the word in sentences. With this kernel of key words, the child practises making sentences and completing a variety of word games. The child writes the sentences made in an exercise book which, like the books used in many community classes, is specifically for this purpose (see Gregory 1995 for a fuller description of work with linguistic minority parents).

It is important that any homework expected of parents should all be demonstrated explicitly at the parents' meeting to which interested siblings should also be invited. Caregivers who do not manage to attend the session will almost always respond to a home visit by the teacher. At the same time, parents are invited into the class to complete this work with a group of children in their mother-tongue. If all (or almost all) the children speak the same mother-tongue and bilingual support is available, an ideal opportunity arises for a bilingual approach using the same 'key words' and sentences in both languages, for evidence available indicates that even incipient biliterates have advantages over emergent bilinguals who have no tuition in their mother-tongue (Fitzpatrick 1987). Some projects using this approach are already under way in Germany, where a Turkish community class teacher works alongside the German teacher so that children complete work in German and the mother-tongue (Holscher 1995). Home–school links depend upon the energy and perseverance of teachers and take a long time to establish. Only in retrospect and over the long term does it become obvious that every minute was one well spent.

Working from the 'Inside-Out': a simple procedure

With information from the initial questions in mind and with essential resources in place, a simple framework links practice with theory. Within this framework, the teacher considers the following:

- How can the child be made to feel 'a reader' from the very start?
- Which themes are closest to the child and the family?
- Which key experiences from the host culture should be explicitly introduced and how?
- Which emotions are important in the child's life and how can they be linked with early reading?
- Which key words might be essential in each of the above?
- Which chunks of language will be vital?

The plan below provides an example showing how teachers can begin to provide emergent bilinguals with lexical and syntactic clues in the new language and how these are embedded in the semantic knowledge of the host culture. An example of a plan in Appendix 3 suggests ways in which different themes may be developed using a combination of 'Inside-Out' and 'Outside-In' approaches. The starting-point of the plan is to introduce experiences which excite children and to recognise their fears upon entering an unknown world in a new language while showing that the classroom is a safe haven in which to experiment and where fears can be reconciled. Each theme, therefore, sets out with an adventure which is based upon experiences from the home or school culture. Themes are endless, but there are common key interests as children begin school: loves, hates, new babies, accidents, illness, fears, journeys and other adventures.

A daily 'Inside-Out' reading session may have the following pattern:

1. Start with an 'adventure' or drama which draws upon the child's emotions: fear, love, hate, sympathy or simply the excitement of guessing the unknown, e.g. Dina (a puppet) is in hospital following an accident.

2. Initially, 'model' the experience through the puppets. They use (sometimes hesitantly and sometimes needing the children's help) essential chunks of the target language which are to be introduced and practised. This explicit modelling is particularly important where most of the class are beginners to the new language. The chunks (or structures) of language practised will form the basis for early class 'Big Books' for reading together. As the theme is developed together orally, children are encouraged to experiment and the language used is less controlled.

3. After the scene has been enacted by the puppets, the children offer their own parallel experiences and key words are noted by the teacher. They then re-enact the scene shown by the puppets. Sometimes, the teacher will use a song she has found or invented which practises these particular language chunks. The children will act out the song, often using the dressing-up clothes or other props as they do so.

4. During the early stages, one or two sentences (later more) are written on strips of card using the language chunks which the teacher wishes to practise and containing the children's key words. Two copies of each sentence are made: one is cut into separate words which fit into the teacher's word stand or can be attached to the magnet-board; the other remains intact as a sentence and is stored with a collection of past class sentences.

5. The class reads the sentence cut into individual words in chorus after the teacher first and then individually. As the teacher changes children's key words, the child who originally 'owned' the word is given the chance to read the sentence first. During the early stages, one or two replacements are sufficient, but these increase rapidly as the children gain in confidence as readers. The teacher is careful to refer to terms like 'word', 'sentence', 'full stop', 'question mark', etc. as the children work and, where relevant, calls children's attention to letters which recur.

6. The children play games with the words, e.g. one child removes a word while the other children close their eyes and then guess which word is missing or the words are jumbled by a child and need to be reordered.

7. Finally, the sentence is entered in the class news-book and illustrated by the child whose key word it contains. These big sturdy books, together with the class sentence, past sentences, word cards and plastic stand are easily accessible for the children to practise with each other during free moments in the day.

8. At odd moments during the day when the class is assembled together, take the pile of key words. Choose a word and ask the child to whom it 'belongs' (or any child who volunteers) to read the word first and then to use the word in a sentence or question. This is very important in helping children to both 'chunk' the language and to pick out individual words in the chunks.

Throughout the reading sessions, some points to remember:

• Do allow children time to respond. The temptation to assist an emergent bilingual quickly is great, but sometimes reduces children's confidence in trying to pronounce words themselves.

- Do recognise the value of reading in chorus before asking a child to read alone. Imagine again the 'Ventafocs' example and the difference between joining in with friends and having to pronounce strange words alone.
- Do understand the child who is too shy at first to take part actively in class reading. Listening is an essential part of early second language learning and some children need much longer than others before beginning to speak.
- Do remember the 'magic' teacher-assistants, the puppets: they will succeed where 'normal' mortals fail.

IN SUMMARY

In this chapter, we have seen ways in which the teacher may explicitly 'scaffold' the learning of emergent bilinguals using an 'Inside-Out' approach to beginning reading in school. From the framework offered, we see how explicit 'scaffolding' takes place through:

- recognising children's existing linguistic skills and cultural knowledge and building these into both teaching content and teaching strategies;
- limiting the size of the reading task by introducing explicitly common new lexis and language 'chunks';
- modelling chunks of language orally and in an idealised way through the puppets and/or songs and socio-dramatic play;
- devising home–school reading programmes which recognise the role of both parent and child as mediator of different languages and cultures and which families feel comfortable with.

A final unique feature of the 'Inside-Out' approach is that it is not designed to be used in isolation but to be only half of the reading programme. It is the other half, looking from the 'Outside-In', to which we now turn.

Further reading

Ashton-Warner, S. (1963) *Teacher*, London: Penguin (reprinted in 1980 by Virago Publishers, London).
Cochran-Smith, M. (1984) *The Making of a Reader*, Norwood NJ: Ablex.
Freire, P. (1973) *Education: The Practice of Freedom*, London: Writers & Readers' Publishing Corporation.
Mackay, D., Thompson, B. and Schaub, P. (1978) *Breakthrough to Literacy*, London: Longman.

5

Introducing the Unknown: the 'Outside-In' Approach to Reading

Six-year-old Sunit and Kamlyit are studying a crab which they have brought back from a trip to the seaside.

Sunit: We went in our rocket.
  We saw a giant crab in the sky.
Kamlyit: The claws were open.
  It was crushing the sun.
Sunit: But the sun was too hot.
  It burned the crab.
  Crab breathed out onto sun.
  And it turned colder.
  And the crab could hold the sun.
Kamlyit: And crush it.
  And eat it.

Excited from their trip into an unknown world of shells, waves, seaweed and jelly-fish, Sunit and Kamlyit are imagining an even more adventurous journey they might make. Eighteen months ago, they appeared unable to understand simple instructions given by their teacher in the new language; now, they have a range of lexis and syntax at their fingertips and are able to 'map' these onto new experiences taking place in the target language. Sometimes, experience and language might narrowly miss each other as when Sunit saw the sea for the first time and shouted excitedly to the others 'Look, that big puddle!', but he was soon able to relate all the illustrations and stories he had seen and heard about the sea to its reality.

How are these children now able to use a new language so impressively? Let us focus more closely on their achievement in terms of the lexis and syntax the children use. They both realise that the past tense is usually used for story-telling and they can use both regular (burned, breathed, turned) and irregular forms (went, were, saw, was, could) as well as the past continuous form (was crushing). They have also mastered the comparative forms of adjectives (colder) and are comfortable with some prepositions (in, onto). Finally, they have a fascinating array of lexis suitable for dramatic story-telling (rocket, giant crab, claws, crush, burn, breathe, eat, etc.). Kamlyit particularly loves 'crush' which he uses twice. A glance at these words shows how they are likely to fit into Ashton-Warner's 'key vocabulary'; they belong to a world of fear and violence, yet the children know that it is all imagination and that they are in the security of the classroom. Yet how might the children invent a story so confidently using such suitable lexis when we know from Chapter 3 that CALP (cognitive academic language proficiency) can take children many years to master in a second language?

Looking closely at the children's text, some features seem familiar to their teacher. She knows that they have often entered the world of giants; 'Jack and the Beanstalk' was a favourite story. They certainly have 'chunks' of language containing comparatives and superlatives in their repertoire from 'Goldilocks and the Three Bears' and 'The Three Billy Goats Gruff', etc. Yet, their story seems even more familiar to their teacher. Suddenly, she remembers that a longer theme of work the term before centred on the Anansi Spider stories from Africa. Remarkably, the children have used the lexis and syntax of one spider story (*Anansi the Spider* by Gerald McDermott) which they had listened to many times on a tape with dramatic sound effects (Western Woods tapes) and woven their own meanings into it.

Sunit and Kamlyit are not unusual. What they show us is the immense influence of the written story heard time and time again in enabling emergent bilinguals to make a new language and new world their own. In a book called *Coming to Know* edited by Phillida Salmon (1981), Margaret Meek writes of the value of reading or telling stories as 'handing down the magic' from one generation to the next. This chapter examines the magic whereby written stories can provide a unique 'scaffold' for beginner bilingual readers in building up graphophonic, lexical and syntactic clues. The chapter is divided into three sections. The first asks: what is an 'Outside-In' approach to reading and what is the magic which storybooks are able to feed into all the knowledge centres as young children begin reading? The second section briefly examines the role of story-reading by the teacher to the whole class which I refer to as the Outer Layer of the approach. The third section turns in more detail to the Inner Layer of the approach where children read and study texts themselves and offers a framework for structuring children's story-reading in the classroom. In each section, we see ways in which 'explicit scaffolding' as outlined in the Introduction to Part Two of this book can guide our teaching strategies when working with an 'Outside-In' approach to reading with emergent bilingual children.

I. HANDING DOWN THE MAGIC IN A STORY

Hearers of folk fairy tales, without being aware of it, experience a sort of initiation not unlike that in the customs of some primitive peoples . . . the folk fairy tale transposes the initiation process into the sphere of the imagination.

(Lüthi 1970, p. 103)

Unlike most spoken conversations, written stories are structured. This structure is often referred to as a 'story grammar' (Lüthi 1970). Put simply, texts have beginnings, middles and ends, identifiable 'chunks' of texts which act together as parts. Luke (1993a) shows how 'Goldilocks' can be 'parsed' using a story grammar template:

> *Three bears at home (setting/main characters) » Bears leave home; Goldilocks arrives (initiating event/main character) » Goldilocks is hungry (problem #1) » Father Bear's porridge (attempt #1) » too salty (outcome #1) » Mother Bear's porridge (attempt #2) » too sweet (outcome #2) » Baby Bear's porridge (attempt #3) . . .*
>
> *(Luke 1993a, p. 36)*

Carol Fox (1988) and Henrietta Dombey (1988) show how a familiarity with this 'grammar' transforms the language of young children who store story-language from books in memory for retellings of their own stories. In this way, they are able to call upon 'chunks' of language which will later help them in predicting written versions of the same texts. When five-year-old Josh declares in his telling of a story 'What was his dismay when he got up there? There was gnashing of teeth', he shows that his language repertoire is ready and waiting to predict the texts of books he cannot yet read. Seven-year-old monolingual Ernest finds summarising or answering questions on a story very difficult. When asked by an adult 'What happens in a story?', he replies 'They live happily ever after'. Upon being pressed 'Who does?' he says 'Poor people'. Nevertheless, when asked to *tell* the three bears story, he launches into a long and accurate account:

> *She knocked on the door and nobody answered. And so, she pushed the door open and she saw three bowls. She tasted one bowl, but it was too lumpy. She tasted the second one and it was too cold. She tasted the little one and it was just right. And she ate it all up . . . Daddy bear said (in a deep voice) 'Someone has been sitting in my . . . eating in my . . . eating out of my porridge.' (In a higher voice) 'Someone has been eating out of my porridge.' (And higher still) 'Someone has been eating out of my porridge and they have eaten it all up.' And he began to cry.*
>
> *(Applebee 1977, p. 55)*

We begin already to see the scope of semantic, syntactic and lexical clues he should bring with him as he begins to read the text. The contrast between 'conversation' and 'stories' is apparent even with emergent bilinguals' simplest retellings. Compare, for example, the conversation between an adult and five-year-old Parag, who is new to the language of school. As they look at a fish in a tank together their talk might run something like this:

> *Child: This, (pointing to fish)*
> *Adult: What? Fish?*
> *or: What's this?*

Other questions by the adult wishing to continue the conversation are plausible, such as: Where's the fish? Whose fish is that? Is it yours? How many fish are there? What colour is it? What's the fish doing? etc. Little reflection is needed to show that the child's answer is likely to comprise a single word and that the conversation will, at the very most, be limited. In contrast, five-year-old Ikhlaq is glancing through the story of *Topiwalo the Hatmaker* (Harmony Publishing) and making his own story:

> *Night-time*
> *I see a monkey*
> *On the roof of my house*
> *He was eating a banana*
> *Monkey eating banana*
> *Banana eating monkey*
> *I said*
> *Why are you eating that banana?*
> *And I kicked him off*
> *into the water*

Even in such a simple narration, the book supports Ikhlaq in setting the scene and giving his story a structure (a beginning, middle and end). Edie Garvie (1990) refers to stories as 'vehicles' for teaching about a new language and culture. A story, she says, is 'going somewhere and the learner wants to reach the end of the journey' (1990, p. 31) and this is precisely what distinguishes Ikhlaq's story from Parag's conversation starter above.

Traditional tales simultaneously transcend and unite cultures by depicting universal morals and truths. In *Stories and Meanings* (1985), Harold Rosen neatly coins stories as being 'the common possession of humankind – part of the deep structure of the grammar of our world'. Within the 'security which experiments' provided by the classroom, world-known traditional tales help all children develop not just linguistic, but sensory and emotional acuity. For example, Perrault's 'Cinderella' (or was it, perhaps, first of Chinese origin? we simply do not know) not only invites children into the world of cinders, hearths and poverty as well as that of the glamour of the ball, but also gives hope to the lonely child. Likewise, the 'Ugly Duckling' story gives hope to many a child who cannot express fears openly. In contrast, children who lead only safe, secure and protected lives vicariously learn of fear, want and pain, etc. In this way, there is for all children a two-way process, whereby children both bring their own experience to the book and at the same time, take what the author and illustrator have to offer. What they take is believed to be permanent and 'for ever'. Children's words show us that the fact that stories are inscribed in books gives them an immutability they might not otherwise have.

Here are five-year-old Lisa and Ernest again:

Adult: Where do stories come from?
Lisa: From a book . . .
Adult to Ernest (who says he dislikes Sleeping Beauty*): If you were telling* Sleeping
    Beauty, *could you change it so that you like it?*
Ernest: No.
Adult: Why not? . . . Is it all right to make changes in stories?
Ernest: No.
Adult: Why not? . . . Do you think you could tell it better?
Ernest: No.

Adult: Why not?
Ernest: Because you can't rub out the words.

(Applebee 1977, p. 52)

The 'initiation process' offered by important tales of all ages will be of a special kind for young children entering the school from a very different world. Of course, certain experiences must be first-hand for them to become meaningful. We can reflect back to the fireworks in the British reading tests for seven-year-olds referred to in the Introduction of this book. It is not easy to replace the real experience of fireworks through illustrations, or even text. Remember Tony and his difficulty with Rice Krispies and marmalade for breakfast? Tony may eventually learn the rules and corresponding lexis for a European breakfast, but a thousand story-readings will not replace the experience of trying it himself. Likewise, Sunit's joy at realising that the sea is something different from a 'big puddle' had to wait until he saw it for himself. Nevertheless, we know that the classroom cannot begin to provide real-life experiences for everything young beginner bilinguals will meet in their new world. Gradually, the stories Tony and Sunit will learn about in books will fill the gaps and allow them vicariously to gain access to new and sometimes strange experiences and practices. Stories, then, act as mediators of language and culture to children entering a new world in the classroom.

Tajul shows how he uses story-books as a springboard to find out about the eating habits of the new culture when he can speak only a very few words of the host language. Reading *Meg at Sea* with his teacher, he asks 'English eat octopus?'; *The Hungry Giant* (Storychest) gives him the opportunity to ascertain that 'stick loaves' can also be bread rather than big 'fingers' which is his first hypothesis. None of this would be possible without the story-book as support or 'scaffold' in Bruner's (1986) terms. The 'Outside-In' approach to beginning reading, then, takes the world of story-books as its starting-point. Like its partner, the 'Inside-Out' approach outlined in Chapter 4, it is designed to be only half of the reading programme. Examples showing ways in which both approaches may complement each other can be found in Appendix 3. Figure 9 summarises ways in which story-books act as the key to developing the vital knowledge centres as children begin reading.

An analysis of other important tales using this framework would show how they feed immense funds into knowledge centres providing clues to the young reader. *Semantically*, they introduce children to different ways of life, to new experiences and cultural practices, yet they draw upon universal morals and values (greed/generosity; cruelty/kindness; cowardice/courage, etc.). *Syntactically*, they provide difficult yet memorable chunks of language which are often reinforced by rhymes and repetition ('Run, run, as fast as you can . . .'; 'Mirror, mirror on the wall . . .'; 'Fee, fi, fo, fum . . .', etc.). *Lexically*, they reinforce difficult collocations and lexical sets (plough/field; sow/corn; scatter/seed, etc.) *Orthographic/graphophonically*, they draw children's attention to patterns of letters and sounds through rhymes ('run as fast as you can . . . gingerbread man'; 'b-ake/c-ake', etc.). The final section of this chapter will offer different ways to structure stories using this framework.

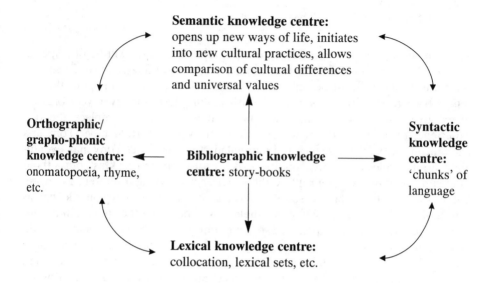

In practice, this may look as follows:

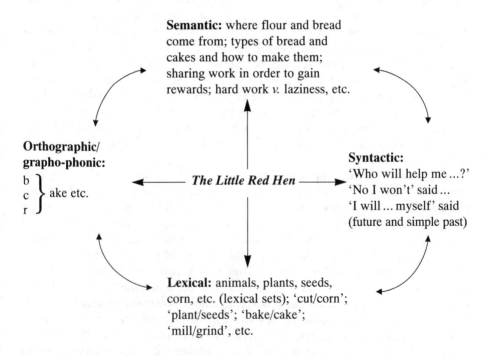

Figure 9   Story-books are the key to development of knowledge centres.

II. THE 'OUTSIDE-IN' APPROACH: THE OUTER LAYER

It is important to distinguish between the Outer Layer of this approach, where the teacher reads a wide variety of books to the children, and the Inner Layer, where the children read and study texts closely for themselves. Teachers in classes where all (or almost all) children are emergent bilinguals will probably choose books from the inner layer selection for class story-reading. But class story sessions where monolingual children and those embarking on a new language are learning side-by-side give emergent bilinguals the opportunity to be 'bathed' in the story language of books. If a story is memorable and contains important messages to children, they will understand the overall meaning and gradually be able to memorise chunks of the language it uses to communicate.

Of course, it is impossible to tell what makes a particular book 'magic' to an emergent bilingual or monolingual reader. Teachers know of five-year-old children who consistently choose to study books portraying families from their own cultural origin, regardless of the difficulty or density of print. It is the illustrations which are 'magic' to them. It is undeniable that stories depicting characters from the home country of children's families and dual language texts also have a magic which often cannot be explained. One Early Years teacher speaks of the popularity of the Bhondoo the Monkey' books (Amena Jayal), a series of flimsy paperbacks from India. The stories of a monkey who is always falling into trouble have immense appeal to her children of Asian backgrounds.

In their study of dual language texts, Viv Edwards and Sue Walker (1995) point out that concern by teachers over aspects such as quality of paper and illustrations are not always shared by children. Indeed, some deliberately chose a 'poor' quality picture dictionary from India because its illustrations seemed 'more adult' than its glossy Canadian counterpart. Discussions with a group of monolingual English-speaking parents of five-year-olds in East London reinforce the notion that choice of books may be very individual and not necessarily conform to critics' view of the 'good book'. Mothers who know nothing of teachers' concerns over choosing high-quality books for children reminisce nostalgically about their own past affection for books which schools have long ago discarded as boring and inappropriate (Gregory (1996). Indeed, readers of this book may themselves harbour secret guilty memories of a particular book which now appears to have no apparent virtues within the educational establishment.

Choosing books for the Outer Layer: two examples

What sort of stories might be particularly valuable for emergent bilinguals in this wider collection and what distinguishes them from other texts? Below is an example of one quite difficult story which has been particularly successful in holding the attention of children at story-time in classes of mixed emergent bilingual/fluent monolingual speakers.

The story is called *The Clay Flute* by Mats Rehnman and has been published in Sweden, the UK, the USA and Australia. A beautifully told and illustrated book set in the Arabian desert, it tells the sad tale of a poor boy, Abeli, whose only possession is a clay flute which his father has taught him to play. Jealous of his skill, Krixikri the desert witch smashes it and changes him into a little monkey. The story tells how Abeli is traded from one person to the next until he falls in love with the Caliph's daughter. Upon her marriage, he plays so sweetly and sadly that all the earth is moved to his will. In a fit of jealousy, the Caliph and his soldiers try to kill him. Abeli escapes and collapses in exhaustion in the forest. He is finally found, tied up and taken home by a poor bedouin. That night, the bedouin's daughter takes pity on him and removes his ropes. His playing moves her so deeply that she bends and kisses him. At that moment, he changes back into a young man and both live happily ever after.

Short excerpts from the text show the complexity of lexis and syntax:

Once upon a time there was a musician who lived in a little village far from here, at the edge of the great desert. When the sun was high in the sky, he'd take out his flute and play . . .

When he played his flute, snakes and lizards came out to dance in the desert sand.

One night when the moon shone over the mountains, he heard a horrible song. Krixikri, the desert witch, appeared riding on her wildcat . . .

She grabbed the flute and tried to play. But the note that came out was so sharp that stars fell over the desert. 'Be careful!' shouted Abeli. The witch laughed and blew again, even more shrilly. The flute couldn't bear the horrible tone and it broke . . .

(After many adventures, Abeli is heartbroken when requested to play at the wedding of the Caliph's daughter.)

(Abeli) played so that the wind tore at the clouds and the sky filled with birds. He played so that the river rose over its banks and entered the palace in waves . . .

Then the Caliph shouted 'Stop, stop! . . .' And the soldiers drew their swords and rushed forward . . .

He has lived happily ever since with Dunja. And wherever the wandering bedouins make camp, he sends them cooling rains and makes the desert bloom.

(Rehnman 1989)

What makes this story successful in spite of its difficult language? When children are asked, they say 'I liked the little monkey' or 'I liked the little girl at the end' or 'It's a nice story because it's happy and sad' or 'I liked the pictures'. As adults, we prefer to find more logical reasons, such as:

- It portrays important universal values of courage and kindness. Children may identify with the little grey monkey or the kind child.
- It shows the victory of good over evil.
- It shows a world far from present reality, yet with everyday feelings children may experience anywhere.
- Although the language is difficult, it is rich in imagery and uses many words which might be personal 'key words' for young children (witch, horrible, grab, scream, kiss, tear, sword, heart, etc.).
- The story moves purposefully and clearly.
- The illustrations are inspiring.

Compare this text with one which appears at first sight to be considerably simpler. It is called *Don't Blame Me!* by Paul Rogers. Like *The Clay Flute*, it is a large hardback book with pastel shaded impressionistic illustrations and large print. The story aims to make children laugh. Set in a typical Devon village, Jethro the painter is painting the pub sign of 'The Jolly Sailor' when some yellow paint spots drop onto Mr Herring's wedding suit as he is on his way to his daughter's wedding. A momemt later, wild Captain Crab storms out because he sees his boat disappearing out to sea. He knocks Jethro off his ladder causing him to put a black streak across his sign. When Jethro remonstrates, Captain Crab calls 'Don't blame me! Blame Mrs Pengelly's goat which has eaten through the rope tying my boat.' The rest of the story continues as Mrs Pengelly blames a shout from Dick Trevelyan for frightening her goat, etc. until the fault is traced back to Mr Herring who, of course, blames Jethro for dribbling the yellow paint on his suit. Each page has a short text and there are two refrains: 'Don't blame me!' and !. . . to give . . . a piece of his/her mind'. Short excerpts illustrate the nature of the narrative:

> *Mr Herring was happy and proud. It was the day of his daughter's wedding. As he came out of The Jolly Sailor, he didn't see Jethro up the ladder. He didn't notice the dribbles of yellow paint . . .*
>
> *Captain Crab rushed out, ranting and roaring and STREAK went the brush, right through Jethro's work. Down came Jethro to give Captain Crab a piece of his mind . . .*
>
> *'Don't blame me!' said Captain Crab. 'I was having a quiet drink when – what do you think? I saw my boat had drifted out to sea! That no good goat of Mrs Pengelly's had eaten right through the rope . . '*
>
> *'Don't blame me!' said Dick. 'I was quietly cleaning windows when Jim Merrymeet's horse, Bessie, whipped the ladder from under me! . . .*
>
> *(and finally, as Jethro realises the fault can be traced back to him)*
>
> *'Yellow paint?' said Jethro. 'Floundering flatfish! Then I know who's to blame!'*
>
> *And feeling ever so foolish, off he went to the Jolly Sailor, where the bride gave Jethro a piece of her . . .*
>
> *. . . wedding cake!*
>
> (Rogers 1990)

Although this story amuses monolingual English classes, it rarely holds the attention of a beginner bilingual child. Adults can only suppose why this might be:

- It is very culture-specific (the pub, people's names, etc.).
- The language is very colloquial and the humour rests upon understanding the finer nuances of the language. There is little sign of any really important words which might form children's personal 'key words'.
- It relies upon humour itself for success as the story is not memorable, nor does it follow a clear path of events.
- The illustrations are not clear from a distance, nor is the pastel shading familiar to many children from Asian cultures.

None of this denies the quality of the book itself; it is simply that the experiences it portrays are specific rather than universal. This brief analysis of two stories illustrates the complexity of choosing books for story-time which will inspire and encourage both fluent monolingual and emergent bilingual children as they begin reading together. The examples above show that the superficial complexity of language contained in a story is not necessarily the most crucial factor, yet the story must make sense to the child. Our problem as teachers is that we can never be sure exactly how much of a text need be understood for sense to be gained.

Choosing books for the Outer Layer: some criteria for book selection

Nonetheless, story-books suitable for an Outer Layer of the 'Outside-In' approach to beginning reading in the classroom should fulfil certain criteria. The approach relies upon memorable stories and texts from all times and all places in the same way that children's own 'key words' fed the 'Inside-Out' approach outlined in Chapter 4. The most suitable stories and texts have often withstood time and many have been translated into different languages. Teachers know that most memorable stories contain universal truths, values and morals, fear and 'security which experiments'. A concise list of books which are generally available in English speaking countries can be found in Appendix 2. Below are questions which teachers might consider as they choose books for their story-book collection.

- Will the story interest the children? Is it *memorable*?
- Will the story motivate the children by drawing on their personal experience or emotions? Will it *develop their imagination* and/or *appeal to their sense of humour*?
- Is there a *strong and exciting or appealing storyline* which will hold the children's interest in spite of not understanding all the language used?
- Will the story *arouse their curiosity* and help them respond positively to the target culture, language and language learning? If there are specific cultural references, are they clear?
- Is the language level *appropriate*? Is it *clear and unambiguous*? Does it make sense without relying on children's ability to understand complex structures and/or colloquialisms? Is it *memorable*, i.e. does it contain features such as *rhyme, onomatopoeia, rhythm* and *encourage appropriate use of intonation patterns* which will help children's pronunciation?
- Is there any *natural repetition* to encourage children to participate in the text, facilitate memorising and provide pronunciation practice? Does the repetition enable children to predict what is coming next in the story? Is the amount of key lexis and syntax which will need to be introduced and practised manageable?
- *Do the illustrations relate to the text* and support children's understanding? Are they clear and attractive? Do they lend themselves to discussion about the story? Are they big enough for all the class to see if necessary?

Some practical questions:

- Is the story available in *different versions*, so that a more difficult version can be used for storytime and a simpler version for the children to read themselves in 'structured story' sessions?

- Is there an *audiotape and/or videotape or computer programme* available for use with the story which children can listen to alone in the listening area or borrow to take home?
- Is the story available in *dual language* versions and are all the languages spoken in the class available?

Finally, some general points:

- Does the story have a *high learning potential* in terms of learning about universal morals, truths and values, about the target culture and customs, about the world, and learning about learning generally?
- Does the story provide a *starting-point for related language or cross-curricular activities* and lead to follow-up work such as role-play and drama, art and craft, etc. in order to reinforce lexis and syntax in a meaningful way?
- Do you like the story yourself? Do you find it memorable and enjoy reading it? If not, discard immediately.

Reading the story

We require an education in literature . . . in order to discover that what we have assumed – with the complicity of our teachers – was nature is in fact culture, that what was given is no more than a way of taking.

(Howard 1974 in Heath 1982, p. 49)

Howard's words originally introduced Roland Barthes' volume *S/Z*. Here, Barthes describes the way in which readers use their knowledge of the world (their codes of knowledge) to frame their understanding of written narratives. In Part One of this book, we saw how easy it is wrongly to assume that our own codes of knowledge and ways of taking from texts are 'given', i.e. 'natural' rather than learned. Tony, Nazma and their classmates showed us that 'reading' called up a very different way of relating to books and other types of print.

In Chapter 2, Sarah Michaels' work (1986) showed how two different ethnic groups of children bring to classroom 'newstime' their own narrative style ('topic-centred', focused on one topic, or 'topic-associating', a series of implicitly linked episodes) which they had learned from home. The teachers unconsciously favoured the children who shared their own 'topic-centred' style, yet neither teachers nor children were aware of what was actually happening; the black 'unfavoured' children simply decided after a short time that they hated 'newstime' and that it was 'rubbish'. By the end of Chapter 2, our families provided strong evidence to suggest that children enter school with a very different 'sense' of reading; some, like Jessica, will share the sense held by their teachers, others will be unable to slot story-reading as it takes place in school into a familiar home practice. We concluded that children need to learn appropriate 'recipes' for successful participation in class reading sessions. Some already have these at their fingertips from home; others do not. For those who do not, teachers will need to make these 'recipes' explicit. For ultimately the teacher mediates the culture and its 'recipes for belonging'.

The difficult question for teachers is: what needs to be made explicit about participation in story-reading and how might teachers go about making it so? One way of finding out is offered in a study by Marilyn Cochran-Smith (1984) of story-reading interactions in a private Philadelphia nursery school. Cochran-Smith observed carefully what was taking place between these 'school-oriented' four-year-olds and their teacher during story-reading sessions (referred to as 'rug-time' interactions) and found that they were typified by a definite pattern and rules which distinguished them from other ('off-the-rug') interactions. These consisted of the following:

1. Children must recognise that the teacher must not be interrupted while reading the book. Upon *discussing* the text, however, they should show active involvement.
2. The teacher 'shapes' the child's response to the text: 'This is sad', etc. In other words, she encourages the children to respond to the text as part of a reading audience.
3. The teacher explains the syntax and meanings of the text.
4. The children are asked to infer from the illustrations and words to make sense of the book *as a whole*.
5. The teacher asks the child to call upon 'text-to-life' information to gain meaning from the text (invites child to see the relevance of the text to real life situations).
6. The teacher asks the child to call upon 'life-to-text' information to give meaning to the text (invites child to bring knowledge from life to understand the text).

These children are already familiar with the rules from home story-readings which means that many may now remain implicit in the classroom. Nevertheless, they are rules which are enforced regularly in story-reading sessions during two pre-school years which means that the children are 'socialised' into print before they can even read a word.

What hints might this study offer to teachers working with children who are unfamiliar with the storytime rules? The simple framework offered below is drawn from close observation of teachers whose story-reading sessions are particularly successful and where emergent bilinguals are making remarkable progress.

- *Overall rule*: Explicitly 'model' what reading actually is and what the fluent reader does. This will mean showing what the reader can bring to and take from the text, but above all it will mean making clear to children the difference between what is actually written on the page and what is teacher/child comment on the text (Gregory 1993).

How might this be done? Divide the reading into stages:

Stage 1. Setting the story in context: This may be talking to the children about the place where the story is set, why you like the story, other stories by the author, introducing one of the characters or the theme and relating it to your own or the children's lives, etc. The aim is that children are on tenterhooks to hear the story.

As one monolingual child pleaded to his teacher, 'I'm really dying to hear the story now.'

Stage 2. Reading the story: Tell the children 'Now I'm going to read the story . . .'. The story should then be read as well as possible (slowly and clearly yet with lively intonation). There are to be no interruptions during this time. The teacher may point to items in the illustrations, but she does not leave the text.

Stage 3. Talking about the story: After reading the whole text, tell the children clearly that what is to follow is *talk* about the story, not reading it. Show the illustrations, asking the children to relate text-to-life and life-to-text. Ask how they feel about the characters, etc.

Stage 4. Re-reading the story (if required).

When the class has an adequate number of fluent target language speakers, the technique of 'reciprocal teaching' described by Palincsar, Brown and Campione (1993) can provide useful focused practice for talking about a text. This takes place in four stages:

Stage 1. Asking questions: The teacher or one child (the dialogue leader) begins the discussion by asking questions about the content of the text. The class discusses these questions, raises additional questions and, in the case of disagreement or misunderstanding, re-reads the text.

Stage 2. Summarising: To identify the gist of what has been read and discussed. Discussion takes place to achieve consensus on the summary.

Stage 3. Clarification: Children offer words, etc. they do not understand and these are clarified by others.

Stage 4. Predictions: The leader asks the class to predict what might come next in a text – or, if a whole story has been read, what might happen to different characters in the story.

However, the key to initiating emergent bilinguals into the host culture and at the same time building a common classroom culture of story-reading in school must lie with the choice of text. Susanne Langer in *Feeling and Form* (1953) reminds us that stories start with our own memories. The teacher's aim must be to harness not only 'real' memories but those which might have been . . . This is why memorable texts will often use the same 'key vocabulary' brought by the child to the 'Inside-Out' approach to reading. *The Clay Flute* touches on two themes of great significance to the child entering a new world: magic or immortal powers and long and dangerous journeys. They are, of course, the stuff of many folk tales. Little wonder that it provoked these stories from six-year-olds:

> *Tarlochan reflecting: I was looking at the star*
> *With my telescope*
> *God's fire came down and burnt me up*
> *God picked me up*
> *And I was saved*
> *I killed God.*

These three boys are painting pictures for the story:

Nabeel: The sun is God's front door
  At night he presses a button
  And the dark goes

Haryinder: God's voice is very quiet
  You can hear him in your head
  The wind is God's blowing

Sunit: The wind is God's wings moving

III. THE 'OUTSIDE-IN' APPROACH: THE INNER LAYER

The creation of meaning is of a dialogic nature. Whenever we talk, we use the words and phrases of others that become our own when we use them to say new things, at new times and in new places.

(Bakhtin 1986)

For emergent bilinguals, the clearest words are often those from simple story-books. Spoken words disappear suddenly from the mouth of the speaker and return transformed by a different context while the text of a book remains constant and can be listened to over and over again until it becomes the child's own. In this way, we might say that a dialogue takes place between the child and the text. Yet for emergent bilinguals who share knowledge of neither the story nor the language in which it is told, the teacher plays a vital role as mediator in the dialogue. As with the 'Inside-Out' approach, the nature of the teacher's task will be different according to how many children are already expert in the target language in the class. Where the teacher is the only (or almost the only) fluent speaker of the new language and where some children are having very different reading lessons in their community, the teacher will need to be far more explicit in her teaching than where only a few emergent bilinguals are present who can imitate and be helped by their more fluent peers.

Below are two different frameworks which fit within the aims of the 'Outside-In' approach. The first is known as 'collaborative reading'. It comes from Australia and is most successful when emergent bilinguals are supported by a number of native speakers or children who are fluent or competent in the new language. The second I call 'structured story'. It was devised to be used with children like Nazma and her friends whose complex and copious outside-school reading was introduced in Chapter 2. The 'structured story' approach is designed for classes or groups where the large majority of children are just beginning to learn to speak and read the new language simultaneously. Both frameworks are suited for group and class work and are equally relevant for children from any cultural and linguistic background.

Collaborative reading

In 'Beginning reading with children's literature' (1993), Len Unsworth and Mary O'Toole explain that the origins of their programme lie in their aim to learn 'more about "the teaching role of the text and its writer" (Meek 1982, p. 20); the ways in which adults "scaffold" young readers' interactions with texts; the successive approximations which characterise young children's oral reading development; and the essential relationship of these aspects of learning to read' (p. 95). They stress how important it is for teachers to examine the social processes whereby children become early independent readers and to take these as a starting-point for classroom work. Important aspects of these processes, they maintain, are:

- the incorporation of appropriate written language in an enjoyable, functional manner into the normal social routines that a child experiences;
- the collaborative exploration of written language with an experienced reader in these routines;
- the provision of recurrent, enjoyable and supportive contexts where the same texts may be 'revisited' over time;
- access to quality children's literature.

Obviously, resources will be important – from a dynamic classroom library, a reading corner, listening area, a 'publishing' (writing) area to links with parents and the wider community. However, the key to successful collaborative reading lies in careful planning within a structured framework. They offer a planning outline for 45-minute daily sessions over about two weeks for children who are well into their first year or at the beginning of their second year in school. The theme is a selection of books by Pat Hutchins. What follows below is a summary of the overall design of each session followed by a brief summary of one reading session to illustrate how their design works in practice.

The design

Unsworth and O'Toole decided upon using different books by Pat Hutchins (see Appendix 2) because they are supportive of novice readers yet at the same time offer multilayered meanings which invite different interpretations. These included *1 Hunter, Goodnight Owl, Don't Forget the Bacon, The Wind Blew* and, of course, *Rosie's Walk*, a tale of timeless brilliance, thoughtfully analysed by Margaret Meek in *How Texts Teach What Readers Learn* (1988), a tale which, she says, 'has taught hundreds of children that stories include what the reader knows and what the text needn't say (Meek 1991, p. 122). One longer text (*The Very Worst Monster*) was also chosen to emphasise that children's reading development can benefit significantly without them necessarily being able to read all of the text in every book which is the focus of the lesson. However, the authors suggest that themes such as 'bullying' (*Willy the Wimp* and *Willy the Champ* by Anthony Browne), illustrators, books without words, poems, etc. may comprise similar units.

They are careful to stress that the stages within each session should remain flexible and not become rituals. Generally, however, they will fit into the following pattern:

- orientation to collaborative reading
- introduction of the new book
- collaborative reading of the new book
- exploration of text meanings
- consolidation of text processing
- extension reading/writing activities

Orientation: This stage calls upon material which is very familiar to the children (rhymes, chants, poems, songs). Gradually, these can be displayed in large print and a child points to the words appropriately. The aim is for maximum participation in a group and to give confidence to less fluent speakers. Later, familiar stories can be retold or briefly dramatised or children's writing shared. This stage occupies about 5 minutes of the session.

Introduction of the new book: The aim in this stage is to arouse children's interest in the book by drawing attention to its external features such as the cover design, name of author, etc. Children use picture or title clues to guess what the book might be about, etc. The teacher also builds upon the children's developing sound-symbol knowledge in identifying the name of the author and the title, e.g. Whose name begins with the same letter as the author? Where have we seen that word before? The teacher may write the author's name and the title may be written large on the black/white board sounding it out as she does so. This stage also needs about 5 minutes.

Collaborative reading: There are 5 steps in this section:

1. The teacher's initial reading of the book (to provide a model for the children).
2. Initial discussion with the children about the story (teacher poses some general questions and then asks the children to listen again for answers and see what else they notice).
3. A second reading with informal participation by the children as a group (teacher pauses in appropriate places for children to join in reading).
4. Follow-up discussion drawing on further observations about the story to scaffold-directed participation in a third reading, planning of systematic participation by children in third reading – different groups read different refrains or choruses (Trip, trap . . . etc.) or sound effects.
5. A third reading with teacher-directed participation by the children chorally in small groups or as individuals as appropriate.

The object is to engage children in the reading of the story in a supportive context. This section takes about 15 minutes.

Exploration of meanings: This is 'talk around text' time. It is to encourage children to question texts, pose problems, etc.; for example: 'Did Rosie the hen know that the fox was following her? (*Rosie's Walk*); 'Was there really a monster?' (David McKee: *Not Now Bernard*). The first steps in this stage will no doubt be taken by fluent target language speakers, but each of their comments offers a model to others. This stage lasts about 5 to 10 minutes.

Consolidation: Here children are given structured opportunities to deal directly with print. Work for small groups is designed to develop graphophonic, lexical and syntactic clues. One group is targeted for intensive teacher interaction each day. This section lasts about 15 minutes.

Extension: There should always be a 'bank' of activities for children to choose upon completing their work. Harder activities should have been practised by the teacher with the whole class before asking individuals to complete alone. Unsworth and O'Toole suggest 'captioned collages', e.g. depicting the scene where a mass of objects are flying in the sky (Pat Hutchins: *The Wind Blew*), by drawing the background, pasting on relevant articles and labelling them using captions from the book. Other extension activities might include constructing and inserting 'speech balloons' into stories, recording stories or a storyboard (matching illustration and text and sequencing photocopied pages from the story).

The session summarised below is an adaptation of the fourth in their series. It takes place towards the end of the first week:

Orientation: Ask the children the names of the three other Pat Hutchins book which have been read (*1 Hunter*, *Rosie's Walk* and *Goodnight Owl*) and vote on the favourite. This is then read again and the children are encouraged to join in. Then simple poems on 'wind' are read out ('Dark, windy night' by Anne English, 'Wind song' by Lilian Moore in *My Very First Poetry Book*, Oxford University Press).

Introduction: Ask the children to find *The Wind Blew* from the display. Read and discuss the title and ask children to predict the story from the cover illustration and the title.

Collaborative reading: Mention the dedication. Upon the second reading, use the repetition and rhyme as a way into *oral cloze* (pause just before the end of the second line for the children to complete).

Exploration: Encourage the children to notice how the illustrations tell the story before the text and compare with the illustrations in *Rosie's Walk* and *Goodnight Owl*.

Consolidation: The children are divided into four groups:

1. The children listen to a tape of the story and follow with the book. On some pages, the text has been affixed on a card leaving spaces to form a rhyming cloze:

> 'It grabbed a shirt left out to dry
> And tossed it upward to the —'

The reader waits a moment for the child to respond and only then carries on reading.
2. Labelling: a group has a photocopy of the third last page of the book with arrows from the objects to boxes. Children either look through the book or use word cards made from the book to label the object.

3. Similar to the group above but labelling the characters of the story.
4. A captioned collage (see description in the general section above on 'Extension').

Extension: Provide the children with the text for each page on separate cards and invite them to sequence differently so that the story will still make sense.

> We become literate by behaving as the literate do, making efforts under their instruction, at home, at school and in our encounters with writing in the world.
>
> *(Meek 1991, p. 6)*

'Collaborative reading' is based upon the belief that literacy learning is a social process and that children's ideas on reading are built from the practices they observe and participate in as members of a community. In Part One of this book, we became aware of the wealth of community literacy activities which young children engage in and bring with them into school. Within the 'collaborative reading' framework, it is the teacher's responsibility to provide access to socially valued literacy practices which may be very new and different from those found within the child's own community. In their role as expert, as mediator of what for many children may be a new cultural practice, teachers must balance explicit teaching with allowing opportunities for children to think independently and to become experts themselves. Similar to Bruner's notion of a 'joint culture creation' (1986) between teacher and child which we examined in Chapter 2, Unsworth and O'Toole maintain that what counts as reading in each classroom will be constructed by teacher and pupils working together on a common understanding of the reading task.

Structured story

The teacher is introducing Nazma, Shabbir, Louthfur and their friends to *The Three Billy Goats Gruff*. It is the first of a series of traditional folk and fairy tales they will read and study during their second year in school. All the class are Bengali (Sylheti dialect) speakers and English is generally not used at home. Consequently, the children's spoken English is still very limited. The teacher has several versions of the story (see Appendix 2) which will be read to the class at storytime. She has chosen the cheapest but most robust version for the structured story sessions (Ladybird 'Read it Yourself'). There are various reasons for her choice: it will be used for her home reading packs; its sentence structure is simple and clear, moving purposefully through the story using rhymes and repetitions; last, she can cut up a second book for magnet-board figurines. She knows, however, that her oral work must focus on the past tense, since this is the tense normally used as we retell stories. She is interested to see how far the children will distinguish the two tenses as they tell the story and read the text.

The teacher first tells the story in English using the figurines as she does so. She tells it a second time hoping the children will respond to an oral cloze 'Trip, trap, trip, trap, over the — '. She learns from this and her questions that the children can say very little from the story in English. She tells the story in a similar way in Sylheti. The children's faces come alive. The teacher is surprised, however, that none know the word for 'goat' and only some the word for 'bridge' in their mother-tongue. Nevertheless, their interest is lively and they actively join in retelling the story and talking about the text.

After ten sessions of about one hour, the children's retelling in English is transformed. They are also able to read the story and have made their own small books using a talking computer programme and rewriting the text. What does the process of coming to know a story in a new language look like? Brief excerpts from sessions near the beginning, in the middle and towards the end of the unit illustrate this:

1. The beginning: *'Take One' of the acting and the teacher tells most of the story herself. She asks the children to join in using English if possible; if not, Sylheti:*

Teacher: Trip, trap. Trip, trap. Next the middle-sized Billy Goat Gruff went a little further on the bridge and said, 'I want to eat some grass as well.' So off he went.
Reshma: Trip, trap. Trip, trap.
Teacher: . . . Why did he want to go, Shabbir?
Shabbir: Eating grass.
Teacher: So why did he want to go?
Shabbir: Go and eat.
Teacher: Say it as if you are the goat.
Shabbir: I eat the grass. (said hesitantly and in a monotone)
Teacher: So off he went. Trip, trap. Trip, trap over the bridge. Suddenly, up jumped the troll and he said . . .
Nazma: I eat you!
Teacher: I want to eat you!
Nazma: I want to eat you!
Teacher: What does he say?
Nazma: My brother is big. You eat my brother.
Teacher: What does the troll say?
Louthfur: OK. Go on.
Teacher: So off he went. Trip, trap. Trip, trap. Over . . .
Resma: . . . the bridge.
Teacher: Now, suddenly, up looked the Billy Goat Gruff and he saw his brothers on the other side of the bridge. He decided to go over and what did he say? Why did he want to go over? Try to say it in English? What did the big goat say when he saw his brothers?
Shahina: (in Sylheti) They've gone over there, so why shouldn't I?

2. The middle: *The children read the text sentence by sentence after the teacher, first in chorus, then individually. This task is very popular and the children's intonation in the new language improves remarkably. They also complete various word focus games, e.g. the teacher has a pile of cards with words from the story. The child reads the word, then puts it in a sentence:*

Teacher: Nazma, find me 'grass'. (she does so) Now give me a sentence.
Nazma: Little Billy Goat Gruff likes to eat grass.

or they look for words in the text:

Teacher: Shabbir, find me the word 'bridge'. (he finds it) How many times do you see that word on the page?
Shabbir: Two.
Teacher: Read me that sentence.
Shabbir: The big troll has a home under the bridge.

or they play an 'opposites' game, whereby each in turn takes a card, hides it from the others and says:

Shahina: It's the opposite of 'up'. (holding 'down')

The pace of this game increases rapidly with practice

3. Near the end: *The children read the story onto tape. Afterwards, they retell the story in their own words in English and in Sylheti:*

Shahina: (as most of the children, she reads the text almost perfectly, using native-like intonation patterns) Here is just a small sample of the text:

Reading
'*. . . Middle-sized Billy Goat Gruff looks up. Little Billy Goat Gruff is over the bridge. He says, "He has some grass. I can go over the bridge for some grass." Middle-size Billy Goat Gruff is on the bridge. Up jumps the troll. He says, "I want to eat you up." "No, no!" says middle-sized Billy Goat Gruff. "Here comes Big Billy Goat Gruff. He is big and fat. You can eat him up" . . .'*

Retelling in English
'*. . . The big goat saw both his brothers on the other side of the bridge. He said. "The little goat and the middle goat are eating grass, so I will go and eat grass. I can go over the bridge." Trip, trap, trip, trap, trip, trap. The big one goes onto the bridge. Suddenly a troll jumps up and says, "I want to eat you!"*
The troll . . .
Teacher: Did he fall down into the water? What happened?
'*. . . He went up. The troll . . . fell into the water. Trip, trap, trip, trap, trip, trap. The big goat went over the bridge. They played and ate and said they liked it there.'*

Retelling in Sylheti
'*. . . The middle goat saw that the little goat was over and he asked if he could go over the bridge. So he went. Trip, trap, trip, trap, trip, trap. Then something like a troll jumped up and said "I want to eat you." "No, no," the middle one said. "My big brother will come and he is big and fat, so you can eat him." So the troll said, "OK, you can go. Then he went and the big one came. He saw that his little brother and middle brother were eating flowers. So he went. Trip, trap, trip, trap, trip, trap. The goat went. Up on top, the troll came and said, "I want to eat you up" . . .*

The children are obviously still more confident and use more sophisticated syntax in their mother-tongue – 'he asked if he could . . ', 'He saw that . . . were eating', 'Up on top', etc. – and have no hesitation using appropriate tenses. Yet their English retelling is competent and they are able to use present, future and past tenses appropriately most of the time. This contrasts enormously with the start of the sessions where their few hesitant English words are highlighted by Shahina's brief but complex answer in Sylheti, 'They've gone over there, so why shouldn't I?'. It also contrasts with their considerable difficulty in telling their news, etc. where their speech is sometimes still marked with very basic errors (Me go . . ? (Can I go?); hims name . . . (his name); shes book . . . (her book), etc.). How might structured story-reading link spoken and written language so that emergent bilinguals can draw upon one to inform the other?

As with 'collaborative reading', the teacher plays a crucial role as mediator. But now she is aware that for some children she may be the only role model for the new language. Reshma, for example, understands and seems to speak more Hindi than English, picked up from watching videos. The role of television and

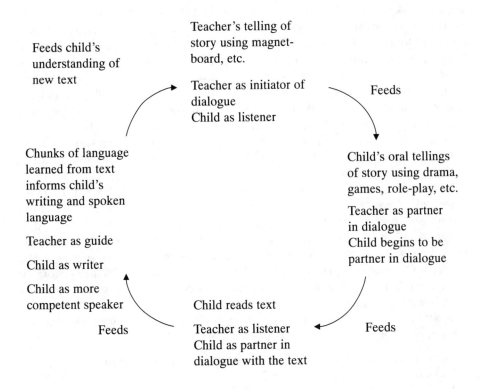

Figure 10 The inner layer of the 'Outside-In' approach is circular in nature.

video in children's language development should not be underestimated, but television may play a relatively small part in some emergent bilinguals' busy lives. The teacher has observed closely the difficulty and occasional embarrassment experienced by the children when they cannot pronounce or 'get their tongue around' words which they then abandon saying. She knows from observation at mosque and Bengali classes that the children love choral recitations and have excellent memories of words including those in Arabic which they cannot understand. All of this knowledge will be built into 'structured story-reading'. It is a simple method best suited to group but also adaptable to class work which complements the 'Inside-Out' approach outlined in Chapter 4. Below is a framework for 'structured story' with emergent bilinguals.

1. Choosing books and stories

In the English-speaking world, a number of stories with simple, clear repetitive texts are now available. An excellent collection of texts for emergent bilinguals available in the UK is suggested by Viv Edwards from the Reading and Language Information Centre, University of Reading (other titles may be found in Appendix 2). Traditional folk and fairy stories and fables are particularly valuable for affective, cognitive and linguistic reasons. They introduce children and their families into a new cultural heritage, yet contain familiar morals and values the world over. In *The Uses of Enchantment* (1975), Bruno Bettelheim gives us a comprehensive analysis of the deep moral questions contained in fairy tales which appeal to all children. Why should the queen want to kill Snow White? Why does Hansel and Gretel's stepmother hate them? and so on. We know that fables (The Hare and the Tortoise, The Lion and the Mouse, etc.) appear in different guises (Kaluli the Hare in Zambia, The Hunter and the Deer in India, etc.) and are well-known and loved across cultures.

Nevertheless, it must be remembered that the aim of 'structured story' is for emergent bilinguals actually to read the texts and that some of these will form the basis of home–school reading packs. This means that teachers will need to adapt some excellent but difficult stories (*The Hungry Caterpillar* by Eric Carle is likely to fall into this category) by making their own versions (perhaps 'Big Books'). Original complex texts (which will include more difficult versions of traditional folk stories) will be read by the teacher during class story-reading or 'collaborative reading' sessions.

Teachers may find it helpful to consider the following questions when choosing a book upon which to base 'structured story' work:

- How memorable and appealing is the story for young children?
  Does it have a repetitive element?
  Is the plot easily understandable?
  Will it introduce children into valued (whether old or new) stories?
- Does it already exist as book, audio and/or videotape or computer disc version? (see Appendix 2)
  Are dual language versions already available (texts and tapes)?
  Is a suitably simple written version already available?
  If not can one be made?
  Are more complex versions available for use during class story-reading sessions?
  Can parents or other members of the community be invited to make illustrated dual language versions of traditional tales from across the world?

Once a book is found or one has been written:

- Is the language accessible and suitable as early reading material in a new language?
  Is the text of a good size to be seen by the children?
  How much text is on the page?
  Are the illustrations clear?
  Can magnet-board figurines be made easily?
  Will it provide children with useful 'chunks' for their spoken language development?

Does it have a memorable rhyme or refrain?

Can songs be linked to it?

- Will it provide links with the 'Inside-Out' approach? (Use of 'key' words, such as those relating to fear, etc. and experiences, which can be expressed through dance, music, cooking, etc.)
- Will it be accessible to parents and be familiar to siblings? (Does it have a moral which is important in both cultures; can links be made with stories known by parents?)
- Generally, how much potential does it have in developing the 'knowledge centres' as outlined in Chapter 3 needed for learning to read?

2. Resourcing 'structured story' in the classroom

We must remember that the 'Outside-In' approach is but half the suggested reading programme. All the resources needed for the 'Inside-Out' approach outlined in Chapter 4 should be available for use during this work. However, some will take on a special importance during 'structured story'. A key addition is the story-pack upon which the approach rests and which I describe below.

(a) The basics

The 'basic' is a pack of resources with work and ideas relating directly to each story. Depending upon the size of book, it will probably be contained in a plastic folder. A second and different pack will be available for children to borrow. There are no strict rules on the contents of the pack and dual language versions may on occasions prove impossible, but packs will usually contain the following:

(i) An outline of suggested sessions for teachers as well as a list of focus lexis and syntax for children (see the section 'Structured story: a simple procedure' below).

(ii) Figurines for a magnet or flannelboard. These depict the story and may be self-made or cut out from a second version of the book.

(iii) An audio-tape of the spoken version of the story in English and the children's mother-tongues on one side and the story as it is read (using a sound to mark off where a child turns the page) in English and other languages if dual language stories are used on the other.

(iv) A second tape I refer to as the 'Listen, Discuss and Do' tape. On this tape, the teacher tells the story and pauses frequently asking the children to draw something from the story. The children have a worksheet either with six empty squares for their drawings or items which they need to discuss in some way with others in the group.

(v) Possibly a video of the story or relevant computer software. A video of children acting the story might be included.

(vi) The story itself. Dual language versions using the children's mother-tongues should be included wherever possible.

(vii) Word cards for the magnet or flannelboard with focus lexis from the text.

(viii) Simple '*cloze*' cards with sentences from the story where children need to find the appropriate word and letter/sound search cards for graphophonic/orthographic focus.

(b) Drama resources

In being who we are not, we can call upon a whole set of features we would not normally have . . . In play we are one head taller . . .
(Vygotsky writing about play in Mind in Society *1978)*

Drama is a type of play and like play it involves a kind of learning about self which results in a change of the self (Gregory Bateson 1955). Drama takes on a special importance during 'structured story'. At first, children find it difficult and need to repeat phrases after the teacher. With practice they become more adventurous and experiment with the new language in ways where they would otherwise not dare. For each story, devote a lot of time to drama, for it takes many 'rehearsals' before children say confidently what they mean. For each story, provide a set of props and dressing-up clothes. Video practices for discussion with the children and final performances if possible.

(c) Community resources

'My favourite story is "Heidi". I think I'll write that.' Jeanette has three young children in the school where she is an active member of a writing group set up by one of the teachers. Her friend talks about 'The Little Mermaid' and the group discovers that Nilmani, the Gujarati speaking member of the group, also knows the story. Both work together to produce an illustrated dual language version for the school. Jan chooses 'The Hare and the Tortoise'. The story is also familiar to her husband, a Twi speaker from Ghana, and he works at home with her on a book and audio-tape. She illustrates the story herself. After a short time, the group are working together on simple dual language versions of traditional tales, supported by audio-tapes, for use by both themselves and the teacher during 'structured story' sessions. Within a year, the group have received funding to cover the costs of their work and one afternoon per week of a teacher's time to work with them.
(Gregory 1984)

The community is an invaluable resource for 'structured story' with emergent bilinguals. Benefits for both children and the community (often, but not always, a group of mothers) are mutual (see Figure 11).

In some European countries, projects for dual language materials have received major local education authority support. Pamela Oberhuemer and a team of teacher educators from the Institute for Early Childhood Education and Research in Munich, Bavaria, Germany, have produced a series of audio- and videotapes of traditional Turkish and Italian stories, in which some characters constantly speak Turkish (or Italian); others German. Yet the texts are written so that even monolingual German listeners have no difficulty in understanding the meaning of the new language. The materials have been devised for pre-

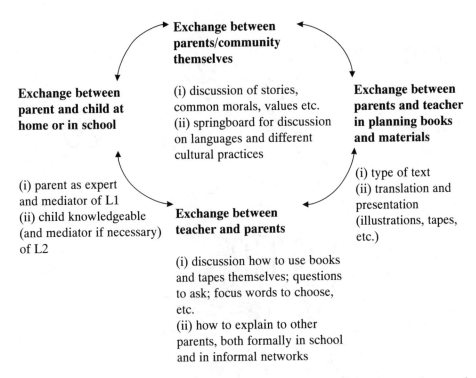

Exchange between parents/community themselves

(i) discussion of stories, common morals, values etc.
(ii) springboard for discussion on languages and different cultural practices

Exchange between parent and child at home or in school

(i) parent as expert and mediator of L1
(ii) child knowledgeable (and mediator if necessary) of L2

Exchange between parents and teacher in planning books and materials

(i) type of text
(ii) translation and presentation (illustrations, tapes, etc.)

Exchange between teacher and parents

(i) discussion how to use books and tapes themselves; questions to ask; focus words to choose, etc.
(ii) how to explain to other parents, both formally in school and in informal networks

Figure 11 Language and cultural exchanges between community, teachers and children.

school (pre-6) intercultural education. Yet they show the potential gains for those who write and design them in terms of linguistic, cultural, social and educational awareness. Parents become experts and gain confidence in passing their expertise to others. Take Jan, for example, whom we met at the beginning of this section. Jan presented her illustrations of 'The Hare and the Tortoise' (see Figure 12) to the group with the excuse 'They're not very good . . .'. One year later, she had become illustrator of a series of published children's books.

(c) Book corner

As in any Early Years classroom, this should be an attractive and comfortable area for children to sit and browse or for 'collaborative reading' and/or 'structured story' to take place. Fewer, more carefully chosen books are better than a disarray of numerous books which the children never use. A display of books by the same author/illustrator or on the same theme (see 'collaborative story') together with children's self-made books should regularly change to reflect the current story which is presented. By limiting the number of books displayed, children quickly become familiar with their stories and recognise the value each individual book holds.

The Hare and the Tortoise

سیر اور کچھوا

in English and Urdu.

Figure 12   Community work on children's dual language stories.

(d) The listening area

The 'structured story' packs are housed in the listening area which has a tape recorder and the magnet/flannelboard. It will be close to the computer and writing area where children compose their own stories. Children are encouraged (using headphones) to listen to the spoken stories in their mother-tongue and English, to follow the text using the book and to tell the story to their classmates using the figurines and the board. They may also complete the 'Listen, Discuss and Do' work in this area, although this may sometimes be completed as a whole-class activity first. In the writing or computer area, they make their own books based on the structured story they are discussing.

Art, music and cooking will all be included in the storywork wherever possible.

3. Working with 'structured story': a simple procedure

Understanding 'structured story' is not difficult if the reader returns to Chapters 2 and 3 in Part One of this book. From these chapters, we learned about common features of reading practices taking place in children's community classes and the special linguistic and cognitive strengths brought by emergent bilinguals to learning to read in a new language. Chapter 2 described the literacy practices engaged in by different emergent bilinguals. From Tony's family (originally from Hong Kong) we realised that practice and perfection along with an eye for exact detail were important. His family also showed the reverence attached to the book. This was shared by all the other families we met in Chapter 2, including Nicole's family whose mother now treasures every children's book in English she can find. We learned in Chapter 2 that all of the children learned through very explicit reading lessons, often involving repeating words after the teacher before practising them with peers. We also saw that the children were able to participate in group oral work for comparatively long periods of time. Chapter 3 gave examples to illustrate the advanced metalinguistic strengths of bilinguals, even at an early stage of using two languages. We also saw evidence of their excellent memories and their eye for detail in print. Of all the cues needed for reading, we learned that word or 'lexical' clues are the strongest, while syntactic and semantic clues will lag behind until children can match language with experience.

'Structured story' aims to build upon strengths brought by emergent bilinguals into school as well as recognising their specific weaknesses. It recognises important principles of successful second language teaching, namely, that bilingualism is multidimensional (involves psychological and social issues as well as linguistic ones); that children can transfer learning from one language to another (*interdependency principle*) so long as second language learning is *additive not subtractive*; that children need *comprehensible input* matching language to experience to best facilitate their learning (Gregory 1994b). At the same time, it works within theories of early childhood learning promoted by Vygotsky (1962) and Bruner (1986) outlined in detail in Part One of this book. Specifically, children are given very explicit guidance (by choral repetition, etc.), yet they take control over learning by devising their own games and drama scripts. They also write their own stories, but only after they are confident orally to know what they want to write. But what might this look like in practice?

Stage one: telling the story

1. Tell the story using the past tense to narrate (other tenses as appropriate) and clear simple language with the help of the figurines and magnet/flannelboard. The story is taped for the children's later use and kept in the story-pack.
2. If possible, tell or play a tape of the story in the children's mother-tongues (this is obviously easiest if all the children have the same mother-tongue). If not, the tape can be heard at home or with classroom assistants who speak the child's language.
3. Tell the story in English again, asking the children to fictionalise themselves as the characters ('and little Billy Goat Gruff said . . .') or using oral cloze ('I'm going to eat you — !). If this is difficult, let the children repeat in chorus or invite the children to speak in their mother-tongue. Participation is important here rather than accuracy.

Stage two: acting the story

1. With the children, make various props/costumes for the story, referring to the language of the story as these are made.
2. Narrate the story. Individual children play different characters and everyone joins in with a refrain (trip, trap . . . over the bridge; Grannie, what big eyes you've got! etc.). It may well take three or four sessions before children are confident in their role and contribution. Video a final version if possible.

Stage three: listen, discuss and do

1. Prepare the children for listening sessions on the tape in the story-pack.
2. Complete the listening work, having simple or more difficult versions of the task if possible.

Stage four: across the curriculum

Extend oral work into other curriculum areas if possible, e.g. music and dance or cooking (Hansel and Gretel), taking photographs of the children to make a class/ group book on what they are doing. Cooking can be especially valuable (cakes, biscuits, etc. for both Little Red Riding Hood and Hansel and Gretel) and the results used during drama sessions.

Stage five: reading the story

1. *Providing the context*: read the story from the book highlighting individual key words which are attached in turn to the magnet-board (these words are kept in the story-pack). The children read the words (after the teacher if necessary). After reading, ask the children to spell some of the words. Point to similarities in meaning and orthographic and phonic likenesses between the words, e.g. below and under; small and little.
2. *Word focus*: remove all the words from the board. Then either give a description of the word chosen or ask a question to which it is the answer, e.g. What is under the bridge? (showing the word 'water') Can you spell it? How does the Big Billy Goat Gruff sound? (show 'loud') What does little Billy Goat Gruff like to do? (show 'play') This is to prepare the children for the 'Guess the word' game.
3. *Guess the word game*: (this is to fix the word in context in spoken language). (i) The words are placed face down. (ii) A child secretly chooses a word. (iii) S/he gives the other children a clue without saying the word, e.g. goats like to eat this (grass) or this feels wet (water), etc. (iv) The others try to guess the word. This is difficult and needs practice with the whole class and the teacher taking the first few words before children can work in groups.
4. *Opposites game*: (focuses the children on important adjectives and prepositions in the story). The 'opposites' word cards are placed face down on the table. One child picks a card and says 'It's the opposite of "little". The other children guess the word and go on to use it in a sentence, e.g. The wolf was *big*

and bad. The children repeat using other cards (wet/dry; dirty/clean; big/little; under/over; up/down, etc.). You may need to give several examples at first, but once children understand the term 'opposite' there should be no difficulty.

5. *Emphasising intonation*: the children read the story sentence by sentence after the teacher, first in chorus as a group and then individually. The choral reading is important when children are very hesitant in a language as even the shyest gain confidence. This stage is important to enable the children to gain correct pronunciation and intonation patterns without having to concentrate on the reading itself. If possible, support this through songs and rhymes using the text of the story.

6. *Building up a text*: the children are asked to read one word in a sentence and then read the whole sentence, e.g. 'goat' – 'Big Billy Goat Gruff goes over the bridge'. During this, build upon the children's knowledge of metal-anguage, e.g. use terms like 'word', 'sentence', 'letter', etc. 'How many sentences are on that page?' 'What makes a sentence?' 'Read me the second sentence on that page.' 'How many full stops are there on that page?'

7. *Picture description*: only at this late stage are the children confident in describing different pictures. Begin by asking 'Show me . . .', then ask 'Tell me what is happening in this picture'.

8. *Story-reading*: ask the children to read the whole story individually or in pairs (or groups if work is completed with the whole class). Try to tape some of their readings so that you can pick up on individual or group difficulties to give extra practice.

9. *Final story-telling*: ask children to tell the story using only the figurines. Tape their tellings. Notice whether forms of language read accurately can be carried over into their tellings. Notice also their use of tenses, adjectives, pronouns (s/he; his/her; him/her, etc. which are difficult for children who have Asian languages).

10. *Story-telling in other languages*: if you are able, ask children to tell the story in their mother-tongue using the figurines (you may need to tape this and ask colleagues or parents for assistance). Compare children's capabilities in both languages.

Stage six: writing the story

(Children are only asked to write the story when they have adequate 'chunks' of the target language to enable them to approach the task confidently.)

1. *Cloze cards*: these are at various levels of difficulty and aim to familiarise and reinforce the structures of English syntax before children go on to write their own story. Some will also provide graphophonic and orthographic practice.

2. *Story-writing*: either use photographs from drama, etc. to make a class/group 'Big Book' or make individual story-books. You might try using the Talking Pendown computer software programme. Use the word cards and a Breakthrough to Literacy blank project folder (Longman) as a basis for a wordbank for the children.

Stage seven: extension into collaborative reading and class story-reading sessions

Search for different versions of traditional stories to use during class story-reading (e.g. Paul Galdone's 1973 version of *The Three Billy Goats Gruff* and various other traditional tales, Anthony Browne's 1983 version of *Hansel and Gretel*, etc.).

IN SUMMARY

In this chapter, we have seen ways in which teachers may explicitly 'scaffold' the learning of emergent bilinguals using an 'Outside-In' approach to reading. The first section took as its starting-point the 'magic' that a good story-book holds for all children. We saw how stories provide a valuable set of 'recipes' for coping with a new life in school and how they act as unique 'scaffolds' to children's learning in a way that conversation cannot. The second section examined story-reading by the teacher (referred to as the Outer Layer of the approach). This is where teachers tackle valuable but difficult texts 'bathing' children in a magic where story and text intertwine and understanding comes somewhere in-between. In addition, criteria were offered for choosing storytime books and a suggested framework for story-reading based on explicit 'scaffolding'. The third section outlined two different approaches for 'scaffolding' children's own reading of texts: (i) 'collaborative reading' (which relies on an adequate number of children who are competent in the target language); and (ii) 'structured story' where most or all the children are emergent bilingual.

From the frameworks offered, we saw how 'scaffolding' takes place through:

- linking spoken and written language through the use of drama, music, cookery, art etc.;
- defining the rules of class story-reading sessions so that children begin to realise the difference between 'reading the words' and 'talk about text';
- 'modelling' reading and enabling children to repeat manageable 'chunks' of text in chorus first;
- increasing the language demands on a child gradually.

Like the puppets in Chapter 4, we saw in this chapter ways in which stories can provide a bridge to a new culture. Five-year-old Derrick Wu illustrates this clearly as he tells us of his journey to rescue Abeli the monkey with the aid of his kite:

> *In Hong Kong there are lots of kites*
> *I had a butterfly kite in Hong Kong*
> *A bird did eat it*
> *I told my grandmother*
> *She say 'Go next door'*
> *I make another kite*
> *In secret*
> *Out of paper and wood*
> *If it hasn't got a tail, it can't go high*

I could make a kite
And go to Hong Kong
And fly it
I could go in a helicopter
You come into the playground and you
Say 'Good-bye'
I go to Hong Kong and fly kite
Then come back

As he begins his volume of traditional Jewish stories, A. B. Singer writers, 'The present is only a moment . . . Today we live, but by tomorrow, today will be a story. The whole world, all human life, is one long story . . .'. How much of Derrick Wu's 'story' is from life and how much comes from the many stories he has heard read? We shall never know, nor, perhaps, do we need to.

Further reading

Edwards, V. and Walker, S. (1995) *Building Bridges: Multilingual Resources for Children. The Multilingual Resources for Children Project*, The University of Reading: Multilingual Matters.

Garvie, E. (1990) *Story as Vehicle*, Clevedon: Multilingual Matters.

Gregory, E. (1996) Learning from the community. A family literacy project with Bangladeshi origin children in London, in S. Wolfendale and K. Topping (eds.) *Parental Involvent in Literacy – Effective Partnerships in Education*, London: Croom Helm.

Unsworth, L. and O'Toole, M. (1993) Beginning reading with children's literature, in L. Unsworth (ed.) *Literacy Learning and Teaching*, Melbourne: Macmillan.

6

Listening to Children Reading

Husna and Naseema are reading Each, Peach, Pear, Plum *together. Despite the attractions of the illustrations, their eyes are drawn to the print and they read quickly and fluently. Husna points carefully to each word to help Naseema who is more hesitant. 'Each, Peach, Pear, Plum, I spy Tom Thumb. Tom Thumb in the cupboard, I spy Mother Hubbard. Mother Hubbard down the cellar, I spy Cinderella. Cinderella on the stairs, I spy the three bears . . .' Husna breaks off with 'I can count to ten in Bengali: Ek, dui, teen, chaar, panch, chhoy, shaat, aat, noy, dosh.' 'Gosh?' asks the teacher. 'Mmm. But this is ten/dosh, not like gosh in* Oh my gosh, my golly . . .' *As they reach the page featuring the magnificent plum pie, the teacher interrupts and asks 'Can you show me the plum pie in that picture?' The children stare blankly at the teacher and the page. Eventually, Husna points quickly to something nondescript in the background. The teacher shows them the pie and allows the children to get back to their reading. They finish the text and are impatient to change the book for another.*

(Gregory and Kelly 1992, p. 144)

Husna and Naseema, Tony, Kalchuma and Fozia began to show us some of the reading strategies used by emergent bilinguals in Chapter 3 of this book. In the excerpt above, the children use their well-developed metalinguistic awareness and excellent memories to make sense of the task. It might be a different kind of sense from that gained as they read their Bengali books where they mostly understand the meaning of the words. It might be a different kind of sense from the melodious reciting of an Arabic prayer. Their sense will often not be ours. But, as we saw in Chapter 2, 'sense-making' is very personal.

Robin Campbell and Theresa Macdonald (1983) show how young monolingual children often interpret words very differently from adults. When listening to stories about 'hares' many four-year-olds interpreted them as 'hair' with grotesque results which did not appear to trouble them. The athors concluded that alongside the desire to make sense of things, children have a certain capacity to accept and tolerate the nonsensical. Emergent bilinguals are likely to interpret many words in texts differently from ourselves and we often find this out only by accident. One teacher recalls how she was practising words beginning with 'h' with a class of mainly Sylheti speaking five-year-olds. Aiming to help them put their words into sentences, she asked a child 'Are you happy?' To her surprise (and embarrassment), the child replied quickly and earnestly 'No, I'm Sabina'. The teacher had forgotten that one child in the class was called 'Happy' and this 'Happy' obviously made more sense to the child!

It is often illuminating to ask young children to 'read' (pretend read) books before formal reading tuition begins. Like *miscue analysis* for older children, taped 'readings' reveal to the teacher much about the child's conception of reading and consequently the task ahead for both teather and child. Working in the USA, the American researcher Bussis and her colleagues (1985) give fascinating insights into a class of Afro-American children's learning strategies during their first years of schooling. The initial intention of the team was to focus only on analysing young children's strategies as they began reading. However, they found that the way children approached the reading task was very similar to the way they tackled all their school work and that children divided into two groups: those whom they referred to as 'convergent' learners and those who took what they called a 'divergent' approach. 'Convergent' learners were children who wanted their work to be neat and tidy, who preferred to be told words rather than experiment, who were often perfectionist and careful. Their approach was reflected in their art work which was often neat and careful and even in PE where their clothes were left folded carefully. In contrast, 'divergent' learners enjoyed experimenting and risk-taking, were often flamboyant in their art work and generally untidy.

Fozia and Kalchuma's 'readings' already show distinctly different features:

Kalchuma: (reading Mr Bump *by Roger Hargreaves)*
  Mr Bump is go to gone bump.
  Mr Bump is go to gone.
  Mr Bump is to all down.
  He went there to bump.
  Mr Bump to . . . what's in there missing?
  Mr Bump go stick . . . his stick, there, stick. (means a 'sticking plaster')

(she continues in the same way with a number of books)

Kalchuma has a very careful methodical approach in everything she does. Although her English is still very limited, she is aware that the new language comprises separate words (which she separates very definitely) and structures which she wants to practise until they are correct. She is concerned at not knowing the word for 'plaster' and, although she guesses 'stick', she is not happy until she is told the correct word. It certainly appears that Kalchuma is a 'convergent' learner who likes to practise what she knows again and again. Interestingly, her 'readings' bear strong similarity to those of children working with 'Breakthrough' materials (see Chapter 4), yet she has never been introduced to this approach.

Compare her 'reading' to that of Fozia, working beside her in the same class:

Fozia: (reading Mr Funny *by Roger Hargreaves)*
(turning the pages and 'reading' fast and fluently with very good intonation)
There's some writing. Mr (?) (Funny) have a sleep in bed. Now a mummy wake up. It's
home time. Daddy wanna sleep at. He close his mouth. You better choose . . . you better
choose any colour that you want books . . . Now they're saying 'Good-bye' and in the
sun . . . and dinner-ladies (pointing to a picture of Mr Messy and Mr Tidy together) come
out. Now finish it.

Fozia's spoken English appears to be at about the same level as Kalchuma's, yet the two children have very different styles of learning. Fozia uses all the resources she can as she 'reads' the text. 'Home time', 'close his mouth', 'you better choose', 'dinner-ladies' are all expressions she would have heard from the teacher in the classroom. She experiments, loves play, is flamboyant and untidy. Her approach, therefore, appears more 'divergent' in character.

How can teachers take account of individual learning styles in a whole-class situation? Bussis and her colleagues recognise that it will be impossible for teachers to analyse each child's learning style and provide appropriate individual programmes. Nevertheless, they stress what *can* be done as follows:

- Recognise *your own* learning style because your teaching style may well veer in this direction and do not assume that all children will share your own style.
- Make sure that class/group reading tuition includes approaches which suit both styles of learning.
- Do not force children to adopt an approach which is alien to their personalities (refusing use of a rubber, for example).

However, the children in the American study were all of the same ethnic background and were all learning to read in their mother-tongue. What effect might it have if children bring very different patterns of learning from home into school? Can experience and cultural factors override individual learning styles? We simply do not know. However, we may suspect that both past and present learning experiences in different contexts may well affect children's sense-making. Both Tony and Jessica showed features typical of 'convergent' learners. From Jessica's 'reading' in the Introduction of this book, we see that she was timid, liked to be told rather than guess and, like Tony, wanted everything neat, tidy and accurate. Nevertheless, she was well able to cope with the 'divergent' approach of her teacher because she knew exactly what was expected of her – it matched her home reading experiences. Our comparison of the reading of these two children showed clearly that what might be successful teaching for one child may leave another floundering.

Let us return to Husna and Naseema, whose reading opened this chapter. There is a crucial difference between emergent bilinguals and monolinguals as they set off to become readers. When monolingual Jessica 'reads', '. . . He put some yoghurt on his Rice Krispies and they went "Snap, Crackle, Pop!" . . .', she is bringing all her knowledge of language and life generally to bear on the text. When Husna and Naseema 'read' '. . . Mother Hubbard down the cellar . . .' they are bringing a knowledge of reading but cannot yet use the words in everyday life. So we see that monolingual children use their knowledge of spoken language to learn to read as they enter school; emergent bilinguals *read to learn spoken language from their reading*. In other words, reading will be a means to learning the target language. Husna and Naseema highlight the strengths and weaknesses of many emergent bilinguals. Remembering words and learning sounds are not often a problem. The problem is rather understanding the meaning of those words and making the text 'their own' by being able to transfer 'chunks' of it into their own speech.

Our question in this chapter is: How might teachers enable this transfer to take place? How might the teacher develop the understanding of children like Husna and Naseema and what ways will be most helpful to record their progress? Chapters 4 and 5 have shown the teacher working with whole classes or groups of children. In this chapter the focus is on the teacher and the individual child. Most of the children we meet are already familiar from Chapter 2. Nazma and Shabbir will show the progress they have made from age five-and-a-half to seven, during eighteen months in school. All the children are still in the early stages of learning a new language and all are learning in British infant classes. Nazma, Shabbir and Louthfur are in a class where all their class-mates are learning to speak a new language. Half of Tajul and Tony's class are fluent monolingual English speakers. The context for the children's learning has been outlined in the last two chapter. The teacher is following 'Inside-Out' and 'Outside-In' approaches and the children are comfortable with learning in this way.

The chapter is divided into three sections which approximate to three stages in children's early reading. The first section offers a framework for reading with very young children before formal literacy tuition begins. Tajul is four-and-a-half as he reads with his teacher in the classroom. The approach suggested owes much to examples of 'scaffolding' we have from caregivers reading with very young children. It assumes that adult and child will be working on a one-to-one basis in an informal classroom. The second section focuses on listening to reading when using an 'Inside-Out' approach. Nazma at five and Louthfur at seven show how different the task may be for each child during the first school years. The third section moves to a more advanced stage. Nazma is now six. We see how the story-books she reads serve as funds of knowledge for entering a new language and culture. Yet it is the teacher who plays a vital role in mediating unknown words and phrases from the text. In this section we see ways in which she goes about this, while at the same time encouraging children to begin to work independently. The teacher is aware of the special strengths and weaknesses brought to reading by emergent bilinguals and uses explicit strategies which recognise these.

I. INDIVIDUAL READING WITH VERY YOUNG EMERGENT BILINGUALS

George (four years and a monolingual English speaker) is 'reading' The Tale of Peter Rabbit *(Potter, B. 1902, Warne, London) with his mother:*

George: Do you have to start here? (points to title)
Mother: Well . . .
George: Or where the picture is?
Mother: Well, that's the name of the story.
  What's the story called?
George: Peter Rabbit.
Mother: That's right.
George: Is that Peter Rabbit?
Mother: Yes, that's a picture of Peter Rabbit.
  Come on, you read the story.
  I'm really looking forward to this . . .

                                                    (Unsworth and O'Toole 1993, p. 139)

Although George has heard this story regularly over the year before this taping took place, he is still unsure whether we read the pictures or the words as he asks 'Do you have to start here . . . or where the picture is?' His mother tells him explicitly as she points to the words 'That's the name of the story' and immediately questions him again, 'What's the story called?' But George is still hesitant and wants confirmation when he asks 'Is that Peter Rabbit?'

Children who arrive in school familiar with the stories and language of numerous story-books appear impressive. But it is important to remember that their performance does not come 'naturally' but is rather the result of years of 'finely tuned' tutoring by caregivers. In his longitudinal study of 128 pre-school children in Bristol, Gordon Wells (1985) discovered that some children entered school already benefiting from hundreds of hours of story-reading by caregivers. To gain a clear picture of what this means, we need to imagine these hours as representing highly focused language and literacy tuition. In Chapter 2, we saw how caregivers across the world give guided tuition to their young children in the cultural practices of the group. Where these practices and the language they are expressed in overlap with those expected by the school, children will be particularly privileged in the classroom setting. George's questions remind us of those of Tony when he reads his 'Mr Men' books to his teacher and constantly asks her to repeat names (Tony asks four times: Who's that? Teacher: Mr Fussy).

It is not possible for the teacher to give Tony the kind of attention reserved for infants by their caregivers. Nevertheless, the higher adult/child ratio in preschool settings allows a unique opportunity for emergent bilinguals to participate in one-to-one story-readings in the target language with adults. Older children will benefit equally from working in this way if interested adults assist teachers in the classroom. But what can we learn from the structure of caregiver/child interactions?

Learning from caregiver/child story-readings

Studies on caregiver/child story-readings were mentioned briefly in Chapter 2 when we glimpsed the reading practices taking place in Nicole's home (our English family living in France). We saw that children had close encounters with texts which were carefully 'scaffolded' by adults. These features are apparent in

George's interaction with his mother. The examples below are taken from the complete version of their story-reading (Unsworth 1993, pp. 139–42):

1. Enlisting the child's interest and excitement:
   'This is a lovely story . . .'
   'I wonder what's going to happen in this book . . .'
2. Keeping the child 'in the field' by:
   (a) asking him to predict through questions
       'Shall we find out?'
       'What's happening?'
       'How will he do it?'
   (b) reconstructing the story
       'What happened to Peter Rabbit then?'
       'What did they have for supper?'
       'What happened to Flopsy, Mopsy and Cotton Tail?'
3. Marking relevant features by showing how to derive meaning from pictures:
   'Where are they putting the blackberries when they've picked them?'

In summary, the adult 'scaffolds' the child's learning by:

- explicitly modelling the reading;
- extending the child's utterances;
- simply telling the child or 'filling in' what he does not know.

It is impotant to note that the tutoring is not just one-way. It is a dialogue in which George negotiates through his questions. It is illuminating to see how these further his understanding:

1. He checks his knowledge about print:
   'Do you have to start here?'
2. He checks his knowledge about the story:
   'He won't be captured, will he?'
3. He seeks new information:
   'How come that's where they live?'
4. He asks questions on unfamiliar language:
   'What's "down the lane"?'

How far will all this be relevant to adults and emergent bilinguals who do not share a common language? A framework is offered below to assist adults in Early Years units or classes.

The key aim to the approach is to show children that they *can* read (even if it is at present only the 'full stops', 'question marks' and some labels) and to help them make sense of a text in whatever way they can. The framework below includes:

- What resources are needed?
- How can one-to-one story-readings best be structured?
- What kinds of record can be kept of these early interactions?

Resources

Although children will have access to a wide range of books, and teachers will choose from these at storytime, we know from Chapter 5 (see also Appendix 2) that some books are ideal for teaching the target language to beginner bilinguals. The simplest of these will be 'labelling' books and those with a very simple, repetitive vocabulary, for example the 'Spot' series of books by Eric Hill which are available in dual language versions and can be supported by games, songs and rhymes which repeat the text. For a selected number of books, adults in Early Years classes will have prepared 'story-packs' for use both at home and in school. The adult and child in the classroom may well need only a copy of the book. Nevertheless, these packs will contain explicit suggestions on reading the story, so that a structure will be given to the work of all interested adults using them. Each pack is likely to contain the following:

1. The book in the target language and, if possible, copies translated into children's mother-tongues (the text may be attached beside or on top of the original).
2. Figurines for use with the magnet or flannelboard.
3. Puppets if possible.
4. Appropriate songs (in different languages for home use if possible).
5. An audiotape in the target language (and in the children's mother-tongues too, if possible).
6. A card listing key lexis, 'chunks' of target language, rhymes, songs, other follow-up activities (art, craft, etc.) for use by all adults working with children in the class.
7. (Not in the pack, but also available in the class resources) appropriate dressing-up clothes, appropriate miniature world figures, if possible.

Structuring the story-reading

The examples illustrating the framework outlined below are taken from Tajul reading with his teacher. Tajul is 4 years 8 months. He has just entered school in Britain for the first time. Tajul's mother-tongue is Sylheti (a dialect of Bengali) and he understands very little English. Whenever possible, he sits with an adult 'reading' stories. Tajul has been chosen because he takes excellent advantage of both adults and books to learn a new language. The books he uses are: *The Tiger Who Came to Tea* (Kerr 1968), *Joseph's Other Red Sock* (Daly 1983), *The Hungry Giant* (Storychest 1985), *Meg at Sea* and *Meg's Mumps* (Nicholl and Pienkowski 1972). The adult's aims closely resemble the 'scaffolding' taking place between caregiver and child:

- to enlist the child's interest and fascination for the story
- to 'model' the reading in an explicit way by pointing to labels and appropriate illustrations, individual words, etc.
- to keep the child 'in the field' by extending the child's utterances, etc.

- to mark relevant features so that the child derives meaning from the text by asking questions, directing child to labels, illustrations, etc.
- to encourage dialogue whereby the child asks questions, seeks information, etc.

What might this look like in practice?

Stage I

(i) Enlist the child's interest by:

- talking about the illustration on the cover
- focusing on one or two important 'labels' (objects) and searching for them throughout the book
- telling the child what you like about the book.

(ii) Model the fluent reader by reading the text at least twice, pointing to the words and, where possible, matching important lexis with the illustration.

(iii) Encourage the child to join in with the labels, refrains, etc. wherever possible.

Examples:

Teacher: (reads) 'Joseph's other red sock'
Tajul: There's sock?
Teacher: Yes. Let's see what it says . . . (reads)
  'Joseph's mum called, "Are you awake?" . . .'
  . . .
Tajul: There's dog. (pointing to illustration)
Teacher: Is it a dog or is it a tiger?
Tajul: Tiger.
Teacher: It's a tiger . . . (then carries on reading)
Teacher: (reads from The Tiger who Came to Tea)
  'And he ate all the buns . . .'
Tajul: Eeee
Teacher: 'And drank all the tea . . .'
Tajul: Eeee
Teacher: (reads) 'And he had a look round the kitchen to see what else he could find . . .'

Key-points: Focus on clear modelling and pointing.
         Allow plenty of time for the child just to listen.

Stage II

(i)   The child shares the 'reading'. The child begins and the teacher extends the child's utterances.

(ii) The teacher directs the child through questions and encourages the child to ask questions on the text.

(iii) The child repeats words and refrains after the teacher.

Examples:

Teacher (reads from Joseph's Other Red Sock)
  'I pulled' said Joseph 'and Arthur pulled and Harold pulled and the rabbit pulled . . .'

Tajul: What's that? (pointing to half-hidden figure, only tail-like image visible)
Teacher: I don't know. Turn over and we'll find out. (reads) 'And it flopped and wriggled
  and jiggled. It looked terrible!'
Tajul: Yes.
Teacher: (whispers) *What is it?*
Tajul: Terrible.
Teacher: A terrible monster, I think, don't you?
Tajul: Yes.

(In this excerpt, Tajul and his teacher are reading from The Tiger who Came to Tea*)*
Tajul: (pointing to illustration) *There's tiger.*
Teacher: What's he doing?
Tajul: Eating.
Teacher: Yes. He's drinking tea.
Tajul: Yes.
Teacher: (reads) 'So the tiger drank all the tea and he ate everything on the table.'
Tajul: And he . . . (pointing)
Teacher: He knocked over the jug, mmm.

(Here, the teacher and Tajul are reading Meg at Sea*)*
Teacher: (reads) 'Meg used a magnifying glass to make fire.'
Tajul: Where?
Teacher: There's the magnifying glass (points) *to make fire.*
  There's the fire (points). *Can you see?*
Tajul: Yes. There? (points to magnifying glass)
Teacher: Yes.
Tajul: There's the window. (points to magnifying glass)
Teacher: That's the magnifying glass.
Tajul: Yes.
Teacher: (reads) 'Meg and Owl went fishing . . .'
Tajul: Fish! (points)
Teacher: Yes! That's the fish.

Key-points: 'Labelling' questions are easier for the child at this stage than those
           needing whole 'chunks' for answers.
           Extend the child's one or two word utterances.
           Allow plenty of time for repetition.
           Encourage the child to question and initiate dialogue.

Stage III

(i) The adult relates the story and text to the child's own life and experience,
     investigates the child's understanding of the text and initiates the child into
     the host culture.
(ii) Child and teacher read in unison or alternately (I refer to this as 'chained'
     reading).

Examples:

Teacher: (reads from* Meg's Mumps)
  'Meg let him have a ride on her broomstick. CATASTROPHE.' (pointing to word)
  What's happened to her?
Tajul: She dead.
Teacher: She's fallen off her broomstick, I think, hasn't she?

Tajul: Yes.
Teacher: (reads) 'So Meg had to stay in bed until Christmas.'
Tajul: Yes.
Teacher: So she's not dead. She's in hospital, I think.
Tajul: Yes.

Teacher: (reads from The Hungry Giant*)*
   '. . . and got the giant some bread.'
Tajul: (points to bread) This not bread.
   These are finger.
Teacher: It's supposed to be bread, actually.
   Some bread looks like that. It's not supposed to be fingers. It's supposed to be bread.
Tajul: It's not bread.
Teacher: Well, if you go into Tesco's supermarket, you can find some long thin bread like that.
   What does your bread look like? Does your bread look different from that?
Tajul: No. My bread is square.
Teacher: Oh, your bread is square, is it? Well, some bread is long and thin and some bread is square . . .

'Chained' reading: (teacher and child are reading from Smartypants *Storychest)*

Tajul: (reads) 'Smartypants'
Teacher: Yes.
Tajul and Teacher: (read) 'I am a smartypants, rum, tum, toe. Here is a racing
Tajul: car
Tajul and Teacher: See me
Tajul: go
(Teacher and child continue in this way)

Key-points: Encourage the child to talk about the text and relate it to life.
See if the child can take lexis and 'chunks' of syntax from the text to talk about the story.

Record-keeping

The case studies of young children learning in Part One of this book highlighted the importance of a dialogue between the home and school. Tony's confusion might not have arisen if his parents and teacher had been able openly to discuss his different work and progress in the Chinese and English school. These discussions take time and must, therefore, be built into a record-keeping framework. Such a framework is offered by The Primary Language Record devised by Myra Barrs and her team at The Centre for Language in Education in London. Knowledge about a child's home literacy experiences is at the heart of this approach to record-keeping:

> *The purpose of the discussion between parent(s) and teacher is to encourage a two-way communication between home and school, to let parent(s) share their knowledge of the child, at home and at school, their observations and concerns, hopes and expectations. Regular informal conversations between parents and teachers can help to establish a real partnership between home and school and can create a forum where achievements as well as concerns can be discussed.*
>
> *(Barrs et al. 1988, p. 12)*

Parents are invited to visit the school during the Autumn and Summer term to discuss their children's reading. A summary of this discussion is included on the main record. In addition to the Primary Language Record, two other types of record should be kept:

(i) A record of the adult's strategies in reading with the child (kept as frequently as possible).

(ii) A record of the child's progress through taping a reading session with the adult or two children 'reading' a book together or perhaps telling the story using figurines or puppets.

Below are examples of records which may be kept for each. They may also form the basis for a staff development session in Early Years classes which focuses on reading with individual children:

Record of adult strategies when reading with a very young emergent bilingual

How did you enlist the child's interest in the book?

Did you extend the child's 'labels' or simple utterances? If so, which ones did you choose and how did you go about extending them?

Which relevant features of the story did you draw the child's attention to (labels, refrains, objects in illustrations, etc.)? Did you use questions, directives, 'Look at that cow!', etc.

How did you encourage dialogue between yourself and the child? Were you successful?

What follow-up work did you initiate (if any)? Why did you choose this?

Record of child strategies

Title of book:

A. Social context of reading

- What literacy experiences does the child bring from home? Do older siblings attend mother-tongue or religious classes? Does the child participate/observe these? Do siblings or parents read with the child and in which language(s)?
- Has the child had the opportunity to read the book in the mother-tongue? How well does the child listen in the mother-tongue? How far does the child join in and try to retell the story, etc.?
- Is the child interested in reading with an adult? If so, what sort of materials or books is s/he most drawn to?
- How did the child choose the book to be read?
- Who initiated the reading?
- If it was the child, how did s/he begin?

- Does the child appear to be more 'convergent' or 'divergent' in learning? In what ways is this made apparent?

B. Listening and repeating

- How long did the child concentrate on the task?
- What particular difficulties in pronunciation did the child have?
- Could the child repeat words/phrases/refrains after the adult?

C. Understanding the talk about text

- Could the child point to appropriate objects in illustrations when asked?
- Could objects be named when pointed to?
- Could s/he answer simple questions on the content of the story?
- Could the child retell the story?
- What lexis is the child able to use from the story?
- Could the child use any 'chunks' of language from the book during a retelling?
- Are there any patterns of errors (personal pronouns – s/he; his/her; him/her, etc.)?
- Is there evidence of use of different tenses (past, future, etc.)?

(Examples should be given for the above, wherever possible.)

D. Taking over the language of the book into life

- Could the child relate the story to happenings in real life?

(Give examples where lexis, 'chunks' of language, etc. from the story has been used in different contexts.)

E. Follow-up

What developments would you hope to see by the next reading record?

II. LISTENING TO CHILDREN READ USING THE 'INSIDE-OUT' APPROACH

Readers will remember Nazma, Shabbir, the twins Sabina and Shahina and Louthfur, our group of Sylheti speaking children from the East End of London. In the last chapter, we saw them reading during 'structured story' sessions in their English class. But we first met the group in their homes and community classes in Chapter 2. We learned that none of the children spoke English in conversation with their families and that they lived in an area where mostly their own language was spoken in the street and in the courtyards where they played. We also caught a brief glimpse of them reading to their teachers in their Bengali and Arabic classes. Nazma was repeating words and the alphabet after her Bengali teacher; the twins, Sabina and Shahina, were practising a Bengali rhyme from their reading book and Louthfur was practising sounds in combination with different stresses in preparation for learning to read the Qur'ān.

Observation of the group at work in their different community classes enabled their English teacher to understand why repetition of words and sounds, neatness and accuracy might be so important to these children. For there were distinct rules of participation in the community class lessons, clear even to a stranger unable to follow the language. Tape recordings made of typical mornings in her English class showed her how much more difficult discerning the rules of participation might be. Children were expected to take control of their learning without explicitly being shown how this might take place. Reflecting upon her work, she wondered whether the children might be looking for clearer rules of participation in her lessons. Lacking clear rules, they appeared simply to transfer outside-school learning strategies into their English classes. These strategies did not always seem appropriate to the teacher and consequently did not always receive support. Her growing understanding of children's reading outside school led her both to make more explicit what she expected of the children and to build on skills they were bringing with them into the classroom.

Listening to individual children reading within her 'Inside-Out' approach was one result of this teacher's learning. In Chapter 4, we saw how the class of five-year-olds and their teacher built up together a common bank of important words and sentences relating to occurrences in individuals' lives. The children understood the meaning of the words and sentences because they belonged to their own experience. They learned words quickly because of their excellent memories and their keen eye for detail. These word and sentence cards form children's first reading material alongside the books used in the 'Outside-In' approach. They are explicit evidence to children that they are succeeding in a new task which involves not just learning to read but learning a new language too. In this way, record-keeping using word and sentence cards gives children tangible evidence of their ability to read during the very first stages of learning. Nazma, Shahina and Shabbir read so many words and sentences after six months that they use only books after this time. Louthfur, however, found reading and speaking a new language very difficult and progressed much more slowly.

What follows below is a framework showing how an individual child's reading may be recorded in both the classroom and through work sent home to be practised with caregiver or sibling. It is crucial to remember that the main aim at this stage is to show children they *can* read. And they can. There will be almost no child who fails to read at least their name, 'full stop', 'question mark', 'love' and 'mum'. Most will collect many more words and sentences with extraordinary speed.

Resources

- Class word and sentence cards.
- Class-made 'Big Books' and 'dictionaries' with news, labels for activities (cooking, etc.), song and rhyme books.
- An exercise-book for each child which records words read and sentences made.
- A duplicate exercise-book for the child to take home to practise the words and sentences.

Stages

Flexibility is important. Some children are more confident starting with reading the individual word, putting it into a sentence and moving to read other sentences containing the word; some children find it easier to read a whole sentence first, pick out an individual word in it and then make new sentences using that word. It is best to use both approaches alternately. Work with Nazma, Shabbir and Louthfur show how recording might take place:

The date is 27 November, just two months since five-year-old **Nazma** began reading in her first class. Her attendance has not been regular. Nevertheless, her concentration is avid when participating in class reading sessions. She is particularly attached to the puppets; cares for them by writing notes to the school when they fall sick and spells for Dabir (the boy puppet) who is a little slow in this respect. Reading becomes part of these experiences. Although her spoken English is extremely limited and she has difficulties with pronunciation, she has an excellent memory and rarely forgets a written word or sentence. Her visual is much stronger than her auditory memory. Indeed, she seems to be learning English through the written word. Poorer auditory skills, however, mean that she needs time to repeat words and sentences or to practise saying them with the teacher or another child. Nazma's immaculate drawings and careful, neat approach indicate to her teacher that she follows a 'convergent' learning style.

The teacher has a pile of word cards and a separate pack of sentence cards. Nazma's own sentences will be among these. She writes down words and sentences read by Nazma in her own exercise book:

SENTENCES READ

○	= unknown
----------	= read with help
(SC)	= self-corrects

DATE	SENTENCE (FOCUS WORD UNDERLINED)	SENTENCE OFFERED
27/11	Dabir is in <u>hospital</u>	I go to the <u>hospital</u>
	Is Nazma in <u>bed</u> today? No.	Is Shabbir in <u>bed</u> today?
	Louise is <u>sad</u> today	Dina is <u>sad</u> today
	My baby is <u>happy</u> today	My teacher is <u>happy</u> today
	<u>Krishna</u> is in M a n c h e s t e r	<u>Krishna</u> is my teacher
	My <u>mum</u> goes to the h o s p i t a l	I love my <u>mum</u>

If Nazma hesitates or cannot read a word, the teacher:

- asks her a question to remind her of the context ('Manchester': Where did Krishna go yesterday?)
- asks her to continue reading and come back to the unknown word (My mum — to the hospital)
- points to the first letter or syllable of the word and covers the rest, (adding a question if necessary ('hos – pital': Was Dabir in school yesterday?)

The sentence cards are then laid out and Nazma counts all the 'is' or 'hospital', etc. The same is done with different letters. If there is time, she uses the word cards to make sentences. Finally, her teacher asks her: Which sentence did you like most this week? What was your favourite word? Which news did you think was happiest/saddest?, etc.

A second copy of Nazma's sentences will be taken home. If she can work with her older sister, she will write more sentences using the words underlined. If she works with her mother (who does not speak or write English) or alone, she will practise copying the sentences and spelling and reading the words.

After two and a half months, Nazma has 56 sentences in her book. Of course, they are simple and many of the words are duplicated. Nevertheless, Nazma feels confident that so many words are within her possession and at her fingertips to be used in talk, book-reading and writing.

Shabbir also speaks no English at home. He is the eldest child and his mother says he is teaching her to read a little English. Shabbir is extremely shy and speaks very quietly. He is very keen and enthusiastic to learn but dislikes experimenting or taking risks. Like Nazma, he has an excellent visual memory, but poor pronunciation. His teacher knows that this will not be helped by his shyness and makes every effort for him to participate in songs and rhymes practised in unison with his friends or the whole class. Similar to Nazma, Shabbir appears to prefer a 'convergent' learning style. He often chooses to start by reading individual words. This is how his reading is recorded by the teacher in Shabbir's exercise-book:

SENTENCES READ

----------	= uncertain but knows with help
○	= unknown
(SC)	= self-corrects

DATE	WORD	SENTENCE OFFERED
27/11	Bangladesh	My mum goes to Bangladesh
	sick	My baby is sick
	hospital	Dabir is in hospital
	happy	My mum is happy today

sad   Shabbir is sad today

love   I love my baby

Sometimes the teacher draws Shabbir's attention to how he goes about reading. For example, she asks: 'How did you know that word says "Bangladesh"?' 'Tell me another word that begins with that letter.' If Shabbir hesitates, she gives him a clue ('This word is the opposite of "sad"') and draws his attention to the first letter, perhaps asking for other words which begin in the same way. If the word is unknown, she tells him and puts the word into a sentence.

After word reading, Shabbir's teacher uses the class sentence cards and asks him to find the words he has chosen to read on them. As he does so, she asks him to read those sentences too. Like Nazma, he is asked to identify patterns in words as well as individual letters. Like Nazma, he also remembers virtually all the words and sentences read together in the class.

He takes a second copy of his book home and practises the words and sentences with his mother. She appears proud that he is teaching her and often tells his teacher how clever he is.

Louthfur is also the eldest child in his family. But he is very different from both Nazma and Shabbir. He finds it extremely difficult to concentrate and likes to flit from one activity to another in his English class. He appears to have a very poor visual and auditory memory. After two years in school, his understanding of the new language is very limited and his spoken English not easy to understand. Yet his spoken Sylheti is good and we saw in Chapter 2 how he was able to concentrate for long periods in his Arabic class.

Here Louthfur is working with photographs taken of his family and the area where he lives. His teacher writes the words offered by Louthfur onto a card; 'sweet shop, clothes shop, mosque, church, park, my house, my school'. She then asks him questions whereby the words need to be put into phrases or sentences, e.g. 'Where is your mosque, Louthfur?' Louthfur replies 'Brick Lane.' The teacher writes, asking him to read each word with her as he does so, 'My mosque is in Brick Lane.' She makes a second copy and cuts it up into individual words. Louthfur first matches these to the sentence card and then goes on to make 'My sweet shop is in Brick Lane', etc. using individual cards. He plays a word recognition game by turning over individual cards and trying to put each into a sentence. His teacher then focuses on one of these words, perhaps 'is' or 'in' and both look for the word in favourite books or in class Big Books. The teacher knows that Louthfur has mastered both simple sounds and blends in his Arabic class, so she then asks him to spell some of the words out loud and to try to think of other words beginning with the same sound as one chosen, e.g. 'L' which starts his name. She then completes simple guessing games, e.g. 'I'm thinking of somewhere where you like to play on the swing.' Louthfur guesses 'park'. 'Can you spell it?' asks his teacher.

Louthfur highlights the special problems faced by emergent bilinguals who do not find reading easy. His pronunciation is poor but his hearing is good and his mother-tongue is fluent. His teacher uses her French colleague's idea of clapping out the syllables in longer words. This helps Louthfur hear the separate syllables instead of slurring words together. He takes home his exercise book with his own words and sentences and sometimes a simple story-book or a taped story. But his teacher is aware that there is no one who speaks English in Louthfur's home. His mother confidently helps him with work from his Bengali book, but when confronted with the English shyly smiles and says 'Let's leave it to the teacher. She knows best. Let's leave the English to her.'

III. LISTENING TO CHILDREN READ USING THE 'OUTSIDE-IN' APPROACH

It is a year later and Nazma, Shabbir and their classmates are now six. They have been working on 'Little Red Riding Hood' together. It is their third story using the 'structured story' approach and they have made enormous progress. The story has been told in both English and their mother-tongue and they have listened to the story for a second time in English and begun to discuss it. We join the group at the beginning of the third telling which will be an *oral cloze* telling of the story:

> *Teacher: Now I'm going to tell you the story again and every time I stop somewhere where someone has to say something you have to tell me what that person says. So be ready because I'm just going to pick someone like this (clicks fingers and says a name) and you have to tell me what is being said . . . so listen carefully.*
> *'Once upon a time, there was a girl called Red Riding Hood and she lived with her mum and dad in the forest. One day, she was playing with toys and she had lots and lots. One day, they heard that the grandmother was very ill, so Red Riding Hood's mother said to her . . .' (clicks)*
> *Child: '. . . Take these to your grandma. She is not well.'*
> *Teacher: 'And Red Riding Hood said . . .' (clicks)*
> *Child: 'Yes.'*
> *Teacher: "Good, she said, "Yes." But before Red Riding Hood went off to the forest, her mother said . . .' (clicks)*
> *Child: 'Don't talk with the . . .' (hesitates)*
> *Teacher: What's the word?*
> *Child: 'Strangers'*
> *Teacher: Right. Let's all say that word.*
> *(Children all say 'strangers' together.)*
> *Teacher: No, one at a time.*
> *(Different children repeat the word correctly.)*
> *Teacher: Once more, everyone together:*
> *Children: STRANGERS.*
> *Teacher: Thank you. That was excellent. 'So off went Red Riding Hood to the forest. It was a lovely day and the flowers were out; all different colours. And there were birds in the trees singing. And she had an idea when she saw the flowers. She said to herself . . .' (clicks)*
> *Child: 'Let me take some flowers for grandma. She loves flowers.'*

The children very efficiently retell the whole story in this way. At the end, the teacher says 'Well done! I think you all deserve a round of applause' (everyone claps). After this, the group will act out the story, and complete various word, sound and meaning focused activities before going on to read and write their own versions of it.

Below are three retellings of 'Little Red Riding Hood'. The first is by Nadia, a six-year-old monolingual English speaker who is making excellent progress in her reading. The other two versions are by six-year-old Nazma who has been using the 'structured story' approach described above.

Nadia (before reading the Tony Ross version of 'Little Red Riding Hood'): 'This is the beginning. Little Red Riding Hood's mum said, "I've made some cakes for nanny . . . so, (mmm) Little Red Riding Hood's mum said, "Go and give them to her . . . so she went . . . and then she went far into the woods because her nan lived in the woods and then she met . . . (mmm) she met a wolf and the wolf said, "Come with me" and she said, "No." And then she just walked on and she went to her nan's house and then she knocked on the door and the door was opened so she came in and she went in her nan's room and then little Red Riding Hood . . . no . . . and the wolf was in the bed dressed up as her nanny and little Red Riding Hood said, "What big big eyes you've got" and, well, the wolf said, "Because they're to see you" and then she said, "What big ears you have" and then he said, "To hear . . ." and then the wolf said . . . I mean and then little Red Riding Hood said, "What a big mouth you have!" and he said, "Well, I'm coming to eat you up!" and then . . . and then he scared little Red Riding Hood . . . and then the nan was in the wardrobe . . .'

Nazma is retelling the story *in Sylheti* (in translation below) first:

'One day there was a girl called Little Red Riding Hood and she lived with her mum and dad. One day her mum said, "Take one cake and biscuits to your grandma because she is ill." And then she said, "I will get some flowers." So her mum said, "Don't talk to any boys." She said, "OK. I won't talk to them." On the way, she picked red and yellow flowers. Then the wolf saw her and said, "Will you play with me?" She said, "No, I will not play with you. I am going to see grandma to give her some flowers." Then the wolf ran to grandma's house and knocked at the door. Then grandma said, "Is it Red Riding Hood?" The wolf said, "Yes it is. Open the door." Grandma slowly opened the door and saw the wolf and cried out, "God help me! God help me!" But because no one helped her, she ran into the wardrobe. There was another knock at the door and the wolf opened the door. It was Red Riding Hood. She said, "Why do you have big eyes?" "To see you with." Then she said, "Why do you have big ears?" "To hear you with." "Why do you have big 'teeth' (said in English)?"

Teacher: Someone tell her what the Bengali word for 'teeth' is.
Child: (Daat. (Bengali for 'teeth')

Nazma: 'Then he said, "I want to eat you." She screamed "HELP ME! HELP ME!" Then she ran off and saw a man who was her father. She told her father, "Dad, the wolf wants to eat me." "OK. You stand here and I will go and kill the wolf." Then after he had killed him, they looked for grandma. Then they found her and gave her the flowers, biscuits and cakes. Then grandma said, "Take some apples – one for your father and one for you."

Teacher: That was excellent! Nazma told the story completely, not missing out anything.

After reading, acting, completing oral cloze and many other activities around the story including practising pronunciation by reading after the teacher, etc. Nazma retells it in English.

Teacher: Can you tell us the story without looking at the pictures and in English? Say some of it in Sylheti if you can't say it all in English:

Nazma: 'Red Riding Hood lived with her mum. They had bad news. Her grandma was ill. Red Riding Hood's mother said, "Go to you grandma's house." So Red Riding Hood said, "OK." Before she went, her mother said, "Don't talk to any strangers." And she went into the forest. A wolf saw her, then he said, "Play with me." She said, "My grandma's ill. I've got to go quickly." The wolf went first. He goes to grandma's house and does knock knock. "Who's that?" says Grandma. "It's Red Riding Hood." "Come in." Then she saw the wolf, she runs to the cupboard. Red Riding Hood came a little while later to her grandma's house. "Grandma, what a big eyes you have!" Grandma said, "Better to see you with." And she sid, "What a big ears you have!" "Better to hear you with." "What a big teeth you have!" "Better to eat you with!" Then she run and run and the wolf run after her. She saw a man. Luckily it was her father. "The wolf has come to eat me" she told her father. Then her father said . . . (unclear). Then Red Riding Hood said, "We've got to find grandma." Then she said, "Grandma, grandma, where are you?" Grandma said, "I'm here!" Red Riding Hood gave her the flowers, biscuits and cakes. "You are a good girl. We can all have it for tea" said grandma. Then grandma gave them two apples and they lived happily ever after.'

The crucial difference between Nadia and Nazma is that Nadia's mastery of the English language will inform her reading whereas Nazma's reading itself helps inform her spoken English. Nazma achieves this high standard of understanding and spoken language in two languages through intensive talk within and around texts. Like Verhoeven's Turkish children we met in Chapter 3, Nazma has an excellent memory and is already able to read far more than she can actually express. Words themselves are not a problem; making sense of them is. For Nazma and her classmates, the text is a mediator of the new language. The teacher's task is to make the text mean; to help children transfer what they can read into their active language repertoire. What follows below is a framework which fits into the explicit 'scaffolding' outlined in Chapters 4 and 5. The approach borrows from Catherine Wallace's (1986) miscue charts and from the reading conferences, teachers' diaries and running records of Myra Barrs and her team at the Centre for Language in Primary Education in London (1988). The stages may be used as a basis for regular work with individual children while a trice-yearly reading miscue analysis and taped storytelling record as outlined in Stages 4 and 5 is a realistic aim. Samples of children's writing should be kept with a transcript of the retelling so that teachers may compare children's spoken and written language. This is essential as a constant reminder that although children may read what they do not yet fully understand, they will not be able to write what they cannot yet say. The framework is illustrated by examples from Nazma at age seven reading an adaptation by Fran Hunia of the traditional tale of 'Rapunzel'.

A framework for children's story-reading and story-telling

Stage 1: Before reading

Some suggestions:

- Awaken excitement for the story by talking about why you like it or why the child might find it interesting, e.g. by relating it to the child's own experiences.
- Relate the story to other stories with which the child is familiar and remind the child of these.

- Talk about the title and/or author and introduce the child to any essential unfamiliar words by pointing to objects in illustrations.
- Read the book to the child first, taking care over pronunciation and intonation.
- Ask the child to listen to the story on tape and follow in the book.

The teacher knows that this story will be new to Nazma. She tells her that the title 'Rapunzel' is the name of the princess in the story and asks Nazma to practise saying the name because it is so hard. She tells Nazma that she loved the story as a child because she wanted to have such long hair. She tells Nazma that a wicked witch is in the story and asks if she can remember other stories featuring witches. Finally, she asks Nazma to read the story alone as she wants to tape her reading.

Stage 2: Reading the story

If the reading is to be used for record-keeping, it is easier to tape the child or have a photocopy of the text to mark.

Some suggstions for reading:

- Allow the child to read the text straight through if confident.
- Share the reading with the child, sentence-by-sentence or page-by-page according to the child's confidence.
- If the child lacks confidence, read the text in unison.

If the child hesitates over a word:

- Ask a question to remind of the context. (This is a useful tool because emergent bilinguals are busy focusing on the words and often lose sight of the whole sentence or text.)
- Direct the child to the illustrations. (They can provide valuable clues, but only if the child knows the name of the object pointed to in the target language.)
- Say or direct the child to the first sound of a word or cover part of the word, making it easier to recognise. (This is usually very successful as word and sound recognition are particular strengths.)
- Encourage the child to leave the word out, read on to the end of the sentence and return to the word. (This is often successful for native speakers but is much more difficult for emergent bilinguals who are less able to draw upon semantic and syntactic clues.)
- Allow children time to reflect upon a word.
- Simply say the word to keep up the flow of reading, but ask the child to repeat the word and preferably the sentence (if it does not upset the flow) again.

Nazma has many books to choose from in her classroom. At present, she prefers simple retellings of traditional stories or fables which she often recognises from her Bengali class. One day, as she began to read 'The Peed Peeper', her teacher realised just how much we take this shared cultural knowledge for granted and how important these stories are in giving her access to a new world. Below, Nazma is reading Rapunzel:

√ = correct
(SC) = self-corrects
0 = different word used but meaning unchanged
T = teacher tells
⌣ = omission
went/want = substitution
√C2 = correct on 2nd. reading

√ √ √ √ √ √ √ √ √C2 √ √ √ √
A man and his wife looked into a witch ⓘ s garden. They saw some lettuce.

It (SC) √C2 √ √ √ √ √ √ √ √ √ √ √ √ √
"That lettuce looks good," said the woman. "Yes," said the man. "I will get

√ √ √ Now (SC)√C2 √ √ √ √ √ √ √ √
some for you." "No," said his wife. "It is the witch's lettuce. We can't

√ √ picked/Kipped (SC)√C2 √ √ wouldn't (SC)√C2
have it." She kept on looking at the lettuce. She wanted some so much.

√ √ √ √ √ √ √ √ √ √ √ √
Soon the woman started to get ill. "I will have to get some lettuce for

√ √ √ √ climb-ed √C2 √ √ √ √
you," said the man. He climbed into the witch's garden and took some

√ √ √ √ √ √ √ √ her √C2 √ √ √
lettuce. He took it home and gave it to (his wife.) She was very pleased with

√ √ √ √ √ √ √ √ √ √ √ √
the lettuce. The man climbed into the witch's garden again. This time the

√ √ √ √ √ √ √ √ √ √ √ √
witch was waiting and she saw the man get some lettuce. "That's my

√ √ √ √ √ √ √ √ √ √ √
lettuce," she said. "Give it to me." "Please let me have it," said the man.

√ √ √ √ √√ √ √ √ √ √ √ √
"I want it for my wife. She is ill." The witch said, "You can have the

√ √ √ √ √ √ √√ √ √ √ √ √√√ √
lettuce, but when your wife has a baby, you must give it to me." One day

√ √ √ √ √ √ √ name √C2 Rap- √C2 √ √ come √C2 √
the woman had a baby girl and named her (Rapunzel.) The witch came to get

√ √ √ √ √ √√ √ √√ √ √ √ √ √
her. "Come with me, Rapunzel, I will give you a good home." The man and his

√ √ √ get (SC)C2 √ √ √ √ √ √ √ √ √ look (SC)C2
wife had to give Rapunzel to the witch. They were very sad. The witch took

√ √ √ Kipped C2 √ √ √ √ √ √ √ √ √ √
Rapunzel away. She kept her in a tower. Rapunzel could not get down and she

√ √ √ √√ √ √ √ √√ √ √ √ √ √ √
had no one to talk to. She was very sad. When the witch wanted to see

√ √ wanted (SC)√C2 √ √ √ √ √ √ √
Rapunzel, she went to the tower and said, "Rapunzel, Rapunzel, let your

√ √ √ get (SC)Lit-let √ √ √ √ climb-ed √C2
√C2
hair down." Rapunzel let her hair down to the witch. She climbed up

√ √ √ √ √ √ √ √ √ √ √ come (SC)√C2
Rapunzel's hair and went into the tower. One day a prince came to the

√C2
√ √ √ √ √ √ look-ed √C2 √ √ √ √ √
tower. He heard Rapunzel singing. He looked everywhere for her but he could

not see her and he could not get into the tower. He went home. But he

wanted to see Rapunzel, so he came to the tower again The witch came to

the tower. She didn't see the prince. He heard her say, "Rapunzel,

Rapunzel, let your hair down." The prince saw how Rapunzel let her hair

down. Then he saw the witch climb up it and get into the tower. The prince

waited for the witch to climb down and go home. Then he went to the tower

and said, "Rapunzel, Rapunzel, let your hair down." Then he climbed up it.

Rapunzel was very pleased to see him. They talked and talked. When the

prince was going home, he said, "Can I come and see you again, Rapunzel?"

"Yes," said Rapunzel. The prince kept on coming to see Rapunzel. One day he

said, "Please marry me, Rapunzel." "I want to marry you," said Rapunzel.

"But we can't get married up here in this tower. I have to get down. Can

you help me?" The prince said that he would help. "Please get me some

silk," said Rapunzel. "I will make a ladder so that I can climb down." The

prince got some silk for Rapunzel. He took it to the tower and said,

"Rapunzel, Rapunzel, let your hair down." Rapunzel let her hair down. The

prince climbed up it and gave her the silk. Rapunzel started to make the

ladder. One day the witch came to see Rapunzel. She hurt Rapunzel's hair

when she climbed up it. Rapunzel said, "The prince didn't hurt me when he

climbed up my hair. The witch was very angry. She cut Rapunzel's hair and

took it away. Then the witch waited in the tower for the prince to come.

The prince came to the tower to see Rapunzel. He said, "Rapunzel, Rapunzel,

let your hair down." The witch had Rapunzel's hair and she let it down to the prince. The prince climbed up Rapunzel's hair. He looked for Rapunzel ✓c2.

but he could not see her. He saw the witch and he jumped down quickly. When

the prince jumped down, he hurt his eyes. He could not see. He walked away

sadly. The prince walked on and on. One day he heard a girl singing. It was

Rapunzel. The prince walked up to her. Rapunzel was so pleased to see the

prince that she started to cry. Her tears went into the prince's eyes. The

prince could see again. Rapunzel went home with the prince and soon they

were married.

In addition to the running record completed as Nazma reads, her teacher makes brief notes in her diary:

> *3 June: N. has a remarkable memory and, once told a word, almost never forgets. Uses phonic strategies and still reads word for word but does seem to understand. Reads in a monotone and pronunciation still poor. Needs lots of opportunities to talk about story to others. How much can she retell?*

Stage 3: Focused talk about text

Nazma is paired with a classmate or with a child from an older class on more focused activities, e.g.:

(i)   completing comprehension questions on the story
(ii) working on '*cloze*' exercises
(iii) 'true or false' statements given by the teacher to encourage them to look back carefully over the text
(iv) making up their own story on a similar theme, etc.
(v)   listening to a taped version of the text which has inaccuracies and writing these down.

If possible, native speakers and emergent bilinguals should be paired during these activities for they teach and learn from each other; the art of explaining is as difficult as understanding.

In Nazma's class 'pairing' with a native speaker is not possible and Nazma's teacher is aware that she cannot receive help with her English at home. However, her teacher has taught her the skill of reflecting upon what she does *not* know during 'structured story' sessions. As a result of this practice, Nazma is able to re-read the story to herself at home and, as she does so, to write down all the words which are unfamiliar in her exercise book. The analysis of Nazma's reading below shows that we may well underestimate the extent to which children can teach themselves when taught appropriate skills and a manageable text.

Stage 4: Re-reading the text

At home, Nazma writes down the following unknown words: garden, tower, kept, waited, silk, everywhere. Before she reads the story to the teacher a second time, both study these words and the teacher explains their meaning, sometimes asking the child to use the word in a sentence. She then reads the story a second time focusing on *intonation*. Sometimes both teacher and child read a sentence together, exaggerating this: 'Rapunzel, Rapunzel, let your hair down.'

Approximately twice yearly, the teacher uses a simple analysis suggested by Catherine Wallace (1986) to chart Nazma's miscues:

LM = Level of miscue (graphophonic, syntactic, etc.)
SM = Source of miscue (unknown word, etc.)
LR = Learner response (leave, self-correct, etc.)
TP = Teacher prompt (leaves, tells, etc.)
SC = Child self-corrects on first reading
*   = Correctly read on second reading

No.	Miscue	LM	SM	LR	TP
1.	witch * (witch's)	grapho-phonic and syntactic	does not recognise possessive	leaves	corrects and asks N. to repeat
2.	it * (that)			SC	
3.	now * (no)			SC	
4.	picked/ kipped (kept)	grapho-phonic and semantic	unknown word	leaves	corrects and N. repeats as 'kipped'
5.	wouldn't * (wanted)			SC	
6.	climb-ed * (climbed)	grapho-phonic and pronun-ciation	unknown past tense	leaves	corrects and N. repeats

7.	her * (his)	grapho-phonic and semantic	error in possess. (relates forward to 'her')	leaves	corrects and N. repeats
8.	name * (named)	grapho-phonic and syntactic	unknown past tense	leaves	corrects and N. repeats
9.	come * (came)	grapho-phonic and syntactic	unsure of past tense	SC	
10.	get * (give)	grapho-phonic and syntactic	slip	SC	
11.	kipped * (kept)		pronun-ciation of unknown word		
12.	wanted * (went)	grapho-phonic and syntactic	slip	SC	
13.	get/lit * (let)	grapho-phonic	unknown word	SC	
14.	* climb-ed (climbed)	grapho-phonic	unknown past tense	leaves	corrects and N. repeats
15.	come * (came)	grapho-phonic	unsure of past tense	SC	
16.	looked-ed * (looked)	grapho-phonic	unsure of past tense	SC	
17.	verywhere * (every-where	grapho-phonic	unknown word	SC	points to 'e'
18.	want * (went)	grapho-phonic	unsure that 's' needed if 'wants'	SC	

19.	wouldn't	grapho-		
	* (wanted)	phonic	slip	SC
20.	come	grapho-		
	* (came)	phonic	unsure of past tense	SC
21.	–			
	* (again)		unknown word	omits	points, tells and N. repeats
22.	who			
	* (how)	grapho-phonic and semantic	slip	SC
23.	get			
	* (let)	grapho-phonic and semantic	slip	SC
24.	–			
	* (waited)	doesn't try	unknown word	leaves	tells and N. repeats
25.	talk-ed			
	* (talked)	pronun-ciation	unsure of past tense	leaves	leaves
26.	kipped			
	(kept)	pronun-ciation		SC
27.	come			
	* (came)	grapho-phonic	unsure of past tense	SC
28.	into			
	* (in)	grapho-phonic	slip	SC
29.	kept/ kipped/ quickly			
	* (quickly)	grapho-phonic	unsure of meaning	SC

Three main features stand out from Nazma's reading:

(i) She uses grapho-phonic and lexical clues, miscues because she is uncertain of the meaning of the whole text, but then self-corrects immediately (wouldn't (wanted); now (no)).

(ii) She has difficulty in pronouncing words which means they sometimes cannot be understood (kipped).

(iii) The only words she is unable to read are those she does not understand or where she is unsure of the grammar (come/came; quickly, etc.).

After her second reading, Nazma talks about the story, relates it to others she knows and explains why she likes it to her teacher. Barrs *et al.* (1988) refer to this as a '*reading conference*'. From this, her teacher can see how much of the story has been understood.

Stage 5: Retelling the story

Earlier in this chapter, we saw how easy native speakers find retelling a story, even before they can read. For Nazma, it is the other way round; reading is much easier than retelling. It is important for teachers to record emergent bilinguals' story retellings to highlight areas that they need to focus on in their spoken language programme. Here is Nazma retelling 'Rapunzel' after she has read it twice to her teacher:

Nazma	**Teacher**
1. (hesitates over beginning)	2. *What happened one day?*
3. *The woman wanted the lettuce*	4. *. . . and . . . did she get it?*
5. *Yes*	6. *How?*
7. *The man climbed up and gets the lettuce.*	8. *And how did she feel then?*
9. *She feel very pleased. One day, the witch saw the man taking her lettuce . . . (pauses)*	
	10. *What did she say?*
11. *'This is my lettuce.' The man said, 'Please can I take it. 'My wife is sick.' Then the witch said, 'When you want to have a baby, you have to give it to me.' Then the witch came and take the baby. (pauses)*	
	12. *How did they feel?*
13. *Sad. Rapunzel was big and she lived in a (indistinguishable)*	
	14. *Where did she live?*
15. *. . . in a tower* *She was feeling sad.*	16. *(corrects pronunciation and N. repeats) Why was she sad?*
17. *Because she wanted someone to talk to her. One day, the witch came to the tower. She said to Rapunzel, 'Rapunzel, Rapunzel, let your hair down.' Rapunzel let her hair down. Then the witch climbed up. The prince came and he heard a song . . . One day, the prince saw Rapunzel and the witch was climbing her hair. When the prince came, he . . .*	

18. *What did he do?*

19. He climbed up Rapunzel's hair
    and they was happy

20. *Mmm. How did they feel?*

21. Nice.

22. *Mmm. And what did he say to her
    one day?*

23. 'Please marry me.'

24. *And what did she say?*

25. 'I could marry you but I can't
    marry you in the tower.

26. *So what did she say?
    What did she ask him for?*

27. A silk.

28. *What did she want to make with
    the silk?*

29. A ladder. The prince came with
    the silk to the tower and make a
    ladder. One day, the witch came
    and said to Rapunzel, 'Rapunzel,
    Rapunzel, let down your hair.'
    And she said, 'When the prince
    was coming up, he didn't hurt my
    hair.' Then the witch was very
    angry and cut Rapunzel's hair.
    Then the prince was crying out
    and he couldn't see Rapunzel.
    He see the witch and he jump
    quickly. When he jump, he hurt
    his eyes.

30. *Could he see then?*

31. No

32. *Do you know what we call
    someone who can't see? A special
    word.*

33. No.

34. *Blind.*

35. One day, the prince was walking.
    He heard a girl singing. It was
    Rapunzel. Then they was married.

36. *How did he see again? What
    did she do? Let's find it in the
    book.*

37. (reads) 'Her tears went into the
    prince's eyes.'

38. *So what made him see again?*

39. Tears. (difficulty in pronunciation)

40. *Her tears. Her tears made him see.
    They were magic tears.*

The transcript provides a record of Nazma's achievements in less than two years of school, the only place where she speaks her new language and during which time she has also begun reading in Bengali and classical Arabic. The transcript also shows the teacher what she needs to focus on next. Her notes are as follows:

> *Nazma: Strengths: Is now able to use many past tenses (both regular and irregular, e.g. climbed, lived, wanted; saw, came, was, couldn't, didn't, heard; was feeling, climbing, taking, crying, walking); adjectives (happy, nice, angry, sick, sad, big); prepositions (down, up, in, to); nouns (tower, silk, garden, tears) and 'chunks' of language (Rapunzel, Rapunzel, let down your hair). Many of these she has transferred from reading the story into speech.*

> *Weaknesses: She hesitates on retellings; is unsure how to begin; avoids the future tense and convenient past tenses (got, took, had, kept) as well as other new words (everywhere, started, waited) and 'chunks' (had no one to talk to), etc.*

> *Teacher learns: To focus more on 'openings' of stories; to introduce more indexical words which point to a special part of the situation and would help link Nazma's retelling (I, now, here, there, afterwards, next, tomorrow, this, etc.). Generally, to use more drama around stories, more taped stories and more retelling of stories during class reading sessions.*

IN SUMMARY

In this chapter, we examined a variety of ways in which adults may work with children individually to help them make sense of learning to read in a new language. A simple framework was offered for analysing these interactions which may be used for children's records. Examples showed children at three different ages and stages of language and literacy learning; the pre-school or reception age, the first year of formal literacy tuition and after approximately two years in school. During the first stage, we saw how adults can learn much from caregiver/infant story sharing. 'Scaffolding' involves extending children's utterances ('Fish' – 'Yes, the fish is swimming, isn't it?'), explicitly pointing to objects in illustrations and naming them and allowing plenty of time for both listening and repetition. During the first school year, the teacher's main aim is to show children in whatever way she can that they *can* read and that the task is *manageable*. By the third stage, the teacher focuses on linking reading, understanding and reproducing texts.

A number of principles emerge as important at each stage:

- Make sure that reading taken home by children makes sense to parents and is manageable for them. Recognise that siblings will often read with children at home and introduce '*paired reading*' between older and younger children in the school as excellent practice for this.
- Build up links with community teachers to discuss approaches and materials (stories, etc.) which are familiar to children.
- Never assume that children automatically understand or can reproduce a text which they are able to read. Allow plenty of opportunities for children to listen, discuss and retell texts before they can make them their own.

- Do not underestimate the power of repetition and older children's ability to practise texts *even alone* at home.
- Realise that children may approach reading very differently according to home and community class experiences and according to whether they are convergent or divergent learners. Be explicit in your own reading tuition yet flexible if children's approach to learning does not always match your own. Always try to build upon children's strengths when you see that a particular approach helps them make personal sense of a task!

Further reading

Barrs, M. *et al.* (1990) *Patterns of Learning. The Primary Language Record and the National Curriculum*, London: Centre for Language in Primary Education.
Edwards, V. (1995) *Learning to Read in Multilingual Classrooms*, Reading and Language Information Centre, Reading: University of Reading.
Gregory, E. (1994c) Negotiation as a criterial factor in learning to read in a second language, in D. Graddol, J. Maybin and B. Stierer (eds.) *Researching Language and Literacy in Social Context*, Clevedon: Multilingual Matters Ltd. for the Open University.
Wallace, C. (1986) *Learning to Read in a Multicultural Society*, Oxford: Pergamon Press.

7

Epilogue

Learning . . . a second language is part of a multi-faceted intercultural learning process which takes place by learning with and from those of other cultures and which relates to every aspect of culture.

(Satzke and Wolf 1993)

These words introduce the chapter in the Austrian National Curriculum on the teaching of German to 'non-German mother-tongue speakers'. The introduction goes on to focus on the importance of the school in fostering respect amongst children for every language and culture and the need to prepare children for life in a multicultural society. Successful teaching, it insists, depends upon the ability to 'distance' oneself from the mother-tongue in order to understand the nature of the language learning task for the child. The rest of the chapter outlines in detail a programme of study for early second language learning.

Every country stresses the importance of equality of opportunity in its aims for education. Each country believes firmly in its own curriculum as the means to providing this equality. It is *how* equality is to be realised which is viewed very differently as one steps across national borders. As we saw in Chapter 1, some countries recognise positively a diversity of languages and cultures in society, while others accentuate the need to iron out differences in fostering a unity of nationhood. Yet as they look into the future, international in-service networks show that Early Years educators are voicing similar questions across countries and continents.

One question concerns assessment. Throughout this book, we have seen that the linguistic strengths and weaknesses of emergent bilinguals are very different from those of their monolingual peers. How, then, will teachers adequately assess the reading development of young children using tests designed for monolinguals? But there are other hurdles in achieving fair assessment. One is the unpredictable way in which second language learning progresses. The spoken language of Nazma, Shabbir and even Nicole has not always advanced at a steady pace. It has been interrupted by holidays or illness when it has stagnated or even regressed, made up for by a sudden spurt shortly after the children's return to school.

Another hurdle to fair assessment is voiced by the children themselves as they look back to starting school. The children all remembered feeling 'a bit sad' or frightened, not only because they could not say what they wanted to but because they often felt too scared to voice what they *could* say. We know that some children will have experienced traumas before leaving their country of origin from which they cannot recover overnight. At the age of eight, Nazma and her classmates are able to understand most classroom discussions and converse on many daily events. But reading even simple literature reveals how vulnerable the children are and how precarious is their grasp of whole areas of the new language. Nazma's blank expression as she reads what sounds to the listener to be 'the piece a prick' (the pizza princess) and Shabbir's stumbling over words such as 'emeralds', 'spectacles' and 'brains' as he confronts 'The Wizard of Oz', show us the problem of expecting young emergent bilinguals to perform at the same level as their monolingual peers and how embarrassing for some children mistakes might be. Sometimes, an inability to understand key words might prevent a child from grasping the meaning of a whole text. A quick translation or explanation of these words will enable everything to fall into place. But it is precisely this sort of help that monolingual teachers cannot give. The question of how to provide a fair assessment for children like Nazma has not yet been answered but the obvious difficulties of the task have persuaded many countries to exclude emergent bilinguals from language tests until they are viewed as proficient in the new language.

A second question concerns the role of families and outside-school reading practices in children's lives. The children in Chapter 2 are learning to read within a network of support from different community members. Each reading practice is very separate; its language, materials, methods and participation structures are very distinct. Children will participate in very different practices. Nicole's storybooks, the computer and spelling games, such as Scrabble, etc., contrast sharply with Sabina and Shahina's Bengali and mosque classes. Parents will be more or less knowledgeable about each of these, but school reading is obviously likely to be most alien and most difficult for them to act as initiator or guide, especially when they, themselves, cannot read in the new language.

We have, however, another very important resource; one to which we should pay more attention in both home reading programmes and research studies. Listen to eleven-year-old Fatima as she recalls learning to read in English:

Every day, at home-time, my brother said 'Read' and my parents stayed happy because I was learning a lot. Now I'm teaching my little brother and sister. I remember how my brother taught me well and I'm teaching them the same way. They already know their ABC.

Her words reflect those of many older bilingual children. Older siblings are excellent *brokers* of a new language because they are able to link school and home reading practices. Observations of young children working at home with older siblings are beginning to show how approaches from state and community schools intertwine. Although each pair is obviously unique, this syncretism of literacy practices largely follows a similar pattern: (i) the younger child first reads word by word after the sibling, then gradually reads individual words and completes sentences before reading more and more alone; (ii) the older sibling questions the child on the text in the mother-tongue and gives explanations; (iii) spelling tests. The older children often like their pupils to be exact in their reading and will correct them, drawing attention to an 's' on the end of a word, etc. Yet after reading they go back to talk about the illustrations and how they link with the text. These 'teachers' are vital, for they understand the two worlds of the younger child in a way which is impossible for monolingual teachers. Is there any way we might recognise and build upon what is happening in our home/school reading programmes? We must remember that these 'lessons' take place without any request or intervention from school. Siblings assist each other in this way because they take literacy in the new language very seriously indeed.

A third question concerns the interplay between teacher expectations, home–school relations and home reading programmes. Research studies with Mexican-American families show that the decisive factors for home–school continuity are high academic standards and teacher expectations, supported by a well-defined and explained home reading programme. Nicole's parents would certainly support those findings. Shabbir and his classmates are already thinking about the future. They speak confidently of becoming doctors, nurses, teachers and pharmacists. Whether they manage to fulfil their aims rests upon many factors, not least of which is their teachers' knowledge of the children's ways of learning.

The questions above all reveal just how much we still need to understand about how children learn to learn in a new language. Every time Early Years educators question why children like Tajul refer to magnifying glasses as windows and tigers being 'friends' of lions because they are 'like' them, they add an important piece to this understanding. I hope that this book will be a contribution to their questions and discussions.

Glossary

Additive/subtractive language learning: Second language learning is referred to as 'additive' if the new language is learned without detriment to the mother-tongue. It is 'subtractive' if the aim is to replace the first language with the new one.

Arbitrary nature of language: The relationship between the word (or symbol) and the sound it makes is referred to as arbitrary because there is no intrinsic link between the sound sequence and the word it refers to. Young bilinguals have an early awareness of the arbitrariness of language as they know that an object can be represented by more than one word.

Assimilation (policy of): The policy which aims to absorb immigrants as quickly as possible into the language and culture of the host country.

Bibliographic knowledge: The knowledge of books or written texts in the widest sense. This may be a knowledge of the layout of a book (in English left to right, top to bottom, etc.) or the knowledge that certain words and expressions 'belong' to certain texts, e.g. 'Once upon a time . . .', etc.

Broker: 'Language broker' is the term given to those who mediate a new language (and culture) to other members of their family. Many children in Europe and the USA are language brokers for both parents and younger siblings.

Bussing: The transporting of children by bus from the area in which they live to a school in another in order to create racially balanced classes.

CLPE (The Centre for Language in Primary Education, Webber Row, London SE1 8QW): An in-service and resource centre for all aspects of language in the primary curriculum. It houses a good collection of materials for use in multilingual classrooms.

Cohesive devices: The term used to refer to words which link one sentence (or part of a sentence) to another. Some common cohesive devices are: pronominal reference, e.g. 'I saw John yesterday. *He* was ill'; synonyms, e.g. sick/ill; superordinates, e.g. 'apples and oranges = fruit'; collocational expressions, e.g. 'toast with butter and jam'. Knowledge of these can greatly assist a child in predicting a text.

Collocation: Words which are habitually associated with each other, e.g. cup and saucer; knife and fork, etc. Knowledge of more complex collocations, e.g. 'rancid' rather than 'rotten' butter, come through experiences in a language or can be gained through experiences with written stories, e.g. 'grinding corn; sowing seeds', etc.

Comprehensible input: Language which contains some new element in it but is nevertheless understood by the learner because of linguistic, paralinguistic or situational clues or world knowledge back-up.

Conjunction: A word used to connect words or clauses, e.g. but, and, because, if, although.

Cues (reading clues): Signals sent from five knowledge centres (bibliographic or book); semantic (meaning); syntactic (structure); lexical (word) and grapho-phonic (sound/symbol relationship) to assist readers in predicting a text.

Diglossia/diglossic situation: Terms in sociolinguistics for the use of two or more varieties of language (one a 'high' or standard variety and one a 'low' spoken vernacular) for different purposes or functions in the same community.

Emergent bilinguals: The term used in this book to refer to the first generation of children to receive formal education in the country to which their families have immigrated. They are children who do not usually speak the host language at home and are at an early stage of second language learning. Their ultimate aim is to become bilingual which is defined as being able to function in two or more languages at the same level as native speakers and being able, positively, to identify with both (or all) language groups (and cultures) or parts of them.

European Communities Directive (1977): A Directive from the European Community which strongly supported the principle that the teaching of the mother-tongue improves rather than impairs the linguistic and educational performance of bilingual children and urged all member countries to provide mother-tongue teaching.

Generative words: The term used by Paolo Freire in his work with adult illiterates in Brazil during the 1960s to denote words of high personal value which also generated a variety of phonemic combinations, e.g. sl- ave; c- ave; r- ave, etc.

Grapho-phonic knowledge: Knowledge which enables readers to match written symbols (graphemes) with the sounds we attach to them (phonemes).

Holophrastic stage (of language learning): The first stage of language acquisition whereby a one word utterance can be made sense of only in the immediate situation, e.g. 'doggie' can mean 'Look at the doggie' or 'Doggie wants his food', etc.

Interdependency principle: The principle that a child will be able to transfer knowledge gained in one language to others.

Interlingual/intralingual miscues: Interlingual miscues are those which arise from interference of the mother-tongue, e.g. 'she's' for male and female for Asian children speaking languages where gender is not marked by the relative pronoun. Intralingual miscues arise from the structure of the target language itself, e.g. 'goed' where the past tense rule 'add -ed' is applied to irregular past tenses.

Interpsychological/intrapsychological planes: According to Vygotsky (1962), children's development appears first on the interpsychological (or social) plane in interaction with others and then on the intrapsychological (or mental) plane.

Key vocabulary: The term used by Sylvia Ashton-Warner in her book *Teacher* (1963) to denote the words which are most important to children as they begin reading.

Knowledge centre: According to Rummelhart's interactive theory of reading (1977), we draw upon cues (clues) sent out from four knowledge centres (semantic, syntactic, lexical, orthographic/grapho-phonic) as we set about learning to read. In this book, I add 'bibliographic knowledge' as a fifth knowledge centre.

Lexis (lexical knowledge): Lexis is the vocabulary of a language. Lexical knowledge is the knowledge of words which enables readers to predict which word might follow in a text. This may be through *collocation, pronominal reference*, etc.

Linguistic set: A group of words linked through common association, e.g. 'breakfast' words, 'school' words, etc.

Linguistic stem: The term is used here to mean 'structure'. Ben-Zeev (1977) found that bilingual children were more able than monolinguals to analyse linguistic stems when asked to ignore word meaning and sentence framing and substitute one word for another, e.g. Researcher: 'If "they" means 'spagetti', how do we say "They are good children"?' (Answer: 'Spagetti' are good children.)

Metalanguage/Metalinguistic awareness: A term in linguistics for language used to talk about language. Research studies show that young bilinguals have an advanced metalinguistic awareness as they are able to realise the arbitrariness of language, see word boundaries, etc. at an earlier stage than monolinguals.

Minority language submersion: When minority languages are totally ignored or deliberately suppressed, we refer to the situation as one of 'minority language submersion'.

Miscue analysis: A detailed analysis of the errors made by an inexperienced reader in order to ascertain which cues (clues) s/he can use as well as which may be lacking.

NALDIC (The National Association for Language Development in the Curriculum, SW Herts LCSC, Holywell School Site, Tolpits Lane, Watford WD1 8NT): A national organisation with special interest and regional groups whose members share the common aim to raise the school achievement of ethnic minority pupils.

Oral cloze: Originally from 'close' (to complete a pattern in Gestalt theory). A cloze exercise asks children to supply missing words either orally or in writing, e.g. 'Little Red Riding Hood went to the forest to pick — '.

Oronym: Strings of sound that can be carved into words in different ways, e.g. 'I scream' or 'ice-cream'.

Orthographic knowledge: One of the five knowledge centres called upon by the reader: an awareness of spelling patterns, e.g. 'scr' may begin words in English but 'hlt' may not.

Paired reading: Usually used to refer to home reading schemes whereby caregiver and child share the reading. Usually the child begins reading and signs to the caregiver to continue. Descriptions of successful 'paired reading' schemes can be found in Topping and Wolfendale (1985).

Participation structure: A term used to refer to the nature of turn-taking between teacher or caregiver and child as they interact during reading events.

Parts of speech: A grammatical category or class of words. Traditional grammars of English generally list eight parts of speech: noun, pronoun, verb, adjective, adverb, preposition, conjunction, interjection.

Phoneme: In linguistics, the smallest category of sound which can distinguish two words, e.g. 'p-an', 'b-an' which comprise three phonemes 'b' or 'p', 'a' and 'n'.

Phonological knowledge: The knowledge of sound patterns in a language.

Preposition: One of the traditional parts of speech denoting principally time and space (at, from, through, without, up, down, under, over, in, to, etc.) but also cause and purpose (for) and agent (by, with).

Pronominal reference: Where a pronoun (he, she, it, we, you, they, etc.) refers to a noun which precedes it, e.g. 'I saw Mary yesterday. *She* was ill.'

Qur'ān: The sacred book of Islam.

Reading conference: Child and teacher (or second child) discuss a reading book. An integral part of record-keeping in The Primary Reading Record (Barrs *et al.* 1990).

Reading and Language Information Centre, Bulmershe Court, Earley, Reading RG6 1HY: A major centre for resources and in-service courses for teachers working in multilingual classrooms.

Redundancy: Part(s) of a message which can be eliminated without loss of essential information.

Scaffolding: The metaphor used to describe the way in which both caregivers and teachers structure young children's learning. The notion of a 'scaffold' which can be dismounted piece by piece highlights the child's growing capacity and independence.

Schema: A mental model of the world which enables one to make personal sense of it.

Semantic knowledge: The knowledge of the meaning of words within a culture including their denotations, orientations, implications and ambiguities.

Sense and meaning: In this book, Vygotsky's (1962) definitions are used, whereby 'meaning' denotes the dictionary definition of a word, the way it is commonly understood, and 'sense' the personal meaning attached to a word which will depend upon the personal and cultural experiences an individual has made in relation to a word, e.g. 'flag' may have a positive or negative 'sense' according to an individual's experience within a culture.

Signifier/signified: In linguistics, the word is sometimes referred to as the 'signifier' and the object it refers to the 'signified'.

Speech event: The term used by Hymes (1974) to denote an event for which certain words, phrases and linguistic 'recipes' are necessary. These will be different from one culture to another (e.g. weddings, funerals, etc.).

Superordinates: Terms with a wide reference, e.g. *flower* and *furniture* which will include a number of subordinates, e.g. rose, daisy, table or chair.

Synonym: Words which have similar meanings, e.g. obedient, compliant, etc.

Syntactic knowledge: Knowledge of the grammar of a language (the way in which words combine into units such as phrase, clause and sentence).

Voiced/unvoiced (voiceless) consonants: 'Voice' is the buzzing sound made in the larynx by the vibration of the vocal chords. 'Voiced' sounds are 'b, d, g, z'; 'voiceless' sounds are 'p, t, k, s' whereby 's' can be voiced if it follows a voiced sound (wugs) or voiceless if it does not (bus).

Bibliography

Adams, M. J. (1990) *Beginning to Read. Thinking and Learning about Print*, Massachusetts: Mass. Institute of Technology.

Alladina, S. and Edwards, V. (eds.) (1991) *Multilingualism in the British Isles, Africa, The Middle East and Asia*, London: Longman.

Anderson, A. B. and Stokes, S. J. (1984) Social and institutional influences on the development and practice of literacy, in H. Goelman, A. Olberg and F. Smith (eds.) *Awakening to Literacy*, London: Heineman Educational.

Applebee, A. (1977) What are stories? The children tell us, in M. Meek, A. Warlow and G. Barton (eds.) *The Cool Web*, London: The Bodley Head.

Ashton-Warner, S. (1963) *Teacher*, London: Penguin (reprinted by Virago 1980).

Bakhtin, M. (1986) *Speech Genres and Other Late Essays*, Austin: University of Texas Press.

Barnitz, J. G. (1978) *Interrelationship of Orthography and Phonological Structure in Learning to Read*, Illinois: Urbana.

Barrs, M. *et al.* (1988) *The Primary Language Record Handbook*, London: Centre for Language in Primary Education.

Barrs, M. *et al.* (1990) *Patterns of Learning. The Primary Language Record and the National Curriculum*, London: Centre for Language in Primary Education.

Barrs, M. *et al.* (1993) *Guide to the Primary Learning Record*, London, Centre for Language in Primary Education.

Bateson, G. (1955) A theory of play and fantasy, in J. S. Bruner, A. Jolly and K. Sylva (eds.) *Play*, London: Penguin.

Bateson, G. (1979) *Mind and Nature*, London: Wildwood House.

Ben-Zeev, S. (1977) The influence of bilingualism on cognitive strategy and cognitive development, *Child Development*, Vol. 48, pp. 1009–18.

Bettelheim, B. (1975) *The Uses of Enchantment*, London: Thames & Hudson.

Bourne, J. (1989) *Moving into the Mainstream: LEA Provision for Bilingual Pupils*, Windsor: NFER Nelson.

Bruner, J. S. (1979) From communication to language: a psychological perspective, in V. Lee (ed.) *Language Development*, London: Croom Helm.

Bruner, J. S. (1986) *Actual Minds, Possible Worlds*, Cambridge Mass: Harvard University Press.

Bussis, A. M. *et al.* (1985) *Inquiry into Meaning: an Investigation of Learning to Read*, Hillsdale, NJ: Erlbaum Associates.

Campbell, R. N. and Macdonald, T. B. (1983) Text and context in early language comprehension, in M. Donaldson, R. Grieve and C. Pratt (eds.) *Early Childhood Development and Education*, Oxford: Blackwell.

Carroll, J. B. (1977) Developmental parameters of reading comprehension, in J. T. Guthrie (ed.) *Cognition, Curriculum and Comprehension*, Newark, Delaware: International Reading Association.

Cazden, C. B. (1983) Contexts for literacy: in the mind and in the classroom, *Journal of Reading Behaviours*, Vol. XIV, no. 4, pp. 413–27.

Chall, J. S. (1979) The great debate: ten years later, with a modest proposal for reading stages, in L. B. Resnick and P.A. Weaver (eds.) *Theory and Practice of Early Reading*, Vol. 1, Hillsdale NJ: Erlbaum Associates.

Chomsky, N. (1964) *Aspects of the Theory of Syntax*, Cambridge MA Institute of Technology Press.

Cleave, S., Jowett, S. and Bate, M. (1982) *And So to School. A Study of Continuity from Pre-school to Infant School*, Windsor: NFER Nelson.

Cochran-Smith, M. (1984) *The Making of a Reader*, Norwood NJ: Ablex.

Collins English Dictionary (1992) (3rd edition) London: Harper Collins Publishers.

Cummins, J. (1979) Linguistic interdependence and the educational development of bilingual children, *Review of Educational Research*, Vol. 49, pp. 222–51.

Dombey, H. (1983) Learning the language of books, in M. Meek (ed.) *Opening Moves*, Bedford Way Papers 17. Institute of Education, University of London.

Dombey, H. (1988) Partners in the telling, in M. Meek and C. Mills (eds.) *Language and Literacy in the Primary School*, Lewes: The Falmer Press.

Dombey, H. and Meek, M. (eds.) (1994) *First Steps Together. Home-School Early Literacy in European Contexts*. Stoke-on-Trent: Trentham Publishers/IEDPE.

Donaldson, M. (1978) *Children's Minds*, Glasgow: Fontana.

Douglas, M. (1970) *Purity and Danger*, London: Pelican Books.

Dunn, J. (1989) The family as an educational environment in the pre-school years, in C. W. Desforges (ed.) *Early Childhood Education. The British Journal of Educational Psychology*, Monograph Series No. 4, Scottish Academic Press.

Duranti, A. and Ochs, E. (1995) Syncretic Literacy in a Samoan American Community, *Focus on Diversity*, Vol. 55, no. 2, pp. 1–2, Bilingual Research Centre, University of California, Santa Cruz.

Eco, U. (1980) *The Name of the Rose*, London: Picador.

Edwards, V. (1995) *Reading in Multilingual Classrooms*, Reading and Language Information Centre, Reading: University of Reading.

Edwards, V. and Redfern, A. (1992) *The World in a Classoom*, Clevedon: Multilingual Matters.

Edwards, V. and Walker, S. (1995) *Building Bridges: Multilingual Resources for Children*, The Multilingual Resource for Children Project, University of Reading: Multilingual Matters.

Elkonin, D. B. (1963) The psychology of mastering the elements of reading, in B. Simon and J. Simon (eds) *Educational Psychology in the USSR*, London: Routledge and Kegan Paul.

Fitzpatrick, F. (1987) *The Open Door*, Clevedon: Multilingual Matters.

Fox, C. (1988) Poppies will make them grant, in M. Meek and C. Mills (eds.) *Language and Literacy in The Primary School*, Lewes: The Falmer Press.

Freire, P. (1973) *Education: The Practice of Freedom*, London: Writers and Readers Pub Co-op.

Garvie, E. (1990) *Story as Vehicle*, Clevedon: Multilingual Matters.

Gibson, L. (1989) *Through Children's Eyes. Literacy Learning in the Early Years*, London: Cassell.

Goodman, K. and Goodman, Y. (1978) Reading of American children whose language is a stable rural dialect of a language other than English, *ERIC ED*, pp. 173–754.

Goodman, K., Goodman, Y. and Flores, B. (1979) *Reading in One Bilingual Classroom: Literacy and Biliteracy*, Rosslyn Va: National Clearing House for Bilingual Education.

Gregory, E. (1984) A story . . . a story . . . linking English, English second language and remedial reading lessons through folk tales, *English in Education*, Summer, pp. 40–59.

Gregory, E. (1993) What counts as reading in the early years classroom? *British Journal of Educational Psychology*, Vol. 63, pp. 213–29.

Gregory, E. (1994a) Cultural assumptions and Early Years pedagogy: the effect of the home culture on minority children's interpretation of reading in school, in *Language, Culture and Curriculum*, Vol. 7, no. 2, pp. 1–14.

Gregory, E. (1994b) The National Curriculum and non-native speakers of English, in G. Blenkin and V. Kelly (eds.) *The National Curriculum and Early Learning. An Evaluation*, London: Paul Chapman Publishing.

Gregory, E. (1994c) Negotiation as a criterial factor in learning to read in a second language, in D. Graddol, J. Maybin and B. Stierer (eds.) *Researching Language and Literacy in Social Context*, Clevedon: Multilingual Matters.

Gregory, E. (1996) Learning from the community. A family literacy project with Bangladeshi-origin children in London, in Wolfendale and Topping (op. cit.)

Gregory, E. and Biarnès, J. (1994) Tony and Jean Francois: looking for sense in the strangeness of school, in H. Dombey and M. Meek-Spencer (eds.) *First Steps Together. Home–School Early Literacy in European Contexts*, Stoke-on-Trent: Trentham Publishers/IEDPE.

Gregory, E. and Kelly, C. (1992) Bilingualism and assessment, in G. Blenkin and A. Kelly, *Assessment in Early Childhood Education*, London: Paul Chapman.

Gregory, E., Lathwell, J., Mace, J. and Rashid, N. (1993) *Literacy at Home and at School*, Literacy Research Group, Faculty of Education, Goldsmiths College.

Grosjean, F. (1982) *Life with Two Languages. An Introduction to Bilingualism*, London: Harvard University Press.

Hall, E. T. (1959) *The Silent Language*, NY: Doubleday.

Hatch, E. (1974) Research on reading a second language, *Journal of Reading Behaviour*, Vol. 6, pp. 53–61.

Hatch, E., Peck, S. and Wagner-Gough, J. (1979) A look at process in child second language acquisition, in E. Ochs and B. Schieffelin (eds.) *Developmental Pragmatics*, NY: Academic Press.

Heath, S. B. (1982) What no bed-time story means: narrative skills at home and in school, *Language and Society*, Vol. 6, pp. 49–76.

Heath, S. B. (1983) *Ways with Words: Language, Life and Work in Communities and Classrooms*, Cambridge University Press.

HMSO (1967) *Children and their Primary Schools* (the Plowden Report), London: HMSO.

HMSO (1975) *A Language for Life* (the Bullock Report), Report of the Committee of Inquiry appointed by the Secretary of State for Education and Science, London: HMSO.

HMSO (1985) *An Education for All* (the Swann Report), Report of the Committee of Inquiry into Education for Children from Ethnic Minority Groups, London: HMSO.

Holscher, P. (1995) An intercultural education project in Bavaria. Paper presented to SCCA conference, 27–28 April, London.

Hong-Kingston, M. (1977) *The Woman Warrior*, London: Picador.

Howard, R. (1974) A note on S/Z, in R. Barthes *Introduction to S/Z*, trans. Richard Miller. New York: Hill and Wang.

Huey, E. B. (1908) *The Psychology and Pedagogy of Reading*, NY: Macmillan.

Hymes, D. (1974) *Foundations in Sociolinguistics*, Philadelphia: University of Philadelphia Press.

Hynds, J. (1984) *Learning to Read*, London: Avery Hill College.

Ianco-Worrall, A. (1972) Bilingualism and cognitive development, *Child Development*, Vol. 43, pp. 390–400.

Kelly, G. (1955) *A Theory of Personality*, Mass: The Norton Library.

Lambert, W. E. (1967) A social psychology of bilingualism, *Journal of Social Issues*, Vol. 23, pp. 91–109.

Lambert, W. E. and Tucker, G. R. (1972) *Bilingual Education of Children: The St Lambert Experiment*, Rowley, Mass: Newbury House.

Langer, S. (1953) *Feeling and Form. Philosophy in a New Key*, London: Routledge.

Liljestrom, R. *et al.* (1982) *Young Children in China*, Clevedon: Multilingual Matters.

Linguistic Minorities Project (1985) *The Other Languages of England*, London: Routledge and Kegal Paul.

Luke, A. (1993a) The social construction of literacy in the primary school, in L. Unsworth (ed.) *Literacy, Learning and Teaching*, Melbourne: Macmillan.

Luke, A. (1993b) *The Social Construction of Literacy in the Primary School*, Melbourne: Macmillan.

Lüthi, M. (1970) *Once Upon a Time. On the Nature of Fairy Tales*, NY: Frederick Ungar.

Mackay, D., Thompson, B. and Schaub, P. (1978) *Breakthrough to Literacy*, London: Longman.

Meek, M. (1979) Discussion, 1 December. Institute of Education.

Meek, M. (1981) Handing down the magic, in P. Salmon (op. cit.).

Meek, M. (1982) *Learning to Read*, London: The Bodley Head.

Meek, M. (1988) *How Texts Teach What Readers Learn*, Thimble Press.

Meek, M. (1991) *On Being Literate*, London: The Bodley Head.

Melnik, A. and Merritt, J. (1973) *Reading. Today and Tomorrow*, London: University of London Press.

Michaels, S. (1986) Narrative presentations: an oral preparation for literacy with 1st graders, in J. Cook-Gumperz (ed.) *The Social Construction of Literacy*, Cambridge University Press.

Mills, R. W. and Mills, J. (1993) *Bilingualism in the Primary School*, London: Routledge.

Minns, H. (1990) *Read it to Me Now*, London: Virago Press.

National Curriculum Council (1988) *Introducing the National Curriculum Council*, London: National Curriculum Council.

National Curriculum Council (1990) *Curriculum Guidance 3: The Whole Curriculum*, York: National Curriculum Council.

National Curriculum Council (1992) *Starting Out with the National Curriculum*, York: National Curriculum Council.

Newson, J. and Newson, E. (1975) Intersubjectivity and the transmission of culture: on the social origins of symbolic functioning, *Bulletin of the British Psychology Society*, Vol. 218, pp. 437–46.

Ninio, A. and Bruner, J. S. (1978) The achievement and antecedents of labelling, *Journal of Child Development*, Vol. 5, no. 78, pp. 5–15.

Oberhuemer, P. (1994) Stories make a difference: intercultural dialogue in the Early Years, *European Early Childhood Research Journal*, Vol. 2, no. 1, pp. 35–42.

Palincsar, A. S., Brown, A. L. and Campione, J. C. (1993) 1st grade dialogues for knowledge acquisition and use, in E. A. Foreman, N. Minick and C. A. Stone (eds.) *Contexts for Learning*, NY: Oxford University Press.

Perfetti, C. H. (1984) *Reading Ability*, NY: Oxford University Press.

Piaget, J. (1959) *The Language and Thought of the Child*, London: Routledge and Kegan Paul.

Pinker, S. (1994) *The Language Instinct. The New Science of Language and Mind*, London: Allen Lane/The Penguin Press.

Reid, J. F. (1966) Learning to think about reading, *Educational Research*, Vol. 9, pp. 56–62.

Rogoff, B., Mosier, C., Mistry, J. and Goncu, A. (1993) Toddlers guided participation with their caregivers in cultural activity, in E. Forman, N. Minick and C. Stone (eds.) *Contexts for Learning*, NY: Oxford University Press.

Rosen, H. (1985) *Stories and Meanings*, Sheffield: National Association for the Teaching of English (49 Broomgrove Rd, Sheffield S10 2NA).

Rummelhart, D. E. (1977) Toward an interactive model of reading, in S. Dornic (ed.) *Attention and Performance*, Hillsdale NJ: LEA.

Salmon, P. (ed.) (1981) *Coming to Know*, London: Routledge and Kegan Paul.

Sapir, E. (1970) *Culture, Language and Personality*, Berkeley, California: University of California Press.

Satzke, K. and Wolf, W. (1993) *Lehrplan der Volkschule*, Wien: OBV, Padagogischer Verlag.

SCAA (School Curriculum and Assessment Authority) (1995) *Teaching and Learning English as an Additional Language: New Perspectives*, International Conference, London 27–28 April.

Schieffelin, B. B. and Cochran-Smith, M. (1984) Learning to read culturally: literacy before schooling, in H. Goelmann, A. Oberg and F. Smith (eds.) *Awakening to Literacy*, London: Heinemann Educational.

School Examination and Assessment Council (1989) *An Introduction to SEAC*, London: HMSO.

Schutz, A. (1964) The stranger: an essay in social psychology, in *Collected Papers, Vol. II*, The Hague: Nijhoff.

Scollon, R. (1979) A real early stage: an unzippered condensation of a dissertation on child language, in E. Ochs and B. Schieffelin (eds.) *Developmental Pragmatics*, NY: Academic Press.

Scollon, R. and Scollon, B. K. (1981) *Narrative, Literacy and Face in Interethnic Communication*, Norwood NJ: Ablex.

Sharman, F. and Chadwick, B. (1989) *The A–Z Gastronomique. The Travellers' Guide to French Food and Drink*, London: The Knife and Cleaves Press.

Skutnabb-Kangas, T. (1984) Multilingualism and the education of minority children, in T. Skutnabb-Kangas and J. Cummins (eds.) *Minority Education*, Clevedon: Multilingual Matters.

Snow, C. E. (1977) The development of conversation between mothers and babies, *Journal of Child Language*, Vol. 4, pp. 1–22.

Snow, C. and Ninio, A. (1986) The contracts of literacy: what children learn from learning to read books, in W. H. Teale and E. Sulzby (eds.) *Emergent Literacy*, Norwood NJ: Ablex.

Steffensen, M. S., Joag-dev, C. and Anderson, C. (1980) A cross-cultural perspective on reading comprehension, *Reading Research Quarterly*, Vol. 15, pp. 10–29.

Street, B. (1984) *Literacy in Theory and Practice*, Cambridge University Press.

Tinker, M. A. and McCullogh, C. M. (1962) *Teaching Elementary Reading*, New York, Appleton-Century Crofts.

Topping, K. and Wolfendale, S. (eds.) (1985) *Parental Involvement in Children's Reading*, Beckenham: Croom Helm.

Tosi, A. (1984) *Immigration and Bilingual Education*, Oxford: Pergamon Press.

Unsworth, L. (ed.) (1993) *Literacy Learning and Teaching. Language as Social Practice in the Primary School*, Melbourne: Macmillan.

Unsworth, L. and O'Toole, M. (1993) Beginning reading with children's literature, in L. Unsworth (op. cit.).

Verhoeven, L. (1987) *Ethnic Minority Children Acquiring Literacy*, Dordrecht: Foris.

Vygoysky, L. (1962) *Thought and Language*, Cambridge Mass: MIT Press.

Vygotsky, L. (1978) *Mind in Society: the Development of Higher Psychological Processes*, Cambridge Mass: Harvard University Press.

Vygotsky, L. (1981) The genesis of higher mental functions, in J. V. Wertsch *The Concept of Activity in Soviet Psychology*, NY: ME Sharpe.

Wagner, D. A., Messick, B. M. and Spratt, J. (1986) Studying literacy in Morocco, in B. Schieffelin and P. Gilmore (eds.) *Ethnographic Perspectives*, Vol. XXI in the series Advance in Discourse Processes, NY: Academic Press.

Walkerdine, V. (1981) From context to text: a psychosemiotic approach to abstract thought, in B. Beveridge (ed.) *Children Thinking Through Language*, London: Edward Arnold.

Wallace, C. (1986) *Learning to Read in a Multicultural Society*, Oxford: Pergamon Press.

Wells, C. G. (1985) Pre-school literacy related activities and success in school, in D. R. Olson, N. Torrance and A. Hildyard (eds.) *Literacy, Language and Learning. The Nature and Consequences of Reading and Writing*, Cambridge University Press.

Wells, G. (1987) *The Meaning Makers*, London: Hodder & Stoughton.

Whitehead, M. (1990) *Language and Literacy in the Early Years. An Approach for Education Students*, London: Paul Chapman Publishing.

Wolfendale, S. and Topping, K. (eds.) (1995) *Parental Involvement in Literacy – Effective Partnerships in Education*, London: Croom Helm.

Wong-Fillmore, L. (1982) The language learner as an individual: implications of research on individual differences for the ESL teacher, in M. A. Clarke and J. Handscombe (eds.), On TEOL '82: *Pacific Perspectives on Language Learning and Teaching*, Washington DC: TESOL.

CHILDREN'S BOOKS

(Referred to in the text and not listed in Appendix 2.)

Bernal, M. C. *et al.* (1989) *La Ventafocs*, Vic: Eumo Editorial.

Burningham, J. (1978) *Would You Rather . . . ?* London: Cape.

Colwell, E. (ed.) (1970) *Tell Me a Story*, London: Penguin.

Duncan, J. (1985) *If You Were a Bird . . .* , London: Hodder & Stoughton.

Grimm, J. (1993) *Rumpelstiltskin*, Ladybird Grade II Easy Reader, London: Ladybird Books.

Hargreaves, R. (1976) *Mr Funny*, Thurman Pubs.

Hargreaves, R. (1976) *Mr Impossible*, Thurman Pubs.

Hargreaves, R. (1976) *Mr Messy*, Thurman Pubs.

Hargreaves, R. (1976) *Mr Nosey*, Thurman Pubs.

Jayal, A. (1974) *Bhondoo the Monkey* series, India: Thomson Press.

(1975) *My Big Book of Nursery Tales*, London: Award Pubs.

Potter, B. (1902) *The Tale of Peter Rabbit*, London: Warne.

Rogers, P. (1990) *Don't Blame Me*, London: The Bodley Head.

Ross, T. (1981) *Little Red Riding Hood*, London: Penguin.

The Fireman, London: Ladybird Books.

Appendix 1
Stages of Learning

The emergent bilinguals in this book will be Stage One or Stage Two learners of English (or French) according to the stages described by Hilary Hester in *Patterns of Learning: The Primary Language Record and the National Curriculum* Barrs *et al.* 1990).

STAGES OF ENGLISH LEARNING

The following scale describes aspects of bilingual children's development through English which teachers might find helpful. It is important to remember that children may move into English in very individual ways, and that the experience for an older child will be different from that of a young child. The scales emphasise the social aspects of learning as well as the linguistic. Obviously attitudes in the school to children and the languages they speak will influence their confidence in using both their first and second languages.

Stage 1: new to English

Makes contact with another child in the class. Joins in activities with other children, but may not speak. Uses non-verbal gestures to indicate meaning – particularly needs, likes and dislikes. Watches carefully what other children are doing, and often imitates them. Listens carefully and often 'echoes' words and phrases of other children and adults. Needs opportunities for listening to the sounds, rhythms and tunes of English through songs, rhymes, stories and conversations. If young may join in repeating refrain of a story. Beginning to label objects in the classroom, and personal things. Beginning to put words together into holistic phrases (e.g. no come here, where find it, no eating that). May be involved in classroom learning activities in the first language with children who speak the same first language. May choose to use first language only in most contexts. May be willing to write in the first language (if s/he can), and if invited to. May be reticent with unknown adults. May be very aware of negative attitudes by peer group to the first language. May choose to move into English through story and reading, rather than speaking.

Stage 2: becoming familiar with English

Growing confidence in using the English s/he is acquiring. Growing ability to move between the languages, and to hold conversations in English with peer groups. Simple holistic phrases may be combined or expanded to communicate new ideas. Beginning to sort out small details (e.g. 'he' and 'she' distinction) but more interested in communicating meaning than in 'correctness'. Increasing control of the English tense system in particular contexts, such as story-telling, reporting events and activities that s/he has been involved in, and from book language. Understands more English that s/he can use. Growing vocabulary for naming objects and events, and beginning to describe in more detail (e.g. colour, size, quantity) and use simple adverbs. Increasingly confident in taking part in activities with other children through English. Beginning to write simple stories, often modelled on those s/he has heard read aloud. Beginning to write simple accounts of activities s/he has been involved in, but may need support from adults and other child her/his first language if s/he needs to.
Continuing to rely on support of her friends.

Stage 3: becoming confident as a user of English

Shows great confidence in using English in most social situations. This confidence may mask the need for support in taking on other registers. (e.g. in science investigation, in historical research.) Growing command of the grammatical system of English – including complex verbal meanings (relationships of time, expressing tentativeness and subtle intention with might, could, etc. . . . .) and more complex sentence structure. Developing an understanding of metaphor and pun. Pronunciation may be very native-speaker like, especially that of young children. Widening vocabulary from reading a story, poems and information books and from being involved in maths and science investigations, and other curriculum areas. May choose to explore complex ideas (e.g. in drama/role-play) in the first language with children who share the same first language.

Stage 4: a very fluent user of English in most social and learning contexts

A very experienced user of English, and exceptionally fluent in many contexts. May continue to need support in understanding subtle nuances of metaphor, and in anglocentric cultural content in poems and literature. Confident in exchanges and collaboration with English-speaking peers. Writing confidently in English with a growing competence over different genre. Continuing and new development in English drawn from own reading and books read aloud. New developments often revealed in own writing. Will move with ease between English and the first language depending on the contexts s/he finds herself in, what s/he judges appropriate, and the encouragement of the school.

Appendix 2
Valuable Books Available in the UK for Work with Young Emergent Bilinguals

I. VERY SIMPLE TEXTS PARTICULARLY SUITED FOR 'STRUCTURED STORY' SESSIONS

Bonne, R. and Mills, A. (1961) *I Know an Old Lady*, NY: Rand McNally.
Brown, M. (1995) *Goodnight Moon*, NY: Harper Childrens Audio (Story and Audio Cassette).
Browne, A. (1976) *Bear Hunt*, London: Hamish Hamilton.
Eastman, P. D. (1962) *Are You My Mother?* London: (Collins) Beginner Books.
Ginsburg, M. (1972) *The Chick and the Duckling*, NY: Macmillan.
Gregory, E. and Walker, D. (1987) *The Hen and the Mice: A Tale of Laziness*, Hodder & Stoughton (dual language versions in Bengali, Gujarati, Punjabi and Urdu).
Gregory, E., Walker, D. and Matharu, M. K. (1987) *Gangli Gauri: A Tale of Foolishness*, London: Hodder & Stoughton (a dual language text).
Hill, E. (1980) *The Spot Book*, Series (also in dual language versions).
Hunia, F. (1993) *Hansel and Gretel*, (Read it Yourself) Loughborough: Ladybird Books.
Hunia, F. (1993) *Rapunzel* (Read it Yourself) Loughborough: Ladybird Books.
Hunia, F. (1993) *Red Riding Hood* (Read it Yourself) Loughborough: Ladybird Books.
Hunia, F. (1993) *The Billy Goats Gruff* (Read it Yourself) Loughborough: Ladybird Books.
Hutchins, P. (1968) *Rosie's Walk*, The Bodley Head.
Hutchins, P. (1978) *Don't Forget the Bacon*, Harmondsworth: Puffin.
Kent, J. (1971) *The Fat Cat*, NY: Scholastic.
Mack, S. (1974) *Ten Bears in my Bed*, NY: Pantheon.
Martin, B. (1970) *Fire! Fire! Said Mrs Mcguire*, NY: Holt, Rinehart & Winston.
Murphy, J. (1980) *Peace at Last*, London: Macmillan.
McKee, D. (1987) *Not Now Bernard*, London: Arrow, Random Century.
Piers, H. (1979) *Mouse Looks for a House*, London: Methuen.
Storychest Series, *The Hungry Giant*, Ashton: Scholastic.
Topiwalo the Hatmaker plus tape, Harmony Pubs. Co Ltd., 14 Silverston Way, Stanmore, Middx HA7 4HR.

II. TEXTS RECOMMENDED FOR 'COLLABORATIVE READING' SESSIONS

Ahlberg, J. and A. (1977) *Each Peach Pear Plum*, Harmondsworth: Kestrel/Penguin Books.
Aliki (1962) *My Five Senses*, NY: Thomas Y. Crowell.
Brandenberg, F. (1982) *I Don't Feel Well*, Harmondsworth: Puffin.
Browne, A. (1986) *Willy the Wimp*, London: Methuen.
Carle, E. (1969) *The Very Hungry Caterpillar*, Cleveland Ohio: Collins World.
Cole, T. and Cressey, J. (1976) *Fourteen Rats and a Rat-Catcher*, London: A. & C. Black.
Daly (1983) *Joseph's Other Red Sock*, London: Collins.
Hewett, A. (1970) *Mrs Mopple's Washing Line*, Harmondsworth: Puffin.
Hutchins, P. (1975) *Goodnight Owl*, Harmondsworth: Puffin.
Hutchins, P. (1978) *The Wind Blew*, Harmondsworth: Puffin.
Hutchins, P. (1982) *I Hunter*, London: The Bodley Head.
Hutchins, P. (1986) *The Very Worst Monster*, Harmondsworth: Puffin.
Kerr, J. (1968) *The Tiger who Came to Tea*, Collins Picture Lions.
Moore, L. (1982) *Wind Song*, in J. Foster (ed.) *My Very First Poetry Book*, Oxford University Press.
Nicholl, H. and Pienkowski, J. (1972) *Meg's Car*, London: Heinemann.
Nicholl, H. and Pienkowski, J. (1972) *Meg at Sea*, London: Heinemann.
Sendak, M. (1970) *Where the Wild Things Are*, Gosford, NS Wales: Ashton-Scholastic.
Vipont, E. (1969) *The Elephant and the Bad Baby*, London: Hamish Hamilton.
Wadsworth (1986) *Over in the Meadow*, Harmondsworth: Puffin.
Wagner, J. (1977) *John Brown, Rose and the Midnight Cat*, Melbourne: Kestrel.

III. TRADITIONAL TALES WHICH WILL SUPPORT 'STRUCTURED STORY' DURING CLASS STORYTIME SESSIONS

Barnett, C. (1983) *The Lion and the Mouse*, Oxford University Press.
Brown, M. (1957) *The Three Billy Goats Gruff*, NY: Harcourt Brace Jovanovich.
Browne, A. (1981) *Hansel and Gretel*, London: Julia McRae.
Galdone, P. (1970) *The Three Little Pigs*, NY: Seabury Press.
Galdone, P. (1972) *The Three Bears*, NY: Scholastic.
Galdone, P. (1973) *The Little Red Hen*, NY: Scholastic.
Galdone, P. (1973) *The Three Billy Goats Gruff*, NY: Seabury Press.
McDermott, G. (1972) Anansi the Spider, NY: Holt, Rhinehart & Winston.
Mosel, A. and Lent, D. (1972) *The Funny Little Woman*, Harlow: Longman Young Books.
Rehnman, M. (1989) *The Clay Flute*, Stockholm: R & S Books.
Southgate, V. (1982) *The Shoemaker and the Elves*, Well Loved Tales, Ladybird Books.
Tolstoy, A. (1968) *The Great Big Enormous Turnip*, NY: Franklin Watts.
Wildsmith, B. (1982) *The Hare and the Tortoise*, Oxford University Press.

A more extensive list of books recommended for use with young emergent bilinguals can be obtained from Professor Viv Edwards, Director of Reading and Language Information Centre, University of Reading, Bulmershe Court, Earley, Reading RG6 1HY.

In addition, an excellent list of resources can be found in:

Garvie, E. (1990) *Story as Vehicle*, Clevedon: Multilingual Matters.
Triggs, P. (ed.) (1986/87) *The Books for Keeps Guide to Children's Books for a Multicultural Society, 0–7*, compiled by J. Elkin.
School Books Association/Library Association Youth Libraries, with the help of Lloyd's Bank.

IV. COMPUTER SOFTWARE PROGRAMMES

Allwrite: A multilingual word-processing programme available in Arabic, Bengali, English (and other European), Farsi, Gaelic, Greek, Gujarati, Hindi, Punjabi, Tamil, Turkish, Vietnamese and Welsh. It has been used effectively by parents to support minority languages in schools.

Computer Assisted Language Learning (CALL) package for beginners using HyperCard studio on Apple computers (1995).

Tamil Fonts for Nimbus and Apple computer (1991). Available from The Department of Educational Studies, Goldsmiths College, University of London, Lewisham Way, London SE14 6NW.

Mayer, M. (1983) *Just Grandma and Me', 'Scooter's Magic Castle'* (book and computer disk) Random House: Broderbund Company.

The Talking Pendown computer programme for use with the Acorn computer. Harlow, Essex: Longman.

Appendix 3
Classroom Plans

Plan for linking the 'Inside-Out' and 'Outside-In' approaches within a security which experiments: adventure, fear and safety.

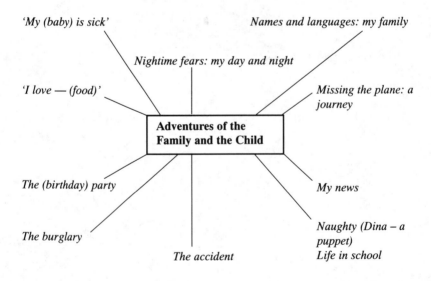

Suggestions for very early lessons for classes or groups with a majority of emergent bilinguals linking 'Inside-Out' and 'Outside-In' approaches. Each example may stretch over at least a week, much longer if it is the starting-point for a curriculum theme.

EXAMPLE 1: NAMES

Aims

Conceptual

- To show children that meaning can be represented symbolically through print.
- That streams of sound can be divided into words and syllables and that there may be a one-to-one correspondence between sound and symbol.
- That print is purposeful.

Linguistic

- That the children should use the following lexis and syntax actively: 'My name is —; His/her name is —; What's your/his/her name?; Good morning; How are you today?; Very well, thank you; I see? I can see —; under, over, around, between' (or most important lexis of stories chosen).
- That the children should understand the texts of the books read, even if unable to use all the words in speech.

'Inside-Out'

Key words

Children's names; names of puppets (plus others suggested by the children of those they want in their book).

Resources

- A photo of each child, the teacher, assistant, headteacher, puppets and anyone in the school who is important in the child's life. Duplicate photos of each child and the puppets – one photo per page to be stuck into the large Class Reading Book and one on the front of each child's personal first reading book. Under each photo in the large book, she has written 'My name is —' (for the children to complete). The teacher also has a 'book about herself' which she completes alongside the children. A child is chosen each day to 'help' the puppets do their work.

THE 'GOOD MORNING' SONG
A very simple introduction to an important 'cultural recipe' of English speaking countries

- The puppets and their abode (a bag, etc.).
- Name-cards for each child plus 'My', 'name', 'is', '.' and either a stand into which these can be inserted or a magnet-board and magnets.
- The sentence 'My name is (name of 1 puppet)' ready on stand or board but concealed.
- The 'Good morning' song.

Plan

1. The teacher introduces the 'Good morning' song simply by singing it to one child. Gradually all the children join in. Then one child sings to another s/he has chosen, etc.
2. The teacher tells the class/group she has two friends who have recently arrived in the host country and are very shy. She tells their names and asks children to sing to them to entice them out of their home. Slowly, the puppets emerge and the teacher models 'What's your name? My name is —' (for each puppet). As the puppets gain confidence, they ask the children their names too.
3. Straight away, the teacher shows the large class book, finds her own photo, reads the text pointing to the words and then writes her name in the appropriate place. The children go through the book and each child reads a page inserting his or her name.
4. The name-cards are introduced (usually familiar), called out and games played (e.g. all in the bag and one child picks one for the others to guess 'Is it my name?'). The puppets name-cards are introduced (these should both begin with the same letter – Dina and Dabir – to initiate sound/symbol correspondence between other names.
5. The sentence with 'My name is (puppet's name)' is shown. The puppet cannot read it (too shy or unable) and needs to be helped by a child. The teacher then takes different names from the bag and the children read 'their' sentence. A game is played where the words are muddled or one is removed. One child is the teacher and the others must guess.
6. The class book is completed by each child and becomes the first Class Reading Book. It is taken to others (headteacher, etc.) to complete and someone 'helps' the puppets. The individual book will also be completed (children copy below teacher or word process from the class book or cards). (Handwriting practice will be in a separate book.)

▲

'Outside-In'

Resources

- Books recommended: *Rosie's Walk* (Hutchins)*
                      Brown Bear (Martin)*
- Other good choices: *Goodnight Owl* (Hutchins)
                      Mr Gumpy's Outing (Burningham)
                      Come Away from the Water Shirley (Burningham)
                      Bear Hunt (Burningham)
                      Grandpa (Burningham)
                      Billy Goats Gruff (varied: see Appendix 2)
                      Where the Wild Things Are (Sendak)
                      Rumpelstiltskin (Hunia)
- Tapes of the stories (dual language versions if possible); figurines for magnet-board; puppets, dressing-up resources.
- Word cards with 'I', 'can', 'see' put together into 'I can see (child's name)' onto a stand or board (concealed).
- A large class book with 'I can see —' written on each page.

Plan

The children read both with and after the teacher (see Chapter 6, 'chained reading').
Rosie's Walk is acted out as the teacher reads and is accompanied by a song 'Little (name

of puppet) dances . . . .'. The puppet dances 'on', 'under', 'around', etc. different parts of the body and the children 'make' the puppet by using their finger (s/he also goes and dances on individual children).

After reading *Brown Bear*, the teacher 'makes' a telescope with her hand and 'spies' through it saying 'I can see (child or object).' The children imitate and each says what s/he can see. A guessing game is played where children guess 'Can you see —?' and one child is 'teacher'. A song is learned, to the tune of 'Frère Jacques' (Can you see me? (repeat) Yes, I can. (repeat) Look at how I (actions, e.g. 'brush my teeth', etc.). (repeat) Just like this. (repeat))

The sentence card is shown 'I can see (puppet's name)' and many others are made using children's names. The guessing game (mixing and removing words) is played. Different children complete the pages in the class book by drawing a picture of a child and inserting the appropriate name.

EXAMPLE 2: FOOD

Aims

Conceptual

Change of state (involved in cooking and food preparation) – melting, dissolving, thickening, rising, etc. Sense of taste (might be linked with other senses). Possibly link with 'growing' (cress, etc.).

Linguistic

Lexis and syntax linked with particular cooking, food preparation and serving activities (recipes, tea-party, picnic, etc.). Important lexis and syntax of stories chosen (decide upon most important lexis and syntax to be practised actively or only understood passively beforehand).

Key words

Names of favourite foods, 'I love —'.

'Inside-Out'

Resources

- Packets and labels of children's favourite foods and drink, preferably brought to school by the children. The name labels are cut off and stuck on cards to be used as word cards (for reading, matching and word games).
- Word cards 'I', 'love', 'says' (plus name cards and any useful extras).
- Ingredients for cooking or food preparation.
- Two large class books (i) to record: 'I love — says Dina' (a page for each child or several children with the label or packet stuck on appropriately); (ii) a book with photos to record the booking/food preparation/tea-party with the class.
- Different restaurants for socio-dramatic area.

Plan

1. The 'Good morning' song is now on large card and one child points to the words as others sing.
2. The favourite food labels are discussed and read by children claiming them.

3. The puppets are woken up and whisper to a child what they love to eat for the other children to guess. The 'guessing game' 'Do you love —?' is played and different children are 'teacher'.
4. Sentences are made (using the sentence stand or magnet-board 'I love —.') and the guessing game (see Example 1) are played.
5. Words beginning with the same letter or having the same pattern are matched.
6. The children complete both the large class book 'I love —' and small individual books (see Example 1 above).
7. Depending upon the focus book chosen for the 'Outside-In', cooking and a tea-party take place (for example, making bread, butter and honey sandwiches if the focus is *The Hungry Giant* (Storychest)) and the second large class photo book completed.

'Outside-In'

Resources

- Books recommended: *The Hungry Caterpillar* (Carle)*
  The Little Red Hen (Galdone) and dual language version *The Hen and the Mice* (Gregory & Walker)*
- Other good books: *The Three Bears* (Galdone)
  The Fat Cat (Kent)
  My Five Senses (Aliki)
  The Funny Little Woman (Mosel & Lent)
  Hansel and Gretel (Browne)
  The Great Big Enormous Turnip (Tolstoy)
  The Gingerbread Man (Hunia)
  The Hungry Giant (Storychest)
  The Three Billy Goats Gruff (Brown, Galdone or Hunia)
- Songs: Many can be invented (for example: 'This is the way I roll my dough', etc. to the tune of 'Here I go round the Mulberry Bush').

Plan

See Example 1 above for a framework. Link with cooking, etc. from the 'Inside-Out' approach.

EXAMPLE 3: ILLNESS/DOCTOR'S/ACCIDENT/HOSPITAL

Aims

Conceptual

Temperature, fever, etc. Relationship between food hygiene and health, sleep, etc.; dental hygiene; emotions during illness; age, etc.

Linguistic

Lexis concerned with illness and visits to the doctor's, hospital, etc.; 'I don't feel well'; 'I'm sick'; 'I've got a tummy-ache/head-ache etc.'; 'Dina (a puppet) is sick today'; 'I had an accident', etc. 'I/my brother went to the doctor's/hospital, etc.' Important lexis of books chosen.

'Inside-Out'

Key words

Sick, ill, well, ambulance, accident, hospital, pill, doctor's, head-ache, tummy-ache, bandage, plaster, etc.

Resources

Dressing-up clothes for hospital, hospital ward or surgery for dramatic play area, song (adapted version of 'Miss Polly had a dolly who was sick . . .' to 'Poor little (name of puppet or child in class) is sick . . .') plus a large version of the song with a gap for different children's names; bed for puppet, plus bandages, etc.; a large class book for photos of the sick puppets, etc.

Plan

1. A puppet's accident is announced and described. A special hospital bed is made, tablets administered, plaster, bandages, etc. applied.
2. The 'Poor little . . .' song is sung and acted out. One child is patient; another dresses up with a bag, hat, etc.
3. Sentences are made relating to the puppets and the children (see Example 1).
4. The class book is completed and individual books are continued.

'Outside-In'

Resources

- Recommended Books: *John Brown, Rose and the Midnight Cat* (Wagner)*
  I Know an Old Lady (Rose & Mills)*
- Other good books: *I Don't Feel Well* (Brandenberg)
  Hansel and Gretel (Hunia)
  Jack and the Beanstalk (Hunia)
  Sleeping Beauty (Hunia)
  Gangli Gauri (Gregory & Walker – dual language versions

Plan

See Example 1.

INDEX OF AUTHORS

INDEX OF SUBJECTS